The Potential of Herbs as a Cash Crop

Richard Alan Miller

Acres U.S.A.
P.O. Box 8800
Metairie, Louisiana 70011

The Potential of Herbs as a Cash Crop

Copyright ©1985, 1998 by Richard Alan Miller

Printed in the United States of America

Publisher's Cataloging-in-Publication
(Provided by Quality Books, Inc.)

Miller, Richard Alan, 1944-
    The potential of herbs as a cash crop / by Richard Alan Miller ; artwork by Connie Nygard. -- 2nd ed., rev.
      p. cm.
    Includes bibliographical references and index.
    ISBN: 0-911311-55-6

1. Herb farming. 2. Herbs--Marketing. I. Title.

SB351.H5M55 1998   338.1'757
                        QBI98-84

This book is dedicated to my Mother and Father
Jack and Katy Miller
for giving me a love of the country.

Richard Alan Miller

Richard Alan Miller is a scientist of extensive and multidimensional expertise. He has been listed in *Who's Who in the West* since 1992 and was named to *Who's Who in the World* in 1996. He did his undergraduate work in theoretical physics at Washington State University, with graduate work including training at M.I.T. and the University of Delaware in solid-state physics. He then spent over a decade in biomedical research and development from some of the most prestigious and technologically sophisticated corporations in the United States. These included the Boeing Company, E.I. duPont de Nemours and Company, and the Department of Anesthesiology of the University of Washington.

Mr. Miller has been published in several international journals for his work both in physics and philosophy, with several books in print on these subjects. He has taught philosophy for credit in the natural sciences divisions at several universities and colleges for more than ten years. He has also taught courses in small farm agriculture, with several books on this subject in print or in process including *Native Plants of Commercial Importance*, *Forest Farming*, *Computers on the Farm*, and *Successful Farm Ventures*. He is also a regular contributor to the sustainable farming journal *Acres U.S.A.* and has published a national newsletter, *The Herb Market Report*. In addition, he has authored or coauthored a series of books in philosophy, alternative health, and self-development. His current research is on the interface between physics and psychology. This is a further continuation of his work in philosophy and the relationship between mind and matter.

He is one of the "new" scientists, recognizing that science should not and cannot be separated from the welfare of the human being. In 1972 he formed the Beltane Corporation, specializing as a regional wholesaler of herbs, spices and teas to the six western states. The company was expanded into three further companies in 1980 to grow herbs and spices as domestic sources of supply. As a physicist he has invented several critical pieces of farm machinery to assist the small farmer in harvesting and processing. As an agricultural scientist he has developed specific farm plans and crop sources to compete with currently imported herbs and spices. In 1987 he formed Northwest Botanicals, Inc. to broker the growing number of new domestic farmers and foragers producing herbs and spices. In this capacity he has been retained as a special consultant to major mass-market firms as well as cottage industries.

Mr. Miller currently serves as a teacher and agricultural consultant from his Grants Pass, Oregon base. For more information on his activities and services visit his website at <http://www.nw.net/ram>.

Connie Nygard

Connie Nygard studied art at the Corcoran School of Art and several schools in the Los Angeles and San Francisco Bay areas. This multi-talented individual is currently a graphic artist and illustrator who lives in the piney woods of southern Oregon where she teaches calligraphy and fine arts within the community. Other books she has illustrated include *The Magical and Ritual Use of Aphrodisiacs* and *Native Plants of Commercial Importance*.

TABLE OF CONTENTS:

Also by Richard Alan Miller

The Magical and Ritual Use of Aphrodisiacs
The Magical and Ritual Use of Herbs
The Magical and Ritual Use of Perfumes
Native Plants of Commercial Importance
The Modern Alchemist

FOR THE RECORD

There is a fiction afloat these days that the large farm is more efficient, that it is the wave of the future. But history says something else, because civilization always goes from food surpluses to crowded cities to hunger. In our own time, automation and cross-border trade with low cost areas of the world have disemployed over seven million people. Nothing makes more sense than to enable these people to find higher wages on profitable farms in sparsely populated rural areas.

Small farms are more efficient than large farms in producing higher value crops per acre and employing more manpower per acre. The efficiency of the small farm is the key in our analysis. Expensive equipment on farms has created a fiction that economics of scale are supreme, but the exact opposite is true.

These are things that public policy ought to examine, but won't, because the business people who write public policy see profit in strip cities now, this minute, and do not look into the future at all. Thus the big operators overwork and mine the soil and view the dinosaur operation as king of the hill, when in fact — and in our own time — the dinosaur farm will go the way of the dinosaur.

The fastest growing unidentified trend in the U.S. today is the increased number of small farms. Not many of these farms turn a profit. They are kept alive with the subsidy of off-farm work. But the units are there, and some few of them are doing the hard think-tank work it takes to make them viable as the national economy continues to falter.

To this end, Richard Alan Miller's insight is a commodity that might well be weighed out on a jeweler's scale. In rippling sentences punctuated by hard facts, he walks the reader through a hands-on course in herb and spice production on the small farm — at a profit. These specialty products, indeed, are a cash crop, and the market has been well established for decades. Foreign producers, after conquering breath-taking transportation costs, have enjoyed this market for as long as the nations of North America have existed. And yet that market rightly belongs to the North American producer.

The book, *Herbs as a Cash Crop,* is full of no-nonsense charm. It is a primer and a post-graduate course wrapped into one. It seems to marry a century old art to modern refinements in a manner so understandable anyone can benefit. No great knowledge of chemistry, botany, entomology or soil physics is necessary to read and understand this book.

But it is necessary for the small farm to do its homework. This means taking Miller's lessons by the nape of the neck and the seat of the pants and repositioning them between the ears of the farm operator. A successful transplant job will see the small farm off and running.

FOREWORD

Some experts say that by the year 2000 more than 85% of gross farm receipts will go to less than 15% of the farmers. This means that out of the 2.4 million farmers today, most of the farming in the future will be done by less than 300,000 surviving farmers. Will you be one of them?

Current reviews of crop categories and their economic outlooks indicate few viable potentials for the small farmer. Alternative crops such as spices and botanicals are feasible, but require information not readily available from such sources as the United States Department of Agriculture (USDA) and the local County Extension Agents.

The purpose of this book is to provide this missing information and a perspective on what is involved for the small farmer when considering these alternative crops. Realistic statistics on current market potentials of herbs and spices are given, with some background and technical approaches, which must be considered. Specific potentials are revealed, including foraging as a life style with good rural incomes.

The objective here is to develop domestic sources of supply for currently imported crops. With access to new breakthroughs in farm machinery and techniques, some 400 new crops currently imported can now be produced domestically. The anticipated benefits are also reviewed.

The method of developing these alternative agricultural crops is reviewed and a small farm management program is described. This includes chapters on specific farm plans, farm machinery and irrigation needs, harvest and dehydration techniques, processing and storage requirements, and — most important — the marketing of these crops. The book is a short course on all aspects of herb and spice farming for the beginner and experienced farmer alike.

The intended audience for *The Potential of Herbs as a Cash Crop* includes those individuals who would like to move to a more rural setting and make a viable income. It also considers those who are already living in the country, but need to put crops onto nonproductive ground. All crops discussed will develop farm income of sufficient magnitude to support land payments and provide jobs not previously available from those areas.

Unlike other "living off the land" approaches, this book features tables to help the reader determine needs, qualifications, and required tools to successfully farm herbs and spices. Insights and classified information are given for the small farmer to process and market his own crops, rather than work through a distributor or middleman. Assets required for successful management are detailed.

Evaluation of resources is critical in determining just what crops are suitable in a given situation. Comprehensive, yet simply stated, this book provides a firm foundation for the potential of herbs as a cash crop and suggests some sources for further research.

CHAPTER 1

The Survival of the Small Farm Through Alternative Agriculture

Historically, in a time of cultural change, a new type of entrepreneur emerges to embody the vision of new ideas with services and
products.

from *The Aquarian Conspiracy* by Marilyn Ferguson

If you are like most of us from the "war baby" generation, you tend to look for a more rural way of life. While some of us are still *preparing* for that move, others have already made that move, often with unfortunate results. There are few industries in the country to provide income producing jobs other than tra-ditional forms of farming. That lifestyle will probably be severely tested for those who do not plan their incomes carefully. There are few jobs and even fewer sources of incomes within the farm community to make those monthly land payments.

The small farmer is faced with a series of major problems, each requiring due consideration before any move is made to the country. The first problem is always to be properly prepared financially. Most of us do not have enough money to simply buy a home in the country and retire without needing some source of continuing income. It is no wonder that we read more and more about the plight of the farmer who has lost his land. With few job opportunities and poor profit margins from traditional crops, yields per acre from the land are not commensurate to land costs.

Because of these and related problems, we know now that each year 100,000 farms are abandoned, and that rural America has sustained a population loss of 40 million people in the last 50 years. Once populated areas occupied by independent small landholders interspersed with small, rural service communities are being transformed into feudalistic estates. This is having a devastating effect on local communities and their ability to be financially self sufficient. This pattern of events has increased the farm size and absentee ownership of the land, thus providing fewer and fewer jobs for that community.

Therefore, the critical first question should be, *Do I have enough money to invest and support my family until the land can pay its costs?* When starting your own farm, you take all the risks. Lessons learned can be very costly. Unless you have had actual, practical farming experience or have completed some work in an agricultural school, you stand against even more difficult odds in surviving on a small farm. Table 1 provides a list of capital investments necessary when starting any new small farm venture, no matter what crop is being considered.

FIRST QUESTIONS

A number of important questions should be asked when considering a farm venture. These must be answered no matter what crop is chosen. For example, what kind of preparation will the farm need before you can plant a crop, any crop? Do you need fencing for livestock, an irrigation system, sheds, barns, or other structures? How much of this work can you do yourself, and what will the materials cost? What would it cost to hire out some of this work, and are such skills even available locally? All these questions must be considered before any venture in small farming has a chance of success.

If you are one of the substantial number of people who feel that the answer to

TABLE 1
Capital Investments Needed to Start a Small Farm

CAPITAL INVESTMENTS	PROBABLE COST SPREAD	UNIT
Land	$ 700 to $ 2,300	Per acre
House	15,000 to 32,000	Total for farm
Barns, Sheds, etc.	1,000 to 10,000	Total for farm
Wire fencing	60 to 120	Per 100 yards
Machinery		
Tractor/Tillage		
Utility Vehicle		
Harvest Equipment	8,000 to 28,000	Total for farm
Irrigation system	150 to 500	Per acre

the city's rat race lies in a rural lifestyle, then proper capitalization is critically necessary for any successful venture. If you think that the prices at the food store are high, check the price tags on items you might need for farming: tractor, tillage equipment, a small truck, equipment for fertilization, spraying, irrigation, and harvest. Water and power cost money, as do skilled and semi-skilled labor.

Let's assume that you can come up with all the cash or credit needed to get your land into production. Now the small farmer faces another major problem. It is the item known as *economy of scale*. Roughly, this means that it doesn't cost five times as much to farm 100 acres of a given crop as it does to farm 20. The same farm machinery needs aside, it is quite possible that costs per acre will be substantially lower on the larger plot. The point is that you'll be competing with large farms, and you will have a built-in handicap. The small farmer will probably have to sell his crop at the same price the larger operator gets, but with lower profits, if any.

The issue for agriculture is less a question of farm size than it is the maintenance of market conditions that assure a sufficient return on the farmer's investment and labor. A review of these factors reveals that the small farm is disadvantaged. Despite the fact that you must bear all the risk of production, must nurture the crop from year to year, often having to wait years before vines and trees reach maturity, you receive too often the least return of all components in the food delivery chain.

Take ketchup as an example. A 14-ounce bottle, which costs the consumer about 59 cents, brings the farmer a little more than 1 cent. In contrast, the wholesaler, or middleman, who is a transient connection between the farmer and the retailer, skims off as much as 40% of the price (or 24 cents) the housewife pays for the market product. Consistent with the average deficient return on the farmer's investment, his earnings — labor included — average less than one-half the national industrial average.

So at this point, it is difficult to resist considering a few philosophical points: anyone who has, or can raise, the capital necessary to buy raw land and develop it into a farm probably does not need an income to make those important land payments. Therefore, any who think of taking over an existing small farm would do well to delve deeply into the reason why that owner wants to sell in the first place.

Can you get away from the city's rat race and be your own boss? Definitely, yes . . . but you may find, as some now have found, that you only traded an urban rat race for a rural treadmill, leaving little time for anything but a bunch of hard work. Instead of owning a small farm, you may find that the farm owns you. How can you compete as a small farm, faced with these points? Table 2 provides a list of annual production costs necessary when maintaining any small farm venture, no matter what crop is being raised.

TABLE 2

Annual Production Costs Needed to Maintain a Small Farm

ANNUAL PRODUCTION	PROBABLE COST SPREAD		UNIT
Land preparation	$ 20 to	$ 70	Per acre
Fertilizers	10 to	40	Per acre
Labor/Weeding	15 to	70	Per acre
Interest/Loan	2,000 to	7,000	Total
Water/Electrical	750 to	2,500	Total
Harvesting	15 to	200+	Per acre

With these important perspectives well in mind, the experienced or would-be small farmer is faced with a fundamental *next* question: "What crops can I grow and market to provide financial security for my family?" Let's suppose that you, as a newcomer, can make enough on your crops the first year or so to keep your family eating, making land payments, and taking care of other necessities. What about the future?

As a family grows in both size and age, it takes more resources to support them. Can you also put money aside to expand your farm and income as the need arises? These tough "first questions" must be asked when considering new crops, along with a new lifestyle in farming.

TRADITIONAL AGRICULTURAL OUTLOOKS

The first products or crops that come to mind are those traditional for the small farm: truck farming, dairy products, fruits, and hay. Unfortunately, these crops have not done well in recent years because supply and demand are fairly well in balance. The current low net farm incomes in the United States have resulted from a combination of increasing farm production expenses and a decline in price for agricultural products. Record crop production, coupled with weak worldwide demand, have resulted in large inventory buildups, further reducing prices.

Profits are best when demand for the product is high and production low, or when the product can be produced in volume. Large corporate firms make their money on volume of sales, relying on the economy of scale principle. Profits from each crop may not be great, but even a small percentage on their large sales make for substantial returns. The small farmer does not have this option. A small farmer's production is limited so he needs to receive top dollar for his crop. His need is best met through producing a unique or rare product of high quality, limiting production to market needs. In this way, the small farmer need no attempt to compete with the corporation which cut pennies through volume sales.

U.S. net farm incomes are the lowest in real terms since the Great Depres-

TABLE 3

Summary of Receipts, Costs and Profitability for a number of Traditional Crops, including several Herbs

CROP	BEETS	CARROTS	CAULIFLOWER	CUCUMBERS	PEAS	SWEET CORN	WINTER WHEAT	ALFALFA	CATNIP*	PEPPERMINT HERB*
Yield/Acre	1140#	30 ton	3 ton	10 ton	2.26 ton	5.5 ton	100 bush.	4 ton	3 ton	2 ton
Market Price	$0.65/#	$28/ton	$337/ton	$136/ton	$180/ton	$54/ton	$4.10/b.	$95/ton	$400/ton	$750/ton
Total Receipts	$741.00	$840.00	$1012.50	$1364.00	$406.80	$297.00	$410.00	$380.00	$1200.00	$1500.00
Preharvest Costs	$741.22	$350.84	$404.02	$1274.79	$203.63	$243.55	$130.97	$50.00	$70.00	$70.00
Harvest Costs	155.22	300.99	200.14	37.66	17.28	15.77	54.24	20.00	20.00	20.00
Machinery	62.62	65.92	69.80	71.11	43.40	50.75	38.48	20.00	30.00	50.00
General Overhead	44.82	32.59	30.21	65.62	11.05	12.97	9.26	15.00	20.00	30.00
Net Profit/Acre	-262.89	89.67	308.34	-85.19	131.44	-26.04	177.05	275.00	1095.00	1330.00

*Cut and baled, as a hay crop.

As indicated, most conventional crops are marginal, at best. Alternative crops such as catnip and peppermint leaf show strong net yields to the small farmer. (Based, in part, on *Extension Bulletin 0776: 1980 Crop Budgets for Northwest Washington*).

5

sion. Net farm income for 1983 was estimated to be $15 billion (without payment in kind. PIK, and 1984 was only at the level of 1982, which was down 24% from a year earlier. The causes are large supplies of traditional agricultural commodities (surpluses of wheat, dairy, corn, etc.), combined with weak demand, resulting in declining prices to the farmer. According to *Acres U.S.A.*, a cheap food policy also figures in the parity equation. The problem is compounded by the fact that production expenses have continued to increase. This has narrowed the gap between production costs and prices received for most traditional crops.

A growing number of diverse studies and farm management budgets for the North American Continent indicates that current agricultural products such as apples, timber, and grains hold no real future potential in marketing or net yields per acre, especially for the small farmer. For example, total meat and poultry consumption declined from 207.6 pounds per person in 1981 to 196.9 pounds in 1982. Farm prices will likely continue to be depressed. Table 3 provides a summary of these trends, showing receipts, costs, and profitability per acre for a number of traditional crops with comparison to two herb crops. Although this list is not complete, it is representative of information available, and organized to reveal critical set-up costs and show why some of these crops are no longer feasible for the small farmer.

The variable costs include fuel, oil, repairs, fertilizers, chemicals, custom work, and labor. Fixed costs include machinery depreciation, interest and insurance. Preharvest and harvest costs are variable, whereas machinery and general overhead are considered fixed costs. These figures indicate the vast advantages the small farmer has access to when he considers alternative crops which have special market niches or limited markets. The potential of herbs and spices as cash crops for the small farmer can be found in numerous studies, but the best bet is to begin conducting your own study by contacting some of the specific agencies listed in Appendix A.

THE CASE FOR HERBS AND SPICES

Recent government and private studies indicate that alternative crops, such as herbs and spices, are quite feasible for the small farm. All see herbs and spices as alternative cash crops and a way to stabilize small farm ventures. The small farmer is not competing with corporate ventures which dominate production in most conventional crops. Some are also seen as a way to provide rural development and create jobs for economically depressed via *cottage industries,* which further process herbs and spices.

With smaller markets than conventional crops, herbs and spices are a natural candidate for the small farm. Ranging from tropical Hawaii to arctic Alaska, North America can grow any herb or spice now grown elsewhere in the world. Hundreds of herbal products are imported into the United States.

Almost all could be exported now that development of new farm machinery and techniques make this possible.

There are many plants, found all over the world, which have medicinal properties. Local cultures have always used these plants in treating almost any physical or mental problem. Many of them, in fact, are the original sources of numerous synthetic drugs used by modern medicine. An example is foxglove, the source for digitalis used in treating certain forms of heart disease. With the current trend toward more natural foods and the increasing costs of medical care, the use of these natural plant substances has shown a marked increase.

Many of the medicinal herbs are native North American wild plants, the use of which were known to the native American peoples for thousands of years. Known as noxious weeds in most cases, these tough, indigenous plants can be grown much more easily in North American than many of the countries which now export them into North America. These imports from Europe and the Mediterranean are usually hardy, drought resistant plants which can be grown under severe conditions.

In fact, periods of drought and poorer soils often stimulate herbs to seek further for nutrients, and in the end produce a more potent product. They may be grown in many varied habitats. There are many which thrive on arid conditions and far too poor soil conditions. These include horehound, Mormon tea, kinnikinnick, American pennyroyal, and yarrow.

Other herbs require only a short period of moisture in the spring, such as mullein and other fast growing annuals and biennials. There are some which prefer rich soil and continuous moisture, such as comfrey, spearmint, peppermint, and devil's club root (a ginseng). The latter are best grown under irrigation. The variations and a wide range of tolerance for soil conditions means that there is some herb suited to almost any piece of ground.

Most herbs are perennials, which makes the initial planting more difficult. but from then on, there is no need to work the ground and plant each year. This saves on labor and machinery costs, and also presents fewer erosion problems and serves to lessen depletion of the soil. Herbs with long taproots will bring up nutrients from below the range of many crops. Thickly planted strands of perennials also provide much of their own weed control after they are well established.

Herbs from all areas are usually closer to a wild state and much more resistant to insects and diseases than the highly bred, traditional, western farm crops. There are numerous herbs such as marigold and garlic which are recommended as border plantings specifically to discourage insects. Others, such as wormwood, plantain, and citronella, are the sources of some commercial insect repellents.

There are reasons, of course, why all the big farmers are not yet growing herbs. First of all, despite long and continued usage as foods, condiments or medicines, almost no herbs have been grown commercially in North America.

As a consequence there is no tradition for such production in the agricultural community for the last 40 years or more. Before that time, almost all herbs used in medicines were collected in the wild (see Chapter 11, which covers foraging). That means that as a cash crop, herbs are unknowns, and farmers prefer to grow crops they are familiar with or can obtain good information on.

Most perennial herbs require two years to reach full production, and there is not the large, long established marketing machinery to guarantee the future market as there is with such familiar perennial crops as fruit, berries, asparagus, and so on. Because of these uncertainties, normal financing is unavailable. The growth of the market has been so recent that there has not been enough time to accumulate the kinds of data required by banks and agribusiness corporations.

Herbs are also frequently unsuited to modern, machine farming techniques. Propagation and planting varies considerably between species but almost always requires hand labor. Chemical fertilizers, herbicides, and insecticides do not produce good results and most cannot be used on a product consumed for medicinal purposes. This means that weeding must usually be done by hand. Harvesting and processing also requires much hand labor. Altogether, these disadvantages have prevented the modern North American farmer from reacting to this new market.

ECONOMIC OUTLOOK FOR HERBS AND SPICES

The USDA Foreign Agricultural Service has published data to indicate that the United States now imports more than ten times the spices and botanicals that they export (USDA Foreign Agricultural Service circulars on tea, spices, and essential oils, FTEA 1, 2, 3-84, April-May, 1984). For example, the United States imports of specific condiments, seasonings, and flavoring materials in 1983 were a record 174,843 tons valued at $229.4 million. United States exports in 1983, on the other hand, totaled 9,987 tons valued at $21.3 million. Why are we importing with such large figures when our economy needs to export? Table 4 contains some specific figures for perspective.

The primary reason is that most spices and botanicals require special dehydration to control the quality of the volatile oils. An example is sage, a major spice used in the meat packing industry. While several firms in California attempted to hand-dry this crop, the United States imported 1,512.7 metric tons at a total value of $3,223,100! The only method for processing this crop in North American now is as an oil by distillation.

The market is large and growing. Accurate figures are difficult to obtain, but there are thousands of tons of herbs used annually in North America. some large chain stores have called herbs "the fastest growing commodity in history." New herb companies, established for less than ten years, are in the several million dollar category, and thousands of retail outlets are thriving. Herb

TABLE 4
United States Imports of Specific Condiments, Seasonings, and Flavoring Materials for 1983

COMMON NAME	IMPORTS METRIC TONS	TOTAL VALUE $1,000	AVERAGE PRICE DOLLARS/POUND
Allspice	755.9	1,600.4	1.40
Anise Seed	652.5	1,156.3	1.10
Basil	1,154.3	1,536.5	1.05
Capsicum	847.9	705.4	0.77
Caraway Seed	3,339.3	3,522.1	0.71
Cardamom Seed	87.1	598.2	12.50
Cassia	8,863.9	8,302.3	0.56
Celery Seed	2,311.2	1,778.0	0.65
Cinnamon	952.5	1,711.0	0.85
Clove	663.6	5,622.1	3.90
Coriander	4,183.6	1,721.5	0.38
Cumin Seed	3,192.7	4,837.5	0.80
Curry	391.7	1,306.1	1.30
Dill Seed	597.6	533.1	0.42
Fennel Seed	1,742.0	2,130.4	0.70
Garlic	382.7	571.4	0.87
Ginger	3,560.5	3,664.1	1.60
Laurel (Bay)	437.1	497.8	0.50
Mace	276.9	1,001.2	3.05
Marjoram	322.7	649.2	1.65
Mint Leaves	134.0	379.1	2.50
Mustard Seed	31,930.6	10,599.9	0.42
Nutmegs	2,061.5	2,954.5	0.78
Onion	14.5	26.0	0.76
Origanum Leaves	3,593.1	6,198.3	0.86
Paprika	5,040.1	7,444.1	0.95
Parsley	313.6	264.7	1.95
Pepper, black	28,346.1	29,296.9	0.90
Pepper, white	3,129.5	4,514.8	1.50
Poppy Seed	3,100.8	4,312.1	0.75
Rosemary	466.4	272.7	0.40
Sage	1,512.7	3,223.1	1.60
Savory	96.4	69.8	0.60
Sesame Seed	42,789.4	39,962.8	0.60
Tarragon	46.4	278.1	9.00
Thyme	893.7	1,297.1	1.10
Tumeric	1,600.1	1,368.6	1.15
Vanilla Beans	977.4	50,811.6	30.00
Mixed Spices	1,338.3	3,270.3	0.80

From USDA Foreign Agricultural Service circular FTEA 1-84 "Spices," April 1984.

teas are carried by most grocery chains, and there is a large national mail order business as well.

Despite this obvious growth, almost all herbs are imported. Many come from Mexico and South America, but others arrive from as far away as Rumania, Yugoslavia and Poland. Much of the peppermint and spearmint comes from Egypt, whereas orange peel is imported from Haiti and Spain. As shipping costs go up and demand increases, prices also increase. Many herbs bring prices that are far higher than could be expected from the cost of producing them. Prices, in general, range from $600 to $2,000 per ton. One to three tons per acre is the average harvest. This kind of return rivals that of the most lucrative farm crops; yet, once established, herbs will continuously produce this high return with lower continuing cash requirements. The primary investment is labor.

Proximity to the market is also less important than with other commodities. Partly, this is true because once they are dried, herbs are relatively easy and lightweight to store and transport. Also, these higher prices make it feasible to ship over long distances. A 10 ton load of herbs is often worth $10,000, whereas a similar load of wheat is generally worth $2,000 or less.

If present trends continue, the herb market should continue to grow for many years. Herbs should have greater potential as cash crops in areas that are not suited to the more familiar farm crops. Areas with limited water and poorer soils can produce as much income per acre with herbs as the most fertile areas with abundant water producing traditional farm crops. In addition, the investment requirements are lower when growing herbs. The primary investment is labor. Machinery costs are less and chemical costs are almost nonexistent in her production. As an ecologically balanced crop, herb production is worth consideration.

A couple of years ago, the *Chemical Marketing Reporter* ran an informative article, *Herb and Spice Growers in U.S. Face Pressures Generated by Land Boom*. According to this report, the United States herb market relies on domestic production for less than 35% of its needs. Three growers produce nearly all the dried herbs from California, which reported more than 1,000,000 pounds dried herb produced as recently as 1978. Among others, these growers produced basil, chervil, coriander, dill, marjoram, oregano, parsley, rosemary, sage, savory, tarragon, and thyme, all of which grow satisfactorily on small farms. Nearly all are aromatic intercrops.

Prices in 1979 were approximately $1,000 per ton for basil, $400 per ton for coriander, $700 per ton for dill seed, $1,000 per ton for marjoram, $2,000 per ton for oregano, $1,000 per ton for parsley, $700 per ton for rosemary, $2,500 per ton for sage, $2,000 per ton for savory, $5,000 per ton for tarragon, and $1,500 per ton for thyme. All of these can be grown by the small farmer, from California to New York, or any other place in the North American continent. The future lies in export, not import, where new money is brought into a community by local agriculture.

The following list of herbs and spices provide only a partial accounting of these crops with market futures (table 5). All can be grown with relative ease in North America and should be considered as excellent alternatives as cash crops for the small farmer. While exact figures on production and domestic

TABLE 5
Partial list of alternative crops (herbs and spices)
with good market potentials for the small farmer

CROP	YIELD/ ACRE (Est.)	NATIONAL USE (Est.)	FARM PRICE	WHOLESALE PRICE	RETAIL PRICE
HERBS					
Apple Mint Herb	2.8 Ton	200 Ton	$800/Ton	$1.20/#	$3.75/#
Catnip Herb	3.0	400	400	1.00	4.20
Chamomile Fl.	0.8	2000	800	1.55	4.45
Chicory Root	2.0	50	400	0.85	2.00
Comfrey Leaf	5.0	400	400	1.00	2.20
Comfrey Root	0.8	80	600	1.40	2.50
Dandelion Root	1.5	50	600	1.40	3.60
Golden Seal Root	0.5	200	2000	11.00	20.00
Lemon Balm Herb	3.0	200	400	1.20	3.70
Peppermint Leaf	0.8	2000	1200	0.80	2.95
Raspberry Leaf	2.0	400	800	0.52	2.15
Red Clover Fl.	0.8	50	1000	1.00	4.00
Spearmint Leaf	1.2	2000	800	0.65	2.20
Strawberry Leaf	1.0	80	600	0.65	2.15
SPICES					
Basil	2.0	150	1000	$1.14	$3.10
Cayenne	1.0	2000	1200	1.40	2.75
Dill Weed	1.5	6000	2000	3.21	5.45
Fennel Seed	1.0	2000	1000	0.86	2.25
Marjoram	2.0	500	600	0.82	2.20
Oregano	2.0	5000	800	1.10	2.05
Parsley	1.5	800	800	2.50	4.55
Rosemary	1.0	150	600	0.98	1.80
Sage	1.5	8000	900	1.20	2.80
Savory	1.5	100	800	1.70	3.90
Tarragon	1.5	600	2000	10.40	15.20
Thyme	1.0	150	900	1.64	2.40

The yields per acre and total national use are estimates based on information from the USDA trade magazines, especially *Chemical Marketing Reporter*, and the author's background in marketing as a regional wholesaler. The yields are for dehydrated product, not produce. There is some variance in prices, depending on the country of origin and the retail cut (see Chapter 7).

potentials are approximations (based only on the author's market knowledge), they are representative of the potentials available to the small farm.

SOME FINAL COMMENTS

Where will you get the know-how when faced with competition from the trained and experienced farmer? Unless you have planned your investment, and prepared your business and operating plan, you stand very little chance against the difficult odds facing you as a small farmer in traditional agriculture. Your only real chance for any kind of success lies primarily in alternative crops. That is what this book is about. It will tell you how to do it with herbs and spices.

You can make it. It is possible to be successful as a small farmer. You can make a decent living for yourself and your family on small acreage . . . if you work smart and work hard. Labor will be the biggest input. Work smart by not even attempting to compete with large agribusiness type crops. Look toward alternatives, like herbs and spices. The small farmer can compete with large farmers efficiently if he is able to take advantage of economies of scale deriving from common purchasing, processing, and even marketing. The heart of this success is the Grange concept, or the profit-sharing cooperative.

Finally, the small farmer can increase his income by on-farm processing of his crops. This can add value to his cash receipts of his crop and broaden his marketing perspectives. This book will explain ways to process herbs and spices on the farm through such things as milling (to interface with manufacturers) and the diverse forms of cottage industries, where such products as herbal salves and lip balms can be marketed directly from the home. When considered from this perspective, even smaller acreages can develop tremendous cash flows. This allows some farmers to consider leasing land rather than having to own it.

The future is quite exciting for the small farmer when he considers alternative agriculture. This book, then, may be considered a *first course* in small farm agriculture, specializing in herb and spice crops. It now lies with you to put these ideas into a viable framework for rural living and livelihood. If the book has been written correctly, it should raise more questions than it answers. It should also direct you toward those questions which must be considered before any venture is attempted.

CHAPTER 2

Some Fundamental
Soil Considerations

The goal ever recedes from us . . . Salvation lies in the effort, not in the attainment. Full effort is full victory.

Gandhi

Soil is the outermost portion of the earth's crust that supports the growth of plants. Soils range from blowing sand dunes to deep muds in river deltas. They include rocky glacial deposits which cover to the plains of the American midwest. Many lack sufficient plant nutrients to sustain agricultural crops, even with tillage.

Defined in simple physical terms, soil is a system consisting of solid, liquid and gaseous elements. The solid phase is a mixture of mineral and organic particles lying in intimate contact so as to provide the foundation for soil. The liquid phase is made up of water. Ideally half of the water is available for plant use, whereas the other half is held in the pore spaces of the soil. Like the atmosphere, the soil gas phase consists of nitrogen (N_2) and oxygen (O_2) in combination with lesser amounts of carbon dioxide (CO_2) and other gases. And there is the life factor in soil.

13

Five basic factors have been identified as responsible for the formation of soil.

1. The parent material which forms a soil tells a great deal about the properties of it. Parent material from which the soils are derived are classified as residual, transported or cumulose. Residual materials (bedrock) are rock deposits that weather in place to form soils. Transported soils are rocks and mineral fragments that have been transported by water, wind, ice or gravity. Soils found at the base of mountains or hills, sand dunes, glacial rock deposits, talus slopes and river deltas are all examples of transported parent material. Cumulose materials are peats and mucks that have developed in place from an accumulation of plant residues that have been preserved by a high water table.

2. Climate helps form soils by accounting for physical and chemical weathering. Physical weathering includes freezing and thawing, heating and cooling, wetting and drying grinding action of rock and soil particles against each other. It also includes winds which move soils (transportation). Chemical weathering is the result of solubility changes (usually by water) and include the processes of hydrolysis and carbonation. Structural changes are also brought about by hydration, oxidation and reduction.

3. The activity of plants, animals, microorganisms, and people have a marked influence on soil formation (biological factions). Burrowing animals such as moles, earthworms and insects are highly important because they exist in such large numbers. Some of the first plants to grow on weathering rocks are lichens, which improve the environment for higher forms of plant life and their subsequent root action on forming soils.

Plants contribute more to soil development and properties than any other biological factor. Through the absorption of water and nutrients and the release of carbon dioxide, roots of plants alter the composition of the soil solution and effect other components that tend to equilibrate with it. Because of the joint activity of plants with the multitude of other soil organisms, principally in the decay of plant residues, the soil is maintained in a highly dynamic state. Lastly, people help to make smaller rock fragments from larger, thus hastening the time required for normal soil formation.

4. Topography, or the lay of the land, is the principle factor in water flow. Steep slopes develop soils more slowly than level areas because of their inability to hold water and transport nutrients. Gently sloping hillsides generally have deeper soils, more luxuriant vegetation and higher organic matter content than steep slopes. Low lying areas receive large amounts of runoff from surrounding hills. If an area is wet at the surface for several months of the year, organic (peat or muck) soils may develop. If the accumulating waters dissolve salts from surrounding soils, the low lying areas may become salt marshes or form toxic salt conditions. However, valleys and other low lying areas are usually covered by deeper, more friable soils than these higher marshlands.

5. The length of time required for soil development is dependent upon the interaction of all the above soil forming factors. Time is continually altering

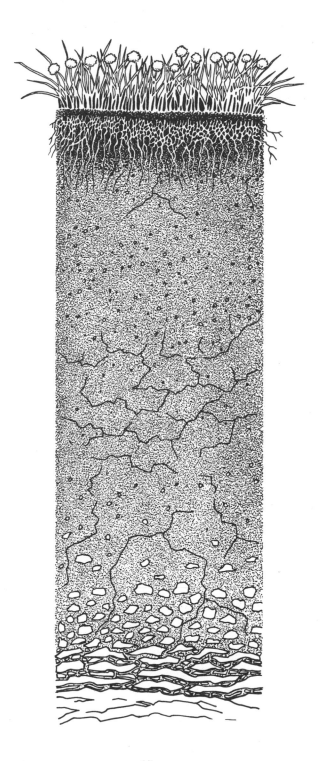

15

these factors through episodes of flooding, volcanic activity, severe wind or water erosion, excessive cold or heat, and drought. Under ideal conditions, a soil to the depth of 6 to 9 inches will develop in 200 years. Under less favorable circumstances (cold, windswept, hot conditions), this process may require several thousand years.

Although soils in general have a number of features in common, various soil types differ markedly. Basic differences relate to the composition of the mineral and organic fractions of the soil body, and to the proportions and arrangement of these components in the profile. For the most part, the diverse nature of soils arise from the wide range of environmental conditions under which they develop.

SOIL HORIZONS AND PARENT MATERIAL

A vertical section (profile) of soil typically exhibits several natural layers known as horizons. These horizons can be distinguished by color, texture, structure, and differences in chemical composition. Soil formation processes are responsible for these soil horizons. Dark, humic material commonly accumulate in the topsoil (A horizon), whereas native materials, iron oxides and humus are washed in small amounts into the B horizon. These have resulted primarily from the native soil forming elements derived from the C horizon.

The C horizon is a loose aggregation of the parent mineral material. This parent material derives from three different kinds of rock, formed respectively by igneous, sedimentary or metamorphic processes. Of these three, igneous rocks are the most abundant, although they do not dominate the surface fraction of soils. Igneous rocks are derived from the cooling of a hot molten mass of rock material called magma. This mass crystallizes into combinations of various types of rock on cooling. This primary material is distinguished from secondary materials derived from metamorphism, or circulating solutions, which serve to alter the pre-existing minerals.

Igneous rocks include granites, gabbros, basalts and other rocks that have metamorphosed. Soils formed from granites contain a full range of particle sizes, some the size of gravel and sand, some as small as particle sizes in the finest clays. Because of its coarse texture and high content of resistant minerals, including quartz, granite is slow to weather. Quartz rocks weather to become the gritty sand found in soils formed from granites. Granite formations supply most of the sand in later generations of sedimentary sandstones and shales.

Sedimentary rocks are formed from mineral and organic fragments derived from rocks which have been deposited by ice, water, or air on the bottoms and shores of ancient fresh or salt water seas. Sand is deposited near the shores, gray mud further out, and limey white mud far from the shoreline. These layers finally surface as dry land when there is geological uplift.

Soils formed from a sandstone parent are sandy, whereas those from shale are clayey. Soils derived from limestone deposits consist largely of insoluble shale materials that were included as gray mud in an otherwise soluble rock mass. They are most commonly clayey.

Metamorphic rocks result from recrystallization of minerals at considerable depths in the earth's crust under conditions of high pressure and temperature. Metamorphic change, whether of igneous or sedimentary origin, fundamentally is a recrystallization of the material. No melting takes place. Essentially no change in the overall composition of the rock occurs. New and different rock forms are produced, but no new elements are introduced into or removed from the rock. The elements which are present are just rearranged into new and different minerals.

SOIL TEXTURE

When speaking of soil, most farmers are referring to the uppermost part of the soil, the topsoil or A horizon. Other layers are also important, but this is where most of the action takes place when growing crops. The B horizon is rich in minerals, continually supplying mineral nutrients to plants growing in the topsoil. Topsoil is an exhaustible resource, being continually worn away by erosive agents such as wind and water. To offset this natural erosion, new soil is continually being added from decomposition of the parent rock material and plant and animal residues. Healthy soil is not inert. Bacteria and fungi teem in good topsoil as they convert the various wastes into usable nutrients for other plants.

The farmer's conduit to understanding soil conditions is called *texture*. Texture means the relative coarseness or fineness of the soil. This is determined primarily by the amounts and sizes of sand, silt and clay particles. While there are diverse categories for texture, the three basic forms used by most farmers are sandy, silty or clayey soils. It is important to remember that few soils are composed of only one soil separate (i.e., sand, silt or clay). Most soils are composed of a combination of various soil separates such as sandy clay loam, silty clay loam, sandy clay, clay loam, etc. Most farmers use "fingertip" feel in determining the nature of soil.

Loam soils are the most difficult to identify by the fingertip method since characteristics of sand, silt and clay are all present, but none predominates. Silty soils form clods which are moderately difficult to break and which rupture suddenly to a floury powder that clings to your fingers. Silt has a smooth, slick, buttery feel when moist. When wet it may have some stickiness from clay particles. Compared to sand, silt produces relatively small pores. Like sand, it contributes little to stable aggregate formations in soils.

Sandy soils are loose and single grained, or gritty. Sand grains do not adhere to each other when wet and individual grains can be seen and felt under all moisture conditions. These soils present the practical problem of keeping what water is available from rainfall and irrigation on the land. Sandy soil requires a farm plan which includes terracing or even contouring to trap and conserve moisture.

Clay, on the other hand, is quite sticky when wet, and has the finest particle sizes. Clay soils form clods that, when dry, often cannot be broken down even with extreme pressure. Clay particles are so small that they are visible only under the electron microscope. Clay is both sticky and plastic when wet. Because of this water retentiveness, they are difficult to work in the early spring. If plowed or worked too early, they mold and then dry to unworkable clods. Clay soils also warm up less rapidly than coarser ones, playing a critical role in seed bed preparations, especially in areas with a short growing season. Clay soils are very slow to wet when water is applied to dry soil. Irrigation must be applied slowly to prevent surface crusting of the soil, which further slows water infiltration.

There are always exceptions to these rules. The degree in which clay soils warm, form unworkable clods, or have slow water infiltration varies among different kinds of clays. Very black clay soils, although fine and possessed of high water capacities, can absorb more heat from the sun than lighter colored ones. Although black soils with a high humus content absorb more heat, they also frequently hold more water. The retained water requires a relatively larger amount of heat to raise its temperature and also to evaporate the water. The net result is that many dark soils are *not* warmer than adjacent lighter colored soils, because of the temperature modifying effects or soil moisture. In fact, they may be cooler except for the first inch or so at the *dry* surface. The critical minimum temperatures for growth of most cash crops is somewhere between 42 to 55 F. The chief factor determining temperature in a soil system is its water retention capacity.

SOIL COLOR

Soil color indicates many soil features. Organic (or humus) material usually imparts the dark, rich brown color associated with fertile soils. Varying shades of red and yellow indicate iron. Red indicates that the iron is oxidized and not hydrated with water. Yellow indicates hydration and less oxidation. White colors are common when salts or carbonates (lime) exist in the soil. Spots of different color (mottles), usually rust colored, indicate a soil experiencing periods of inadequate aeration through the year.

Bluish, grayish, and greenish subsoils (gleying), with or without mottles, indicate longer periods of waterlogged conditions and inadequate aeration. Change in soil color relative to adjacent soils indicates a difference in parent material. Within small regions, color broadly indicates organic matter content differences, darker colors denoting more organic matter. However, between contrasting climatic conditions, color is not a good indicator of organic content.

18

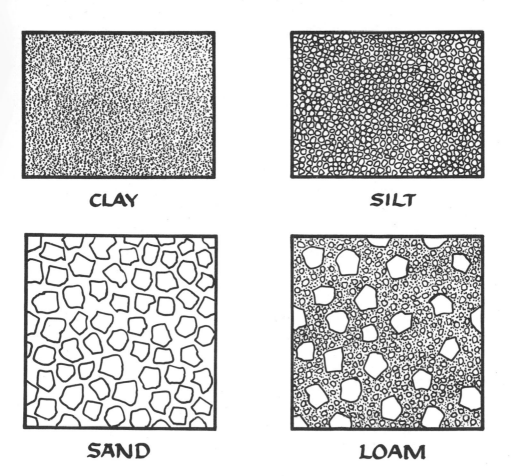

CLAY

SILT

SAND

LOAM

RELATIVE SIZES OF SOIL PARTICLES

PEAT AND MUCK SOILS

Organic (peat and muck) soils comprise .9% of the world's land surface and .5% of the land area of North America. The management of these soils for crop production is quite specialized. Almost all organic soils must be drained to lower the water table, but the depth of the water table must be controlled to minimize subsidence (sinking of the land due to rapid decomposition of the organic matter once drained), and the hazard of fire and wind erosion. Most organic soils are deficient in calcium and must be limed to pH 5.5 to 6.2, depending on the crop. Organic soils are sometimes low in available nitrogen, potassium, phosphorus and micronutrients, and must be corrected with an appropriate fertilization program.

19

HARDPANS

Many soils have dense layers called pans. These interfere with root and water penetration, thereby reducing the effective soil volume from which plants can absorb nutrients, water and air. Naturally occurring pans in North America are generally caused by clay accumulations or by precipitated silica alone or in combination with precipitated iron oxides or calcium carbonate. Plowpans are artificially produced and are widespread in agricultural soils. They are caused by soil compaction due to the weight of plows or cultivation implements just below the level to which the plow penetrates. It is necessary to break up pans by subsoil chiseling below the pan.

SOIL POROSITY

Pore space in a soil is that portion of the soil volume occupied by air or water. Soil particles have irregular shapes and thus leave the pores between the soil particles, which vary and are irregular in shape, size and direction. The relative amounts of air and water in pores fluctuate continually. During a rain, water drives air from the pores. As soil water leaves the pore spaces due to downward percolation, evaporation and transpiration by plants, air replaces the water.

Sands have large and continuous pores which transmit water rapidly. Although clays have more total pore space, they move water slowly unless the soil profile is well aggregated. In a strongly aggregated soil, the aggregates act like sand grains and pack to form many large pores. Well aggregated soils promote water circulation. A soil without structure or aggregation has a very slow water infiltration and permeability rate.

Water moves primarily through a soil by flowing through soil pores in response to gravity. Water generally moves vertically down through the soil, not laterally. Soil pores vary in size from microscopic to visible to the naked eye. The finer the pore, the greater the adhesive force of the walls, and the higher the water will rise from a water table due to the phenomenon of capillary action.

Water movement in fine pores (clay soils, silty clay soils) is very slow due to the size of the pore. With larger pores the water is able to move more quickly, but to a lesser height above a water table through capillary movement. So sandy soils will move water downward, but not upward by capillary action, whereas clay soils move water downward slowly and move water slower through the water table by capillary action.

PLANT NUTRITION

My first teacher in agriculture once said, "There's no such thing as organic farming. All plants live off *inorganic* salts." This view still prevails in land grant colleges, although it is being challenged by many scientists. Still, the physical chemistry of soil is as important as soil structure in any farming venture. A working knowledge of soil chemistry in relation to plant nutrition is fundamental when making plans for the use of land.

Soil is the natural medium in which the roots of most plants grow. Plants absorb both water and food solutes necessary for their well being from the soil. If a soil is fertile, it contains all the chemical elements essential for plant growth, and is alive with microbial action. It is through soil nutrients that the farmer can alter the environment for plant roots and control plant growth (at least partially). The time and kind of fertilizer or soil amendment used, as well as cultivation and irrigation practices, are all directed toward increasing the production of plant products.

ORGANIC MATTER AND SOIL AMENDMENTS

The source of soil organic matter is primarily plant tissue with some contribution from dead animals. Inorganic elements contained in the plant and animal tissue are transformed from plant-unavailable-organic-form to plant-available-inorganic-forms by the action of soil microorganisms. The principle reason for adding organic residues to the soil are —
1. To modify the tilth or friability of the soil, that is, to make it more workable.
2. To add plant nutrients.
3. And to modify the microbial population by providing a mass of energy material for the use of microorganisms.

The amount of organic matter needed to modify the content of a soil is great. To increase the organic matter of a normal sandy-loam soil by 1% requires about 40,000 pounds or 30 to 40 cubic yards of peat material. Humus is the relatively stable fraction of the soil organic matter remaining after the major portion of plant and animal material has decomposed. The addition of organic material to the soil will not result in a permanent increase in soil organic matter. Considering amendments as a whole, their longevity in the soil depends primarily upon aeration, moisture content, temperature and available nutrients. The rate of decomposition is reduced when aeration is limited, under low or excessive moisture conditions, with low temperatures, and when nutrients — primarily nitrogen — are limited.

Rapid decomposition, for several days to several weeks, occurs when grass clippings, manures, or mushroom compost are used as amendments. Leaf molds and humus type composts will last up to six months or more. Rice hulls, redwood bark, fir bark, cedar and cypress may last up to several years. The best approach to using soil amendments is to systematically add as much organic matter yearly as can be conveniently handled (in terms of equipment available), and to continue adding until the soil has acquired the desired characteristics.

When incorporating amendments and organic matter, a uniform soil amendment mixture must be provided throughout the entire root zone. Poor mixing of materials will produce layers or pockets causing problems with air, water, fertilizer and root movement through the soil. Roto-tillers, turning cultivators, discs and harrows are often used for mixing, although discs tend to leave pockets when turning corners, and high speed tillers may separate soil particles into a fine powder.

A common misconception is that all organic matter is good and more is better. Certain kinds of organic matter, such as corn stalks, grain straw and redwood bark are so high in carbon and low in nitrogen that soil bacteria actually multiply in numbers and consume soil nitrogen that otherwise would be available for normal plant growth. Addition of such amendments tends to create a nitrogen deficit.

Organic materials suitable for composting and use as soil amendments include —

1. Rapidly decomposing tree leaves, such as elm, ash, basswood, maple, hickory, alder, apple, peach, cherry, sassafras and sycamore.
2. Grass and legume clippings and sod.
3. Animal manures (except green horse manure).
4. Disease and insect free garden refuse.
5. Table scraps (except meat and bones that may attract rodents and other wild animals).
6. Sewage sludge.
7. And, of course, municipal solid wastes.

Inferior compost or organic materials include —

1. Slowly decomposting leaves and needles from oak, pine and other conifers.
2. Grasses containing viable seed such as annual bluegrass, quackgrass and Bermudagrass.
3. And all paper and wood products except weathered, rotted sawdust.

The primary use of wood byproducts such as sawdust, wood chips, barks and wood fiber is as a surface mulch to conserve soil moisture or when incorporated into the soil, acts to enhance water and oxygen diffusion rates in a right soil. Some fresh wood products, such as red cedar, oak, black walnut and ash sawdust, are toxic to certain plants and should be avoided. Peats, moss peat, and sphagnum peat have not been discussed, although they are used widely in turfgrass, landscape and nursery operations. They are not practical in large scale production agricultural ventures because of the expense, difficulty in mixing into soils, and difficulty in wetting once they have dried.

All organic amendments conserve soil and water. Organic matter on or near the surface increases soil aggregation, reduces the erosive impact of falling rain, increases water infiltration, reduces water runoff, and impedes formation of surface crusts (that slow water infiltration and seed germination) and severe tillage pans (the hard soil layers formed by compaction).

GREEN MANURE CROPS

A green manure crop is grown to be turned under for soil improvement while in a succulent condition. Green manures are used primarily to increase the yield of subsequent crops, as well as to improve the friability of the soil. These effects are the result of —

1. An increase in the organic matter in the soil to balance the losses of organic matter through cultivation.
2. Prevention of leaching of plant nutrients from the soil during periods between regular crops.
3. An increase in the supply of nitrogen in the soil when leguminous plants are turned under.
4. And mobilizing mineral elements.

Turning under a legume as a green manure may be expected to add from 50 to 200 pounds per acre of nitrogen. When either type of green manure increases crop yields, it also hastens depletion of phosphorus, potash, calcium, magnesium and sulfur in the soil. A non-legume also speeds up nitrogen depletion.

The most important green manure crops in this country are vetch, rye, crimson clover, lupines, sweetclover and alfalfa. The green manure must be decomposed before its nutrients become available for plant growth or the organic residues become a part of the soil humus. Young plants and substances high in nitrogen decompose rapidly. As decomposition progresses, it becomes slower because of the comparatively greater resistance of the residual organic matter to decay. Postponement of turning under fall cover crops until spring delays decomposition, conserves moisture and retards leaching, runoff and erosion, but it also sets up competition between the microbe's requirement for food and the plant's need of nutrients.

CROP ROTATION

Loss of organic matter as a result of continuous growth of the same crop has an adverse effect on soil tilth. Growing grasses, pasture, and deep rooted legumes in rotation tends to correct this condition through maintenance of organic matter. The alternation of deep and shallow rooted crops prevents continuous absorption of plant nutrients from the same root zone year after year. In addition, deep rooted plants like alfalfa improve the physical condition of the subsoil when their underground parts decay.

The nitrogen requirements of non-legume crops may be provided by legumes in the rotation scheme, but rotations cannot supply other plant nutrients in which the soil may be deficient. The production of larger crops, made possible by rotation, depletes the soil more rapidly than does continuous cropping. These larger yields cannot continue indefinitely without application of manures and fertilizers.

23

Legumes are more efficient in fixation of nitrogen on soils with low rather than high nitrogen content because they obtain nitrogen from the air only to the extent that the supply in the soil is insufficient. A legume will be more effective as a nitrogen gatherer when two or more crops come between applications of barnyard manures. It is wise to grow legume crops previous to crops that require large amounts of nitrogen.

SOIL pH AND LIMING

A soil's pH is a measure of the relative acidity-alkalinity on a logarithmic scale from 0 to 14. The value 7 is considered neutral, above 7 is alkaline (or sweet), and below 7 is acidic (or sour). Each consecutive number represents *ten times* the value of the preceding number, as they decrease. For example, pH 6 is ten times more acidic than pH 7, pH 5 is 100 times more acidic than pH 7. Soil acidity increases with the leaching of calcium, magnesium, and potassium into the subsoil, and the removal of these nutrients by growing crops. As these elements are removed from the soil particles, they are replaced with acid-forming hydrogen and aluminum ions. Most common nitrogen fertilizers contribute to soil acidity, since their reaction in the soil increase the concentration of hydrogen ions in the soil solution.

Increasing soil fertility is not a matter of simply adding the appropriate nutrient salts. Often the various elements can be found in abundance in the soil, but not in a form which plants can use. The soil pH is important to plant growth for several reasons:

1. Its effect on nutrient availability.
2. Its effect on the solubility of toxic substances (such as aluminum).
3. Its effect on soil microorganisms.
4. And the direct effect of pH on root cells, which affect the uptake of nutrients and water.

A pH level of approximately 6.5 makes a maximum of the nutrients nitrogen, phosphorus, sulphur, calcium and magnesium available. In excessively acidic soils (below pH 5.5), iron, manganese, boron, copper and zinc become more available to plants, whereas the nutrients most available between pH 6.5 and pH 7.5 are reduced. At a pH above 8.0, nitrogen, calcium, and magnesium all decrease in plant availability, whereas molybdenum and boron both increase in availability.

To moderate acid soil conditions, farmers often spread calcium carbonate (limestone) onto the soil. Previously regarded as only a fertilizer, it now is seen as an excellent soil conditioner. Calcium carbonate in the soil acts as a buffer against acid formation, which means that it tends to restrict the development of acidic soils. This occurs due to the increased solubility of calcium carbonate as the acidity increases, which increases the exchangeable calcium in the soil and removes hydrogen ions, which combine with oxygen from the carbonate to form water. Carbon dioxide is released in the process.

24

ESSENTIAL PLANT NUTRIENTS

Eighteen elements are generally considered to be essential to plant growth. Three of the essential elements, carbon, hydrogen and oxygen, are taken primarily from the air and water. The other elements are normally absorbed from the soil by plant roots. None of these elements is any more essential than the others, regardless of the amounts required for plant growth. If any one of these elements is lacking in a soil, plants will not prosper, according to the law of the minimum.

PRIMARY MACRONUTRIENT ELEMENTS

Carbon, hydrogen and oxygen. Carbon forms the skeleton for the trillions of organic molecules found in a plant. Carbon is taken from the atmosphere by plants in the form of carbon dioxide and through the process of photosynthesis is combined with hydrogen and oxygen in water molecules to form carbohydrates. Simple fats are composed of these three elements, whereas proteins contain appreciable amounts of other elements, particularly nitrogen — and to a lesser extent — sulfur and phosphorus.

Oxygen is required for respiration in plant cells whereby energy is derived from the breakdown of carbohydrates. Hydrogen and oxygen form water, which constitutes a large portion of the total weight of plants. Water enters into many chemical reactions necessary for plant growth. Because carbon, hydrogen and oxygen are supplied to plants primarily from air and water, the concern over their supply is somewhat different from that of the other essential elements.

Nitrogen. Ordinary green plants cannot utilize elemental nitrogen, which represents about 78% of the atmosphere. It has been estimated that above every acre of land surface there are about 145,000 to 150,000 tons of this gas. Most of the nitrogen in soils is also unavailable to growing plants because it is tied up in organic matter. Only about 2% of this nitrogen is made available to crops each year. In soils with a proper pH and organic matter complex, the release can be sufficient for most farm crops.

Nitrogen is a component of proteins (an essential part of protoplasm) and also occurs as stored foods in plant cells. It is also a part of chlorophyll, amino acids, alkaloids and some plant hormone molecules. Many soils release around 50 to 60 pounds of nitrogen per acre each season into the air. Clay soils, however, having only 1% organic matter may release as little as 15 pounds; conversely, clay soils with 4% organic matter or sandy soils with around 2% organic matter may release more than 100 pounds of nitrogen.

Many reactions involving nitrogen occur in the soil through the action of microorganisms. Nitrogen is made available to crops from organic matter through two of these reactions, known collectively as mineralization. Mineralized plant nutrients are byproducts of microbial metabolism. Anything that affects the microbial action will also affect mineralization. Among the important factors are water, oxygen, pH, and temperature. The optimum moisture content for maximum nitrification (conversion of ammonia to nitrates) is about 60% of the water-holding capacity of the soil.

Nitrogenous fertilizers, both natural and commercial, are usually the most important fertilizers applied to growing plants. Nitrogen is a mobile element in the plant and can be translocated from mature to immature regions of the plant. An early sign of nitrogen deficiency is a yellowing of leaves, particularly the older leaves; then follows a stunting in the growth of all parts of the plant. A chlorosis (yellow-green color) and "firing" of the tips and margins of the older leaves are early indications of nitrogen deficiency. By way of contrast, an excess of available nitrogen results in vigorous vegetative growth with a suppression of food storage of of fruit and seed development. Many nitrogen fertilizers are available, some — such as calcium nitrate — buffer the acidic effects of nitrogen fertilizers.

Phosphorus. Phosphorus is used in parts of the plant that are growing rapidly, such as meristematic regions and maturing fruits and seeds. Application of phosphorus to soils deficient in the element promotes root growth, hastens maturity and promotes seed production. Phosphorus supplementation is required by most plants under the following circumstances:
1. Growth in cold weather.
2. Limited root growth.
3. And fast top growth.

Phosphorus that is adequately available to the growing plant —
1. Stimulates root formation and growth.
2. Hastens maturity.
3. Aids in cell division and reproduction.
4. Encourages flower development, pollination, and seed formation.
5. Increases legume growth.
6. Increases protein and mineral content in grasses and legumes.
7. Makes plants winter hardy.
8. Increases the percentage of phosphorus and calcium in foods.
9. And aids in legume nodule formation.

Symptoms of phosphorus deficiency in plants include —
1. Slow growth and stunted plants.
2. Purplish coloration of foliage of some plants.
3. Dark green coloration with tips of leaves dying.
4. Delayed maturity.
5. And poor grain, fruit or seed development.

Plants absorb phosphorus largely as orthophosphate ions. The concentration of these ions in the soil solution at any one time is small, making maintenance of this low concentration element of paramount importance to the growth of crops. Soil pH is one of the factors affecting phosphorus utilization which the farmer can easily alter. In most soils phosphorus is at a maximum in

26

the pH range of 5.5 to 7.0, decreasing as the pH drops 5.5 or goes above 7.0. Placement of phosphorus fertilizer is very important. Placing the fertilizer in bands is best accomplished with water soluble fertilizers such as superphosphates. Water insoluble fertilizers, such as rock phosphates are utilized best when mixed with the soil rather than when applied in bands. It is also important to realize that rock phosphates act as slow release fertilizers and will not supply adequate phosphorus for any short season row crop.

Potassium. The primary role of potassium in the cell is that of an enzyme activator. Processes in the plant that appear to require an adequate supply of potassium are —

1. Cell division.
2. Synthesis and translocation of carbohydrates.
3. Synthesis of proteins in meristematic cells.
4. Reduction of nitrates.
5. Development of chlorophyll.
6. And stomatal opening and closing.

Potassium deficiencies greatly reduce crop yields. In fact, serious yield reductions may result without the appearance of deficiency symptoms due to a phenomenon termed *hidden hunger.* Symptoms of potassium deficiency in plants include —

1. Tip and marginal burn, starting on mature leaves as the mobile K + ion is translocated to younger leaves.
2. Weak stalks, plants lodge easily.
3. Small fruit or shriveled seeds.
4. And slow growth.

Potassium deficiency is associated with decreased resistance to certain plant diseases, including powdery mildew in spearmint and root-borer moth damage in peppermint. Root rot and winter kill of catnip are greater with an inadequate potassium supply.

Any water soluble inorganic compound of potassium, such as K-sulfate, K-phosphate, or K-nitrate can be utilized by plants as a source of potassium. Rock forms are slower acting and dependent on the right pH range.

SECONDARY MACRONUTRIENT ELEMENTS

Calcium. Calcium, absorbed by plants as the Ca + + ion is one of the constituents of the middle lamella of the cell walls of plants. Adequate calcium influences plant growth in the following ways —

1. Promotes early root growth.
2. Improves general plant vigor and growth.
3. Increases grain and seed production.
4. Increases stiffness of the straw in grains.
5. Maintains strength and selective permeability of cell walls.
6. Neutralizes oxalic acids produced in plants.

27

7. Increases calcium content of the plant product.
8. Encourages nodule formation in legumes.
9. And regulates the intake of other elements such as phosphorus.

A deficiency of calcium manifests itself —
1. In the failure of the terminal buds of plants and the apical tips of roots to develop.
2. Abnormal dark green appearance of foliage.
3. Premature shedding of blossoms and buds.
4. And weakened stems.

Fertilizer sources for Ca are the same as for P, such as rock phosphate and superphosphate. Other sources include calcium nitrate, gypsum and ammonium nitrate-lime mixtures. Fertilizers are not manufactured as such simply to supply calcium. This element is more economically supplied through periodic applications of agricultural lime with special attention to its calcium and magnesium content.

Magnesium. Magnesium is absorbed in the form of the $Mg++$ ion. It is present in the chlorophyll molecule and therefore is essential for photosynthesis. It also serves as an activator for many plant enzymes required in the growth process. Magnesium is mobile within plants and can be readily translocated from older to younger tissue under conditions of deficiency. It is important in plant nutrition for —
1. Maintaining a dark green color in leaves, resulting in full photosynthetic ability.
2. Regulating uptake of other plant nutrients.
3. Acting as a phosphorus carrier in the plant.
4. Promoting the formation of oils and fats.
5. And it plays a role in the movement of starch in the plant.

Symptoms of magnesium deficiency include —
1. Interveinal chlorosis (yellowing) in older leaves.
2. Curling of leaves upward along leaf margins.
3. Marginal yellowing with a green Christmas tree pattern along the midrib of the leaf.

In more advanced stages of deficiency, leaf tissue becomes uniformly pale yellow, then brown and necrotic. In some species, the lower leaves may develop a reddish purple cast which gradually turns brown and finally necrotic. An important source of magnesium is dolomitic limestone, a material used to supply calcium and magnesium, as well as to correct soil acidity.

Sulfur. Sulfur is absorbed by plant roots almost exclusively as the sulfate ion, SO_4. Some SO_2 may also be absorbed from the air through leaves in areas where the atmosphere has been enriched with sulfur compounds from industrial sources. Sulfur is a constituent of amino acids and is essential for protein synthesis. It is essential for nodule formation on legume roots and is present in oil compounds responsible for the characteristic odors of plants such as garlic and onion.

Sulfur fertilization is required by most legume crops. Sulfur is generally deficient in most Western soils. The most noticeable response to application of sulfur fertilizers are increased root development and a deeper green color of the foliage.

A deficiency of sulfur has a pronounced retarding effect on plant growth. This deficiency is characterized by uniformly chlorotic plants, stunted, thin stemmed and spindly. In many plants these symptoms resemble those of nitrogen deficiency and have undoubtedly led to many improper diagnoses of plant growth problems. Unlike nitrogen, sulfur does not appear to be translocated from older to younger plant parts.

There are numerous old and established sources of fertilizer sulfur. One source for sulfate sulfur is generally as good as any other, so let the cost per unit of sulfur be the determining factor. Plant availability must also be considered. Calcium sulfate, or plain gypsum, has an important role as a buffer for magnesium and a source of sulfur.

TRACE ELEMENTS OR MICRONUTRIENTS

Although micronutrients are used by plants in very small amounts, they are just as essential for plant growth as the so-called primary and secondary macronutrients. Most micronutrients are under homeostatic control. Still care must be used in applying micronutrients to plants since the difference between deficient and toxic levels is small.

Iron. Iron deficiency is believed to be caused by an imbalance of metallic ions such as copper and manganese, excessive amounts of phosphorus in soils, a combination of high pH, high lime, high soil moisture, cool temperatures, and high levels of bicarbonate in the rooting medium. Iron, however, is not usually deficient in most soils.

Symptoms of iron deficiency in plants include —
1. Interveinal chlorosis of young leaves, veins remaining green except in severe cases.
2. Twig die back.
3. And death of entire limbs or plant.

Iron is important in —
1. Chlorophyll formation.
2. Oxidation reduction reactions.
3. And the activity of enzyme systems.

Manganese. The effect of organic matter, lime, and soil moisture have all been associated with manganese deficiency. On soils high in organic matter and near neutral (7.0) pH, crops exhibit varying degrees of manganese deficiency. Considerable amounts of organic matter frequently results in the appearance of deficiency symptoms at lower pH values. Symptoms of manganese deficiency include —

1. Interveinal chlorosis of young leaves, with a darker green color next to the vein.
2. And development of gray specks, interveinal white streaks, or interveinal brown spots and streaks.

Manganese —
1. With iron assists in chlorophyll formation.
2. Is active in carbohydrate formation.
3. Accelerates germination of seeds and maturation.
4. Is active in oxidation-reduction reactions.
5. And affects vitamin content of plants.

Zinc. Plant availability of zinc is regulated by soil pH, soil phosphorus levels, organic matter content and *ad*sorption by clays. Zinc is generally more available to plants in acid than in alkaline soils. Zinc deficiencies have been noted on soils high in phosphate, high in organic matter (particularly animal manures), and clay soils high in calcium and magnesium carbonates.

Zinc is important —
1. To the formation of chlorophyll.
2. In seed production and grain yields.
3. And is essential in the formation of growth hormones.

Zinc deficiencies —
1. Decrease stem length and cause a rosetting of terminal buds.
2. Reduce fruit bud formation.
3. Cause interveinal chlorosis.
4. Cause die-back of twigs after the first year.
5. And cause striping or banding.

Zinc sulfate is a popular fertilizer material that can be applied to the soil or sprayed over vegetables, and field and fruit crops. It is toxic to plants when applied in large quantities. Care should be exercised in its application and precautions should be taken to follow rates that are recommended by local agricultural authorities.

Copper. Copper —
1. Acts as a regulator for several biochemical processes.
2. Acts as a catalyst to help route various nutrient ions into their proper growth functions.
3. And is active in oxidation-reduction reactions.

The availability of copper to plants is conditioned by the amount of soil organic matter, pH, and the presence of the metallic ions — iron, manganese and aluminum. As a rule, copper retention in soil increases with an increase in the organic matter content. The amount of exchangeable copper increases as the soil pH decreases.

Research also indicates that the amount of available copper is related not to the absolute amounts of copper or iron, but to the ratio of copper to iron in the soil medium. Symptoms of copper deficiency in plants include —
1. Stunted growth.

2. Die-back of terminal shoots in trees.
3. Poor pigmentation.
4. Wilting and eventual death of leaf tips.
5. And formation of gum pockets around the central pith in citrus crops.

As with most micronutrients, copper in large amounts is toxic to plants. Excessive amounts of copper depress the activity of iron and may cause iron-deficiency symptoms to appear. Copper fertilizers include copper sulfate and copper ammonium phosphate, both of which may be used as either a foliar spray or applied to the soil.

Boron. Boron has been found to be toxic in Western land desert areas and is associated with high boron waters. Boron deficiencies are generally found in high rainfall areas. Tree crops and legumes in central and northern California and in Oregon and Washington require boron fertilization.

Boron is —
1. Essential for pollination and reproduction.
2. Influences flower and seed formation.
3. Influences oxygen supply to plant tissues and roots.
4. And is closely related to calcium performance.

Factors affecting boron availability to plants includes soil texture, pH and moisture. Coarse textured, well drained, sandy soils are normally low in boron. The fact that boron is retained by the clay fraction of soils does not necessarily imply that plants will absorb this element from clays in greater quantities than from sands when equal concentrations of water soluble boron are present. In fact, plants will take up much larger quantities of boron from sandy soils than from fine textured soils of equal concentrations of water soluble soil boron. Boron uptake is reduced by increasing the soil pH. Boron deficiency is also accelerated under extremely dry soil conditions. Boron is one of the most widely applied of the micronutrients. Commonly used boron fertilizers include borax, sodium pentaborate and boric acid.

Symptoms of boron deficiency include —
1. Death of terminal growth, causing lateral buds to develop producing a "witches broom" effect.
2. Thickened, curled, wilted and chlorotic leaves.
3. Soft or necrotic spots in fruit or tubers.
4. And reduced flowering or improper pollination.

Molybdenum. Molybdenum is required by plants —
1. For the utilization of nitrogen.
2. And legumes cannot fix atmospheric nitrogen symbiotically unless molybdenum is present.

Symptoms of molybdenum deficiency in plants include —
1. Stunting and lack of vigor to the role of molybdenum in nitrogen utilization by plants.
2. Marginal scorching and cupping or rolling of leaves.
3. Whiptail of cauliflower.

4. And yellow spotting of citrus.

Deficiencies of Mo require additions of ounces per acre of Mo to legumes. Mo fertilizers commonly used are ammonium and sodium molybdate and molybdenum trioxide. These materials are mixed with an N, P and K fertilizer, and used as foliar sprays or soil applications.

Cobalt. Cobalt is required by Rhizobia for the fixation of elemental nitrogen by leguminous plants. In general, increases in soil pH decrease the availability of Cobalt. Cobalt is not added to fertilizers. It is required in such small amounts by plants that its application as a fertilizer is difficult because of the small quantities of the carrier that are needed.

Chlorine. Chlorine is required in the photosynthetic reaction in plants. Deficiency is not seen in the field due to its universal presence in nature. Symptoms of chlorine deficiency have only been obtained with nutrient culture studies in the greenhouse. The storage quality of most herbs and the oil quality of spices are lowered by excess chlorine.

Vanadium, sodium and silicon. All have been shown to be absorbed by plants in ionic form, although whether they are essential to the growth of higher plants has not been proved.

Balance is important in plant nutrition. An excess of one nutrient can affect the uptake of another. Visual symptoms of nutrient deficiencies can be a useful tool in diagnosing problems, but assistance from a qualified agriculturalist and/or tissue analysis is advised since problems can arise from factors other than nutrient deficiencies or toxicities.

An in-depth review of nutrient requirements and commentary on salt form fertilizers compared to inorganic rock forms and digested organic materials is available in *An Acres U.S.A. Primer.*

Special thanks to Colleen Clark for her review of this work.

SWEET BASIL
(*Ocimum basilicum* L.)
Labiatae family

As one of the most widely known and used herbs in modern cookery, more than 2,000 tons are imported into North America in a typical year from Egypt, France, Israel and Mexico. A similar market exists in West Germany. With a profusion of varieties, the most common is sweet basil or garden basil. Opal basil (cv 'Purpurascens') or ornamental basil is also quite popular. As an annual, basils are started each year from seed. Because it is very sensitive to frost, most gardeners start it indoors and then transplant it to the garden only after all danger from frost is eliminated.

It can be sowed in 2 foot rows not more than 1/4 inch deep, 12 inches apart in each row. It likes a rich, well aerated soil treated with a manure compost before planting. The soil can be mulched to hold soil warmth and moisture only after sprouts begin to appear. The germination ranges from 4 to 7 days at 70 F. Basil likes full sun and about a six day irrigation schedule. The crop can be manured again when the plants reach a 1 to 2 foot height.

Basil should be harvested before the stems go to flower. The first cutting should take the main stem and at least one node with 2 young shoots intact. The remaining growth will branch out and be ready for another cutting within 2 to 3 weeks, depending on light and water. The harvesting continues until the first frost, when the plants will begin to die back. Since basil is a high oil crop, it cannot be sun-cured but needs special dehydration.

In the cosmetic industry, sweet basil is used as a fragrance ingredient in perfumes, soaps, hair dressings, dental creams, and mouth washes. It is used as a spice in foods and chartreuse liqueur. The oil and oleoresin are used extensively as a flavor ingredient in all major food products. In folk medicines, sweet basil is used for head colds and as a cure for warts and worms. Sweet basil is sold as a crude leaf products, essential oil, and oleoresin.

Spearmint

CHAPTER 3

Some Basic Farm Practices

The seeds of ecological design *are* beginning to sprout, and many of
the hardware components to create an ecologically stable urban community have already been developed and are working. What we have
yet to do is bring together all the threads and weave them into a single coherent design for a new community.
  Sim Van der Ryn, California Office of Appropriate Technology.

Tillage is the manipulation of the soil by means of tools. More detail on these
important implements can be found in Chapter 4, *Basic Farm Machinery.* Tillage serves many purposes. The soil may need to be plowed in order to turn
stubble, manure, and stover left over from harvest. It may be necessary to
bring up minerals from rich lower soil layers, or to cultivate deep ridges for
irrigation. It may be also used to stir the soil and expose it to air and light for
sanitary effect, and it is often the best means to sheet compost weeds and animal manures.

All of these operations affect the soil in one of two ways. They either loosen
the soil and render it more open and friable, or they pulverize and compact it to
make the structure more dense. Lumpy soil needs pulverization, sandy soil
needs to be packed. In planting small seeds, soil is compacted in order to
increase the capillary action and draw moisture to the surface. This aids germination. The choice of the proper tool must be decided by the purpose for
which it is to be used. For example, if the soil is to be turned over literally, then

a moldboard-type plow should be used. If, on the other hand, the farm plan calls for deeper soil turn, then a larger tool is required, such as a chisel plow. The nature of the soil and the purpose of tillage should first be determined. Next the tool should be chosen to best accomplish the job.

All soil working tools can be divided into four general groups:
1. Plows that invert the soil and pulverize it.
2. Cultivators that stir the soil.
3. Pulverizers designed to reduce lumps and level the surface.
4. And compactors that bring soil particles closer together, smoothing the surface.

PLOWING

The plow is the most important tool used on the soil. It operates as a double, twisting wedge, which lifts and inverts a ribbon of soil. By the design of the knives, the furrow slice is also sheared or split into a number of layers, vertically and horizontally. When done correctly, a complete pulverization of the soil also occurs. The key is determining the correct moisture and sun conditions for the best results.

Deeper plowing, below 5 to 8 inches, has not increased yields where the soil profile is naturally open. It can be justified, however, when you wish to improve the shape of taproot type crops. Repeated plowing with a tractor wheel in the bottom of a furrow will develop a compacted layer which limits both water movement and root growth. The modern concept of tillage places greater emphasis on improving the quality of plowing rather than a multiple trip schedule with secondary tillage equipment. These extra passes are used primarily to hide defects in faulty plowing.

There are several important tips to get a better quality plow. The first is to keep tire slippage to less than 10%. This is done by selecting the tractor and plow size combination, determined primarily by soil and topography. When soil building, where some subsoil is to be mixed with the top soil, lowering of plow depth an inch each plowing is plenty. Keeping a straight line of draft is also important, as well as keeping the cutting edges, such as coulters and shares, sharp and in good condition. Nearly half the power required for plowing is used in making these important horizontal and vertical cuts. The cost of maintaining sharp shares and coulters is more than offset by reduced power requirements and tire slippage.

Although moldboard plows are by far the most widely used tillage tool, there are certain soil and crop situations where such things as rotary tillers and disc field cultivators are better adapted. After using a moldboard plow, the soil is left ridged and rough. In an orchard, for example, this furrow and ridge pattern characteristic of the moldboard plow is objectionable. A double disc or rotary tiller is more often used. Moldboard plows can not usually be used on a rocky field, until it has first been heavy disced several times. Field cultivators

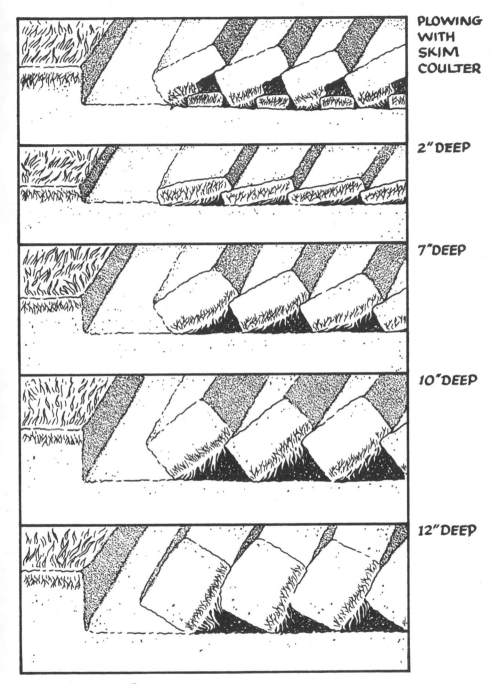

PLOWING
WITH
SKIM
COULTER

2" DEEP

7" DEEP

10" DEEP

12" DEEP

PLOWINGS — 15" WIDE FURROW
    KEEP DEPTH BETWEEN 7" AND 10"

37

are used as a substitute for a plow when surface vegetation and stones are absent.

Fall plowing is not recommended on well-drained soils where the time for plowing is less critical and prolonged exposure to weathering may cause compaction on the furrow slice. Sandy soils usually must be plowed in the fall and again in the spring before planting. Sometimes, they might even be plowed a third time during the growing season. Fall plowing also increases weeds, and gives a greater opportunity for erosion. The longer a bare soil surface is exposed to the weather, the greater the chance water and wind will account for damage.

Land infested with weeds is best plowed in the spring in many parts of the country. Turning weeds under in the fall simply preserves and protects the seed if decay cannot be managed properly. Spring plowing is also appropriate for those soils where winter winds could erode unfrozen open areas. Fall plowing, however, is what most farmers end up choosing for their farm plan, weather permitting. The soil stands a better chance of holding the spring's runoff on the land, preventing erosion and storing up needed soil moisture.

New evidence in small farm agriculture reveals that there are some important advantages to pre-discing a field several times before plowing. In areas where it is difficult to build a good seedbed on blocky soils or thick matted sod cover, this practice has been found to reduce vegetative growth which forms a surface mulch and slows up evaporation until the lower, wetter areas of the field are dry enough to plow. Pre-discing also develops a more uniform moisture condition across several different soil types. This uniformity is essential for even germination of most crop seeds.

The customary rotary plowing schedule is a two phase operation. The farmer goes over the acreage with the rotary hood up, and the rotary blades set just deep enough to cut below the shallow-root level. One week later, a second plow is made at normal plow depths. This two-plow technique is the first in a series of weed control efforts that throw the uprooted grasses and weeds to the surface where they die before being turned into soil on the second plowing. At this point, the field needs to be stoned.

Experienced farmers take a great deal of pride in their plowing and tillage systems. As a new farmer, we all would do well to emulate their work. Straight, evenly turned furrows make even coverage with a seeded crop. The more even the coverage, the fewer the weed problems.

HARROWING

After plowing, the soil is left in a ridged and rough condition. At this point, the soil is now ready for seedbed preparation. Seedbeds contain two zones, a seed zone and the root zone. Unless the seed is surrounded by a zone of uniformly granulated and compacted soil particles, it will not produce uniform stands of a crop. The root zone is the nutrient storehouse for the growing plant during its entire life cycle. Because it is always subjected to longer weathering than the seed zone, it requires less pulverization and firming before planting. Only with late, or fall planted crops is there a need for more firming and pulverization. Firming, in this case, permits more upward movement of moisture from the subsoil.

Light soils can usually be leveled and pulverized by a once-over pass with a tandem disc harrow. Heavier soils, which require stoning, may also require a second lapping or criss-cross type coverage. If stoning is required, a single pass over the field discovers the stones. A second pass following removal of stones smoothes the area. If the seed to be used is very fine, forming a seedbed may require a smoothing with a peg or spike-toothed harrow before seeding. This has the effect of drilling, as the seed falls into the small, evenly spaced furrows made by the spaced peg. The seed is covered as the loose soil falls back into the furrows following the passage of the peg.

Smoothing or spring tooth harrows are also used to kill newly germinated weeds. Often rainy weather will interrupt seedbed preparation, and several weeks might pass before the farmer can get back to the job. Shallow set teeth on the harrow will loosen the rain compacted soil, uprooting young weed starts.

Discs and spring tooth harrows are generally considered the second most important tools in tillage in conventional systems. They perform well over a wide range of soil conditions. In soils that are cloddy, disc and spring tooth harrows tend to bring clods and stones to the surface. This means that they are also depositing the finer particles at some depth below the seed planting zone. This critical pulverization in the seed zone can be made by repeated trips with the harrow, although compaction can also occur in this process. If a good job of plowing has been done initially, shallow secondary tillage is preferred. You need those finer particles in the seed zone in spring.

A once-over with a shallow disc or spring tooth harrow in combination with a roller, or something similar (float, culti-packer, dragged log) can double the proportion of fine granules in the seed zone over two or even three deep discings.

With row crops, it is not necessary to pulverize the entire surface of the field. Only a narrow strip in the vicinity of the seed need be considered. Numerous variations of strip tillage have been developed. Cultivators limit tillage to seed zones and thus represent savings in overall power requirements. Also, a rough, cloddy surface between rows tends to discourage weeds, reduce crust formation, and ultimately encourages water infiltration. Unless strip tillage is preceded by good plowing, however, it will make cultivation and harvest more difficult.

Tillage systems must be determined with the character of the soil in mind. Newer forms of ecologically sound agriculture suggest newer tools and systems based on the regenerative requirement in soil management. Some items of equipment of foreign manufacture are becoming available.

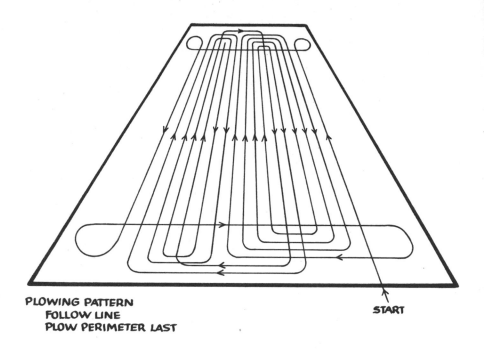

**PLOWING PATTERN
FOLLOW LINE
PLOW PERIMETER LAST**

START

SEEDING AND PLANTING

Seeding and planting should follow seedbed preparations as quickly as possible. This is to take advantage of loose and friable soil. Benefits accrue with a couple of days of gentle rain following the seeding. From this point forward, you should be monitoring the weather and attempting to take advantage of every available weather report. Weather monitoring becomes even more critical during harvest.

Broadcast seeding is the second best technique for the small farmer. The hand cranked, spinner type spreader seems to be the most efficient way to distribute seeds over the small acreage. I personally have found the glitter gun, a tool used to throw glitter on unfinished ceilings, works best for very small seeds such as catnip. Depending on the make, hand held units have a lateral spread of 15 to 25 feet. Assuming a steady pace in walking, you could seed about two acres per hour with one of these units. The importance of adequate and even coverage of the seed must be stressed. A break in broadcast seed coverage provides a fertile ground for the growth of weeds.

Machine powered seeders and drills are particularly favored for stony land, land which has been recently cleared and is still full of roots, and land where the farmer plans to intertill a broadcast green manure crop between the drills. The value of seed press wheels over grain drills has been shown for a variety of soils. A press wheel firms and pulverizes a narrow band of soil directly over the seed. The more positive the seed-to-soil contact, the more uniform the coverage

40

on the seed. This is reflected in the more rapid growth and uniformity of seed emergence.

Machine seeding should be accomplished in shallow furrows, the depth depending on seed size. Very fine seeds, like catnip, should be barely covered, less than 1/8 inch deep. Larger seed, like sage, should be planted 1/4 inch deep. Because of the thin covering over fine seeds there will be some danger of the seed drying out before sprouting. Do not water seedlings later in the afternoon. This will increase the danger of damp-off. Beds should not be allowed to remain wet overnight after seedlings come to the surface.

Hardy perennial flower seeds can be sown from April until the middle of August in most areas. Perennial seeds are sown almost always in later summer because they will produce nice size plants the following spring. These can be easily transplanted into more permanent beds, if necessary. As soon as seedlings develop their secondary leaves and show signs of sturdy growth, they can be transplanted.

Many of the small seedling perennial flower plants should have some protection from the hot mid-day sun while they are still small and immature. A lath frame placed over the bed and braced to stand about 18 inches above the plants will give adequate protection. This lath frame must be in place during the hot part of the day.

Most hardy perennial flower plants are heavy feeders, and as they grow larger will need to be given additional feeding to take care of their requirements. This can be cow manure, compost, leaf mold, and bone meal, liberally applied to the beds. Perennials also benefit from an application of a fish emulsion in early spring. Be sure to watch for signs of disease in mature plants. They can be individually removed to prevent their spread. Keeping weeds down seems to be the best form of disease control.

CULTIVATION

Cultivation is undertaken to break up the soil around weeds and so kill them as they appear. Most crops will require at least two, or even three cultivations before harvest. Most cultivators are edged with sweeps or shovels to weed and loosen the soil between the rows. Disc hillers are designed to throw smothering soil over weeds growing in crop rows. Cultivating row crops requires a great deal of precision because of the proximity of weeds to the crop. When using a two or more row cultivator, the evenness of row spacing becomes even more critical. Poorly spaced rows do not get rid of the weeds. They simply account for destruction of the crop.

The breakdown and oxidation of surface soil particles during clean cultivation presents serious problems. The breakdown of the soil permits a quick rain to seal the soil, reducing aeration and increasing erosion. Compaction of the layer below the cultivator's cutting depth also reduces the root level porosity of the soil. As a general rule, therefore, farmers in the South and Midwest now employ what is known as Faulkner's "trash farming" techniques. This entails keeping the soil covered with a surface mulch of crop residues, while stirring their soils as little as possible.

ABOUT WEEDS

A weed has been defined as "a plant out of place," or "a plant growing where it is not wanted." It therefore follows that a plant may be a weed in some places and not in others. For example, Bermudagrass, considered to be a noxious weed in most fields, is highly desired in pastures of alfalfa used by horses, because a 30% mixture of grass to alfalfa is best digested by horses. The best definition of a weed I have seen is "a plant that does more harm than good and has the habit of intruding where not wanted." Weeds cause a number of direct losses to the small farmer:

1. They lower the selling value of the land. Land overgrown with weeds always sells for a lower price. Weeds increase the difficulty of future cultivation.
2. They reduce crop yields. Competition for water, nutrients, and space all critically reduce crop yields.
3. They increase the expense of cultivation and harvest. Most spices cannot have *any* foreign material, including weeds, in them to be marketable.
4. They reduce the market value of crops. Or, alternatively, increase the cost of processing and cleaning.
5. They harbor fungi and insects that attack young crops. In some cases they poison livestock and livestock products.

Weeds are not always useless, and do have certain advantages. They are, for example, a principle means by which organic matter is added to the soil. Weeds usually contain large quantities of mineral nutrients. When they are returned to the soil, these nutrients become available for more useful plants. They take up soluble plant nutrients on land that is not in cultivation and prevent leaching of those nutrients. They also afford a covering for waste places, checking erosion by water and winds. *Finally, they compel us to cultivate the land.*

The basic habits of life, growth, and propagation of weeds determine the method of their control. Weeds are therefore classified into three groups according to their duration or length of life: annuals, biennials, and perennials.

Annual weeds. Annual weeds are of two kinds, *summer annuals* and *winter annuals.* Summer annuals grow from seed each spring or summer and do not survive the winter. Winter annuals germinate in late summer or fall, live over the winter, and mature and die the next year. They both depend on the seed they produce for propagation. Each plant can produce from 10,000 to one million seeds. They don't all germinate at the same time, and many remain in the soil for years, only coming up when conditions become favorable for them. Cultural control methods of both annuals are designed to promote germination of the annual and then destroy the weed as a seedling. The principle of stubble cleaning is to disturb the surface soil layers immediately after harvest so that weeds may germinate. The young plants are killed by plowing before the next crop is sown. Stubble cleaning is directed primarily at the control of annuals after a cereal harvest.

It is best to stubble clean immediately after the harvest, usually in August. A shallow surface is made by using either a rotovator, disc harrow or cultivator, but the actual degree of weed control is dependent chiefly on the weather. Under moist and warm conditions a high proportion of annual weed seed may germinate, whereas under dry and cold conditions most weed seed will remain dormant.

Not all annual weed seeds in surface soil layers will be made to germinate by stubble cleaning. Many important annuals, including knotgrass and wild oats, germinate in the spring, and can not be cleaned in this manner. Stubble cleaning works best on those annuals with short dormancy periods, or those that germinate in the autumn. Annuals that germinate on uncropped soils during the main growing season may be destroyed prior to cropping by appropriate tillage.

Biennial weeds. Biennial weeds live two years. During the first year they grow rather slowly, producing a taproot and a rosette of leaves close to the ground. During the second year they send up flowering stems that produce seeds, and then die. Such weeds are eradicated by the prevention of seeding and by the destruction of the rosettes that appear in the fall. A common example is mullein. This is a foraged crop which could be swathed, windrowed and baled.

Perennial weeds. Perennial weeds live over winter from year to year either above or below the ground. The underground parts, besides roots, may consist of underground stems, rootstocks, or bulbs. These perennial weeds are often very difficult to eradicate, as when the top is killed the underground parts contain a supply of food material for renewed growth. They are spread vegetatively and by seed. Under field crop conditions, perennial weeds spread mostly by rhizomes. Their rootstock is cut and spread, creating several plants where there was just one.

There are two methods commonly used to control perennials. They are plowing followed by cultivation and collection, or rotovation followed by deep plowing. The first method is carried out initially to uproot the weeds in the furrow slice. Then cultivators and/or harrows are used to drag the weeds out of the furrows for collection. Weeds are then tied together for carting off the field. Under dry conditions, they can be burned in the field.

The second method of rotovation is carried out at intervals of two to three weeks. The objective is to chop up, weaken and exhaust the food reserves in the perennial weeds. Deep plowing is then carried out to complete the kill of the vegetative fragments. Mechanical methods are usually combined frequently

43

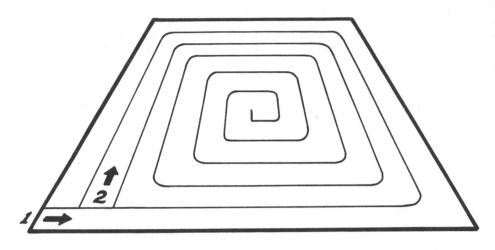

MOWING PATTERN

with chemical methods. Although I do not recommend most forms of chemical herbicides, you should become acquainted with them. They mostly do not work that well, and their cost is almost prohibitive.

WEED CONTROL

There are several methods of weed control and eradication. *Weed control* is defined as the process of inhibiting weed growth and limiting weed infestations so that crops can be grown profitably. *Weed eradication* is defined as the complete elimination of all live plants, plant parts, and seeds of a weed infestation from an area. The more common methods used are cultivation, smothering, mowing, pasturing, chemical herbicides, flaming, crop rotation, and the use of clean seed.

Cultivation. This is a tillage process to destroy weeds with a hoe, plow, or cultivator. It not only includes a kill of the living weeds, but also timing of the operation to prevent the seeds from maturing. In some cases weeds may be destroyed by cultivation or harrowing of meadowlands. This practice is common with alfalfa. However, it is not recommended for meadows infested with grasses with creeping rootstock, like Bermudagrass. Harrowing merely breaks the rootstock of these pests, and growth is invigorated.

Bare summer fallow is sometimes used for cleaning old weed fields. When this method is followed, the land should be plowed in early summer and disced or harrowed often enough during the summer to induce germination of weed seeds and annihilation of the plants that come up. The same end can be achieved in most cases by planting the land to a cultivated crop. Discing appears to provide more control than chemicals when applied correctly. Cultivation, to be efficient in weed eradication, must be thorough and must be kept up late enough to prevent the maturing of any seeds before frost.

Smothering. This is the growing of a heavy, dense cover of some crop such as buckwheat, cowpeas, or soybeans, crops that will outgrow the weeds and deprive them of light, water, and plant nutrients. This is the best way, for example, of destroying Bermudagrass. Usually weeds are very persistent in cultivated fields, but can be smothered out by keeping the land well covered with dense growing crops for two or more years.

Mowing. This can be an important means of weed control when properly handled. Mowing must be done before the seed pods are formed, since many weed plants have the ability to mature seed even after being cut. The frequent mowing required to harvest alfalfa, for example, keeps annuals from maturing seed and tends to exhaust the root reserves in most perennial weeds.

Pasturing. This method is invoked when animals such as hogs, sheep, goats and geese are used to control weeds. Hogs will feed on underground rootstocks of such things as comfrey and Johnson grass. Most weeds are relatively unpalatable to stock and therefore this method is not very effective in many cases.

Chemical Treatment. This method is now used extensively on most farms. Recent studies now indicate problems created by the use of these forms of weed control to be more of a liability to the small farmer than a benefit. Chemical weed killers can be divided into two groups. The first is called a *total* or *non-selective* herbicide, intended to kill all vegetation present. Its use in agriculture is obviously limited and is usually restricted to removing unwanted vegetation from yards, around buildings, and on roads. The second group is called *selective.* These herbicides are used extensively and are intended to suppress and kill some plants without seriously affecting others. In either case, herbicides are dangerous. Used widely in the environment, they can account for deformatives in the newborn, and degenerative metabolic disease conditions in those directly and indirectly contaminated.

Chemical weed killers are applied either to the foliage of weeds or to the soil. Foliage treatments are subdivided according to the way they affect the weeds. A *contact* herbicide treatment destroys plant tissues only by external contact and does not move far from the point of application. By contrast, *growth regulators,* also known as *translocators,* move within the plant to affect tissues away from the point of application, either in the shoots or roots.

Chemical weed killers applied to the soil or *residual* herbicides are absorbed by the roots of seedlings as they germinate, or by the roots of already established weeds and may move within the plant to affect tissues away from the point of contact. Selective herbicides are classified further in relationship to the stage of development of the crop:

1. Pre-sowing or pre-planting treatments. These herbicides are applied to kill weeds and clean the land before sowing or planting crops.
2. Pre-emergence treatment. These herbicides are applied at any time between sowing and emergence of a crop.

LEMON BALM
(*Melissa officinalis* L.)
Labiatae family

Lemon balm is a fairly hardy perennial which is easily started from seed. In farm situations where grasses are a problem, it is most often started from rootstock (similar to catnip). It prefers a fairly friable soil in partial shade. Because the seed is exceedingly small, it should be drilled at a depth of three diameters of the seed (using care not to plant too deep). A fine spray at this time can be used until rootstock begins to develop.

Lemon balm will grow in full sun, although it does much better in partial shade. Row cropping the first sets of rootstock seems best for cultivation of grasses, a major problem with lemon balm. Early mulching with hay is beneficial. Cuttings and root division are the most acceptable ways to establish lemon balm. With root systems that are short and dense, divisions can be made in both spring and fall. Rootlets should contain three to four buds on each, and can be drilled into 2 foot rows like strawberries. In the fall, lemon balm rootstock should be planted early enough to establish before the first frost. Mulch to protect over the winter.

Harvesting is easy, with at least two cuttings per season. It should be cut before it flowers, similar to spearmint. A good deal of fragrance will be lost in even the most careful handling, so this should be kept to a minimum for highest oils. To harvest, the plant should be cut with a side-bar cutter, and tedded up alongside a treeline for partial shade while in a windrow. When dry, it can be baled and stored similarly to catnip. It will tend to brown quickly if there is any night moisture, so look for those dry hot nights as ideal for retaining color and oil.

While the markets for lemon balm are fairly limited now, this is primarily because of its limited availability. When sun-cured correctly, the flavor of lemon balm can sometimes rival lemon grass (an import). This makes its future a possible formula substitution excellent, with availability. It might make an excellent crop for those fields not getting full sun but having good irrigation. Today's market in Europe is much greater than that of North America, although that seems to be changing.

Lemon balm is primarily used as a fragrance herb rather than flavoring. Fresh sprigs are used to top fruit drinks, salads, and some wine preparations. Medicinally the tea is generally used to induce perspiration and cool patients who have fevers. It was also used with salt to heal sores and ease the pain from gout. It is an herb which European trends indicate a growing market. It very well might become a cheaper domestic source for lemon flavorings in tea blends and other food products.

46

3. Post-emergence treatment. These herbicides are applied to the foliage of both crop and weeds after emergence of the crop.

Flame treatment. This form is used to control weeds in cotton and sugarcane fields. Although this requires special machinery, the treatment costs one-third (or less) than cultivation or application of herbicides.

Crop rotation. This method eliminates certain weeds that typically are associated with and dominate a given crop. Certain weeds increase rapidly if a single crop is grown continuously and can frequently be subdued by a change of crops. A complete crop rotation plan is given in Chapter 5, as an example.

Clean seed. Nearly all of our troublesome weeds have been introduced in seeds of various crops, especially in grass and clover seed. Constant vigilance should be maintained, and no seed should be sown without careful examination for weed seeds. The percentage of purity on the tag does not necessarily tell the desirability of the seed. Seed with a purity of 99.9% should be avoided, for example, if the other .1% is a noxious weed such as Canadian Thistle. This could mean a seeding of 2,400 such seeds per acre.

Although great progress has been made in the control of weeds, it should be considered a supplement to, rather than a substitute for, the use of improved cultural practices, such as clean seed, proper tillage and seedbed preparations, timely cultivation, proper amounts and kinds of fertilizers and lime, and newly adapted strains, varieties, or hybrids of crop plants.

SOME TIPS ON HOW TO GROW HERBS

Young herb plants should be given some protection when first set out in the field. When planted, they should be watered in and given a light mulch. Water lightly at least twice each day until the plants have established themselves. All transplanting should be done in late afternoon, and never in the heat of the day. Most herbs and spices are native to hostile environments, where they grow in light, poor soils that have ample drainage. These are the soil conditions you should try to duplicate in your own field in the presence of full sun.

Herbs should never be pushed into a fast, lush growth by over-watering. The essential oils produced by the herbs and spices which give the fragrance and flavors, are more concentrated in herb foliage coming from plants grown in full sun and soil on the dry side. Annuals, because of their rapid growth, can be sown outdoors without starting the plants indoors.

Perennial herb seeds, because of their very hard outer coat coverings, should be placed in the freezer, frozen and re-frozen a couple times. This stratifies the seed coat and enables the seeds to germinate more readily. Once the seed has been frozen and re-frozen, they should be sown immediately. For some herbs, like catnip, the seed should be soaked in water first to soften the casing. If the seed is small, it might also be mixed with an equal part sand before freezing. The sand acts as a "sink" for the cold and allows easier drilling.

Perennial herbs are best started in greenhouses and then replanted in a row crop layout. The second year's crop can then be further divided into a general field crop layout, once the weeds and grasses are under control. Most perennial herb crops require approximately 10,000 plants per acre. Transplants should not be put outside until all danger of frost is past. Some have found that growing seedlings in a greenhouse in the summer is most cost effective. The rootstock is then planted in rows in the fall and prepared for winter via mulching. The following spring's perennial will develop much more rapidly and often can give substantial yields that season.

HARVEST

Good yields are a direct result of good farm practices, and harvest time is when you reap your reward. There are many different types of harvest equipment, most of them highly specialized and quite costly. The small farmer is much better off planting a crop that requires the use of machinery immediately available in the community. The most critical part to harvesting is not what to use, but rather *when* to harvest.

Most perennials, like mints, will lose up to 65% of their root stock when they go to flower. Others, such as several of the spices, should be harvested only after they have begun to flower. To discover the prime times for cutting your crop requires research sometimes not available from local farmers or the County Agent. Coupled with this problem of when to harvest are diverse weather variables. Weather must be considered in any crop requiring dehydration by sun-cure. Harvesting of crops employing second and third cuts is determined more by the length of season and weather variations than the maturity of the crop. In short growing season areas, many have found that final harvests are too short for baling. They then either chop it for hay, or mow it for sheet composting. The new farmer would do well to research his neighbors' practices before he even considers putting seed into the ground.

Herbs raised for their aromatic, seasoning foliage, are at the peak of their flavor when the first flower buds start to appear. Harvesting should be done on a clear day in early morning, as soon as the dew has dried from the foliage. Herbs grown for their savory seeds (like coriander, dill, anise, caraway and cumin), are harvested when their seeds are thoroughly ripened. Seeds are ready to harvest when plants shatter seeds by slight tap of their stems.

IRRIGATION

Water rights have been the plague of man since he first began to farm. There are two fundamental systems of water rights in North America today, *riparian* and *prior appropriation*. Riparian rights are those claimed by the upstream owner of land through or by which a stream may flow. He claims the right to use this water without regard to when or how he might use it. Prior appropriation rights gives the first user of water from a stream a given amount of water.

This right obtains whether he owns the land on which the stream flows or not. Obviously water laws are legal and political dynamite, and the new farmer when setting up a farm requiring irrigation should come to know his local water laws immediately.

The two standard forms of irrigation are a well-pump system, or a water ditch usually owned by the community. There are advantages and disadvantages to each. Putting in a commercial well, one able to pump over 40 gallons of water per minute, is quite expensive. Drilling costs can vary, but the average is about $40 per foot, including the casing. When you realize that most wells have depths from 40 to 200 feet, the cost of a well can be significant. Then you must also pay for the power required to throw the water into your field.

The advantages are that you can depend on your water source during critical periods. Water ditches have been known to break down during critical stages of plant growth. Most water ditches cost about the same as power for a pump-well system in a given season. Typically charges for this ditch irrigation is based on a flat rate per irrigated area, usually ranging from $25 to $65 per acre each season. Politics play an important part in water ditch matters. Often owners do not wish the service, but must pay for it anyway.

All ditch irrigation systems depend on the supply canal or ditch. These supply ditches should always be at least one foot above the highest point of the field. A main line then runs down the length of the field with appropriately spaced turnouts, or risers. Furrow irrigation depends on gravity and can be used for almost all cultivated crops. Water is drawn or diverted from a head ditch that runs across the upper edge of the field to the furrows. The furrows run down or slantwise across the slope of the land, gravity moving the water. Their placement, riser to riser, depends on the slope of the land and head pressure from the ditch.

For best use of the water, this slope usually does not exceed .25% for row crops and can range from 5 to 8% for most cover crops. The length and depth of the furrow is determined by the potential rate of water flow, and the absorption rate of the particular field's soil.

Flood irrigation is used primarily for orchards and other deep rooted crops. This method requires relatively flat land and larger streams of water than those provided for furrow irrigation. Parallel flood strips, usually 50 to 100 feet wide, are created by plowing up bordering terraces to confine the water.

More farmland suffers from lack of water than from an overabundance of it. Two fundamental practices, terracing and contouring, are employed to help control the loss of surface water and the consequent loss of topsoil. Terracing is a method of breaking up a long water wasting slope in a field. A terrace is an artificial shelf that can serve as an absorptive pause in a runoff pattern. It usually is a planned waterway with a ridge on the downhill side that is designed to dispose of an otherwise erosive flood of water.

Contour farming is, in a sense, a form of miniature terrace farming. With the plowing and planting done on a contour line, small ridges form, and later crop stems from harvest act as a deterrent to surface runoff and soil erosion.

TABLE 6
Soil, Light, and Propagation Methods for some Herbs and Spices

HERB	FORM	SOIL	LIGHT	PROPAGATION METHOD	pH	ANNUAL PRECIP. (INCHES)	ANNUAL TEMP. (F.)
Alfalfa (*Medicago sativa*)	HP	Ordinary, well drained	Full sun	Seed			
Angelica (*Angelica atropurpurea*)	HB	Rich, moist	Partial shade	Seed	4.5/7.3	20-51	41-66
Anise (*Pimpinella anisum*)	TA	Ordinary	Full sun	Seed	6.3/8.0	16-67	46-74
Basil (*Ocimum basilicum*)	TA	Rich	Full sun	Seed	4.3/7.5	24-165	45-81
Bay (*Umbellularia californica*)	TP	Ordinary, well drained	Full sun	Stem cut	4.5/8.3	12-43	48-66
Bergamot (*Monarda fistulosa*)	HP	Ordinary, moist	Partial shade	Division			
Blackberry (*Rubus fruticosus*)	HP	Ordinary, moist	Full sun	Division			
Black Cohosh (*Cimicifuga racemosa*)	HP	Rich, forest floor	Partial shade	Division			
Blessed Thistle (*Cnicus benedictus*)	HA	Poor, dry sandy	Full sun	Seed			
Blue Cohosh (*Caulophyllum thalicatroides*)	HP	Rich, forest floor	Partial shade	Division			
Borage (*Borago officinalis*)	HA	Ordinary, well drained	Partial shade	Seed	4.8/8.3	12-51	41-70
Burdock (*Arctium lappa*)	HB	Poor, waste areas	Sun	Division	4.5/7.8	12-51	41-66
Calamus (*Acorus calamus*)	HP	Swamp edges	Partial shade	Division	5.8/7.5	20-165	45-81
Caraway (*Carum carvi*)	HB	Ordinary	Full sun	Seed	4.8/7.6	16-51	43-66
Cascara Segrada (*Rhamnus purshiana*)	HP	Forest floor	Partial shade	Division			
Catnip (*Nepeta cataria*)	HP	Sandy dry	Full sun	Cutting	5.8/7.5	16-51	45-66
Chamomile (*Anthemis nobilis*)	HA	Well drained, sandy	Full sun	Division	6.8/8.0	16-55	45-75
Chapparal (*Larrea mexicana*)	HP	Wet coasts, hillsides	Full sun	Division			
Chervil (*Anthriscus cerefolium*)	HA	Ordinary, well drained	Partial shade	Seed	5.8/7.6	20-43	45-66

Plant	Type	Soil	Light	Propagation			
Chickweed (*Stellaria media*)	HA	Rich, wet pastures	Partial shade	Seed			
Chicory (*Cichorium intybus*)	HP	Ordinary, well drained	Full sun	Division	4.5/8.3	12-157	43-81
Coltsfoot (*Tussilago farfara*)	HP	Rich, moist	Partial shade	Division	4.5/7.5	20-51	41-59
Comfrey (*Symphytum officinale*)	HP	Well manured, heavy	Full sun	Rootstock	5.3/6.8	20-51	43-59
Coriander (*Coriandrum sativum*)	HA	Ordinary	Full sun	Seed	4.9/8.3	12-102	45-77
Cumin (*Cuminum cyminum*)	TA	Ordinary, well drained	Full sun	Seed	7.2/8.3	12-51	48-66
Dandelion (*Taraxacum officinale*)	HP	Rich, wet pastures	Full sun	Division	4.2/8.2	4-112	33-80
Devil's Club (*Oplopanax horridum*)	HP	Wet, forest floor	Shade	Division			
Dill (*Anethum graveolens*)	HA	Light sandy	Full sun	Seed	5.3/7.8	20-67	43-77
Desert Tea (*Ephedra nevadensis*)	HP	Poor dry	Full sun	Division	6.8	26-	-58
Echinacea (*Echinacea angustifolia*)	HP	Dry, open woods	Partial shade	Division			
Elder (*Sambucus nigra*)	HP	Moist forests	Partial shade	Division			
Eucalyptus (*Eucalyptus globulus*)	HP	Moist forests	Full sun	Division			
Fennel (*Foeniculum vulgare*)	HP	Well limed	Full sun	Seed	4.8/8.3	12-102	39-81
Garlic (*Allium sativum*)	HP	Rich, well drained	Full sun	Bulb	4.5/8.3	12-102	24-81
Ginger (*Zingiber officinale*)	HP	Rich, forest floor	Partial shade	Division	4.3/7.4	28-157	64-81
Ginseng (*Panax quinquefolium*)	HP	Rich, well drained	Partial shade	Division	5.0/6.5	28-51	48-59
Goldenseal (*Hydrastis canadensis*)	HP	Rich, well drained	Partial shade	Division	5.5/6.5	28-51	45-66
Hop (*Humulus lupulus*)	TP	Rich, well drained	Full sun	Division	4.5/8.3	12-51	41-70
Horehound (*Marrubium vulgare*)	HP	Well drained, light sandy	Partial sun	Division	4.5/8.3	12-51	45-75
Horsetail (*Equisetum arvensa*)	HP	Sandy, wet clay	Full sun	Division			
Hyssop (*Hyssopus officinalis*)	HP	Well drained, light	Partial sun	Stem cut	6.5/7.3	24-51	45-70
Kelp (*Fucus versiculosus*)		Ocean shores	Full sun	Self			
Kinikinnick (*Arctostaphylos uva-ursi*)	HP	Dry, well drained	Partial shade	Division			
Lavender (*Lavandula officinalis*)	HP	Well drained, light	Full sun	Stem cut	6.8/7.3	20-47	45-70

H – Hardy, T – Tender, A – Annual, B – Biennial, P – Perennial

51

TABLE 6
Soil, Light, and Propagation Methods for some Herbs and Spices

HERB	FORM	SOIL	LIGHT	PROPAGATION METHOD	pH	ANNUAL PRECIP. (INCHES)	ANNUAL TEMP. (F.)
Lemon Balm (*Melissa officinalis*)	HP	Well drained, sandy	Full sun	Division	4.5/7.6	17-61	45-75
Lemon Verbena (*Lippia citriodora*)	HP	Well drained, sandy	Full sun	Division			
Licorice (*Glycyrrhiza glabra*)	HP	Well drained, light sandy	Partial sun	Division	5.8/8.2	12-28	43-66
Lobelia (*Lobelia inflata*)	HA	Dry, open fields	Full sun	Seed	5.0/6.8	24-55	45-61
Lovage (*Levisticum officinale*)	HP	Moist rich	Partial shade	Division	5.5/7.8	20-51	45-64
Mandrake (*Podophyllum peltatum*)	HP	Rich, moist forest	Shade	Division	7.2	24-98	-66
Marigold (*Calendula officinalis*)	HA	Ordinary	Full sun	Seed	4.5/8.2	12-55	42-82
Marjoram (*Origanum majorana*)	TP	Rich light	Sheltered, Full sun	Stem cut	5.8/7.2	20-91	43-81
Marshmallow (*Althea officinalis*)	HP	Rich, moist swamp	Partial shade	Division			
Mistletoe (*Phoradendron flavenscens*)	HP	Moist, oak trees	Partial shade	Seed			
Mugwort (*Artemisia vulgaris*)	HP	Rich moist	Full sun	Division	4.8/8.2	12-165	43-81
Mullein (*Verbascum thapsus*)	HB	Poor dry	Full sun	Seed			
Nettle (*Urtica urens*)	HP	Rich moist	Partial shade	Division			
Oatstraw (*Avena sativa*)	HP	Ordinary, well drained	Full sun	Seed	4.3/8.3	2-164	42-82
Onion (*Allium cepa*)	HP	Rich, well drained	Full sun	Bulb	4.5/8.7	16-109	44-83
Oregano (*Origanum vulgare*)	HP	Light dry	Full sun	Division			
Oregon Grape (*Berberis aquifolium*)	HP	Rich, moist forest	Partial shade	Division			
Parsley (*Petroselinum crispum*)	HB	Rich	Partial shade	Seed	5.3/8.3	12-181	41-79
Passion Flower (*Passiflora caerulea*)	HP	Dry thickets	Partial shade	Division			

Plant	Type	Soil	Light	Propagation	pH		
Pennyroyal (*Mentha pulegium*)	HA	Dry woodlands	Full sun	Seed	4.8/8.3	12-47	45-70
Peppermint (*Menta piperita*)	HP	Rich moist	Full sun	Runners	5.2/8.0	12-157	45-81
Pippissawa (*Chimaphila umbellata*)	TP	Rich, forest floor	Shade	Division			
Plantain (*Plantago major*)	HP	Poor soils	Full sun	Division			
Poke (*Phytolacca americana*)	HP	Rich, low ground	Full sun	Division	4.5/8.0	28-67	46-74
Queen-of-the-Meadow (*Eupatorium purpureum*)	HP	Rich, dry woods	Partial shade	Division			
Raspberry (*Rubus idaeus*)	HP	Rich moist	Full sun	Runners			
Red Clover (*Trifolium pratense*)	HP	Ordinary, well drained	Full sun	Seed			
Rosehip (*Rosa canina*)	HP	Ordinary, moist	Partial sun	Division			
Rosemary (*Rosmarinus officinalis*)	TP	Well drained, light	Full sun	Stem cut	4.5/8.3	12-98	48-77
Rue (*Ruta graveolens*)	HP	Well drained, poor	Partial sun	Stem cut	5.8/8.3	12-102	45-81
Sage (*Salvia officinalis*)	HP	Sandy limed	Full sun	Stem cut	5.1/8.3	12-102	41-77
St. John's Wort (*Hypericum perforatum*)	HP	Ordinary, moist	Full sun	Division			
Sarsaparilla (*Smilax regelii*)	HP	Rich, forest floor	Shade	Division	—	-67	60-77
Sassafras (*Sassafrass albidum*)	HP	Ordinary, woods	Full sun	Seed			
Savory (*Satureia hortensis*)	HA	Light rich	Full sun	Seed	6.3/7.5	12-51	45-70
Scullcap (*Scutellaria lateriflora*)	HP	Swamp, rich moist	Partial shade	Division			
Shepherd's Purse (*Capsella bursa-pastoris*)	HA	Ordinary, well drained	Full sun	Seed			
Slippery Elm (*Ulmus rubra*)	HP	Ordinary, woods	Full sun	Seed			
Spearmint (*Mentha viridis*)	HP	Rich moist	Full sun	Division	4.5/7.5	24-51	43-74
Strawberry (*Fragaria vesca*)	HP	Rich, well drained	Full sun	Runners			
Tansy (*Tanacetum vulgare*)	HP	Ordinary, well drained	Full sun	Division	4.8/7.5	16-51	45-63
Tarragon (*Artemsia dracunculus*)	HP	Well drained, light	Full sun	Division	6.3/7.8	12-51	45-63
Thyme (*Thymus vulgaris*)	HP	Sandy, well drained	Full sun	Stem cut	4.5/7.8	20-102	45-70

TABLE 6

Soil, Light, and Propagation Methods for some Herbs and Spices

HERB	FORM	SOIL	LIGHT	PROPAGATION METHOD	pH	ANNUAL PRECIP. (INCHES)	ANNUAL TEMP. (F.)
Valerian (*Valeriana officinalis*)	HP	Swamp, rich moist	Partial shade	Division			
Vervain (*Verbena hastata*)	HP	Ordinary, moist	Full sun	Division			
Walnut (*Juglans nigra*)	HP	Ordinary, woods	Full sun	Seed			
White Oak (*Quercus alba*)	HP	Ordinary, woods	Partial sun	Seed			
Wild Cherry (*Prunus serotina*)	HP	Moist woods	Full sun	Seed			
Wild Lettuce (*Lactuca scariola*)	HA	Dry waste area	Full sun	Seed			
Wintergreen (*Gaultheria procumbens*)	HP	Dry, wooded areas	Partial shade	Division	4.8/6.8	24-51	46-63
Witch Hazel (*Hamamelis virginiana*)	HP	Moist, forest floor	Partial shade	Division			
Woodruff (*Asperula odorata*)	HP	Moist leafy	Full shade	Division	4.5/8.3	20-55	45-66
Wormwood (*Artemisia absinthium*)	HP	Poor light	Partial sun	Stem cut	4.8/8.2	12-51	41-70
Yarrow (*Archillea millefolium*)	HP	Dry, waste areas	Full sun	Division			
Yellow Dock (*Rumex crispus*)	HP	Rich, swampy areas	Partial shade	Division			
Yerba Mate' (*Ilex paraguaiensis*)	TA	Ordinary, moist	Partial shade	Seed			
Yerba Santa (*Eriodictyon californicum*)	HA	Poor dry	Full sun	Seed			

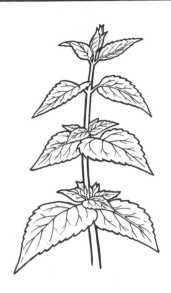

BERGAMOT
(*Monarda didyma* and species)
Libiatae family

Bergamot is generally recognized by its red tubular florets arranged in whorls. It is a hardy perennial, and member of the mint family. It can be a very invasive plant with dense, shallow root systems with many runners. *Monarda didyma* thrives in moist, somewhat acid soils, while the lavender-flowered species, *Monarda fistulosa*, covers the abandoned pastures in limestone areas throughout New England. The lemon bergamot, *Monarda citriodora*, grows in the Appalachian mountains. All are native to North America.

Root division is a most reliable method of propagation. Plants from seed are seldom uniform as they tend to cross-pollinate with wild bergamots. Germination of the seed is about two weeks in diffused light, with viability falling off sharply with seed over two years old. Expect little or no harvest from the first year of seedlings, taking almost one year to establish. Transplanting is most successful at any time of the year except late fall.

Established plantings should be divided every 3 to 4 years, or they will die out due to rapid spreading habits. The roots are easily pulled apart, with only the outer roots being replanted. The center roots should be discarded. Bergamot requires high moisture and fertile (humus-rich) soils. Care must be taken during cultivation because of the shallow root systems of bergamot. In autumn the entire plant should be covered with compost 1 inch deep for both winter protection and a source of nutrients the following year.

Bergamot can be harvested for the essential oil or as a hay crop. Last year more than 35 tons of essential oil was imported into North America from such countries as West Germany, France, and Switzerland. There is a growing leaf market as well. It is extensively used in perfumes, creams, lotions, and soaps. It is also widely used as an ingredient in flavor formulations with fruity citrus notes in most all food categories. It is primarily marketed as an oil, although the crude herb market is growing.

TABLE 7a
The Annual Precipitation of the Capitols of the 50 States

4	8	12	16	20	24	28	32	35	39	43	47	51	55	59	63	>63	inches
										SC							
										RI							
										PA	VA						
										KS	TN						
										WI	NC						
									OK	OH	OR						
									VT	NY	MA		NJ				
		WY	CO					TX	IA	ME	MD	WV	GA				
	NV	UT	ID					NE	NH	IN	KY	NC	WA			FL	
AZ	MT	NM	ND	CA	HI	MN	MI	IL	MO	CT	DE	AR	MS	AL	LA	AK	

TABLE 7b
The Annual Mean Temperature of the Capitols of the 50 States

41	43	45	46	48	50	52	53	55	57	59	61	63	64	66	68	70	72	75	77°F
					UT														
					RI	PA		WV											
		WY		WA	MA	OR		NJ		OK									
VT		WI	NH	NY	NE	OH	NM	MO		TN									
ND		ME	SD	NV	IA	IN	MD	KY	VA	NC	NC		MS		FL				
AK	MT	MN	MI	CT	CO	IL	KS	DE	CA	AR	GA	SC	AL		LA	TX	AZ		HI

From *Botanicals as Environmental Indicators*, Duke, J., Hurst, S., and Kluve, J., *Supplement to the 1977 Herbarist*, © 1977.

56

Once a source of water supply has been established, the cost and methods employed by each farmer are his own. The Soil Conservation Service is an indispensable source of information as to when and how much water a specific crop needs, most economical and efficient ways to deliver the water over your field. The agency can help determine what soil types and slopes are feasible to irrigate.

ECOSYSTEM DATA ON HERBS AND SPICES

Table 6 shows the soil, light, and propagation methods for some herbs and spices. This includes pH, mean annual precipitation and temperature.

Peppermint

CHAPTER 4

Basic Farm Machinery

Before we choose our tools and techniques, we must choose our dreams and values, for some technologies serve them, while others make them unobtainable. —
Rain: The Journal of Appropriate Technology

Machines are made in all kinds of sizes. The reason is, of course, that there is variation in the size of the many jobs to be done on the 8,000,000 farms in North America. Generally, large machinery is associated with a large acreage. It is always a mistake to buy too small a machine. It is also a mistake to buy a machine that is too large for the work to be done. Once the farm plan has been decided, and the power unit for field work selected, the remaining choices become relatively easy.

Plowing or harrowing an acre of land on a 60 acre farm is a different job from plowing or harrowing an acre on a 600 acre farm. The real problem is to select the machine that will do the work economically and in the time that can be allotted to the operation, rather than to select a machine that will do the work in the shortest time possible. On a 60 acre farm much more time can be spent per acre in preparing the land and seeding. A 600 acre farm needs, perhaps, ten times as much grain to be sown during the time available for the same operation.

It is not always easy to fit the farm perfectly with machinery and equipment.

It is for this reason that buying machinery should be done conservatively at the beginning, gradually building your machinery inventory as the need becomes clear. This does not solve those problems where more than one tractor and other equipment might be needed, especially when first developing the soil and building a topsoil suitable for the chosen farm plan. Purchasing these various tools for a small farm is usually economically unwise where small acreage cannot create a sufficient cash flow to underwrite their purchase.

The small farmer, however, has several options or alternatives. He may be able to lease some of the required farm machinery from local distributors, or he can have someone from the local community do custom work for a fee or percentage of his crop. The latter option is quite popular in many rural areas. Commonly 30 to 40% of the crop is given to the custom farmer for his labor and expenses. A neighbor usually charges between $25 to $40 per acre to swath, windrow, and bale one cut of alfalfa. This charge includes labor, wire, and depreciation of the neighbor's equipment.

Cooperative ownership of special machinery and tools is well worth considering as an option or alternative. On many farms there are machines that are not fully used. The typical farm tractor, for example, is used an average of about 500 hours per year, and such equipment as plows, mowers and drills usually average well under 100 hours of use per year. Some of the smaller and less expensive pieces of equipment are sometimes used no more than one full day per year. It must be remembered however, that farming is a job of doing many things, each at the right time, and consequently the ownership of a piece of equipment must be fitted to the job, and not the job to the machine.

Wherever practical, it pays to get more use than many farmers are getting out of their machinery. If you could use your tools twice as much as the average farmer, you would reduce your machine costs by over one-third per day. Thus, a number of profit sharing cooperatives invest in farm machinery for use on sev-

SWATHER

60

eral different fields, rather than encourage individual ownership. This results in spreading the overhead charges — interest, taxes, and obsolescence — over a greater number of working days. Hence, a savings is made to all of the cooperative owners.

The man who is buying a set of equipment to begin farming will do well to buy conservatively. The tractor and only the main tillage tools to go with it should be your first investment. Then add the other items that are necessary — a lowboy wagon and the basic small tools. Hire equipment for harvesting. Add machinery only as you gain both capital and experience in need for and use of equipment. If capital is limited, the first investment in machinery often can be cut down considerably by buying used pieces at farm sales and "bone yards."

TRACTORS

The tractor is the most important investment in modern farming. No other tool is as hardworking and versatile. Since most of the older tractors from the 1940s and 1950s were built to last, you should not feel constrained to buy a newer machine. Some of the better built tractors include International Harvester's Farmall Model H (or M), John Deere's Model B, Allis Chalmer's Model W-30, Case's Model SC, Oliver's Row Crop Model 70, or Ford's Model 9N. With the exception of Ford and Case, all these tractors were factory-equipped with narrow row cropping front ends.

In most respects, the tractor is very similar to an automobile. A diesel engine transmits its power through a propeller shaft to a gearbox, eight or ten speed for most currently built tractors. This power is then transmitted to the drive wheels through a differential gear. This propulsive force (or tractive-pull) depends not only on the force that the engine transmits to the large rear drive wheels, but also on the load on these wheels. If the axle load is too small, the wheels will slip and fail to grip the soil. To increase the load and thus press the drive wheels more firmly against the soil, ballast weights may be mounted at the rear. Sometimes the tires are filled with water and antifreeze instead of air. Often the attached implements drawn by the tractor are designed to develop an additional downward force on the rear axle of the tractor.

Modern tractors are now extensively used for driving various kinds of other farm machinery. Because of this, they are usually provided with three power take-off shafts (PTO). Two of them are mounted under the trailer coupling and rotate at 1,000 rpm and 540 rpm. The power is transmitted to the attached machinery through an articulated shaft. The third PTO shaft protrudes forward and is usually intended for driving an attached grass or grain cutting device. This shaft speed is also 1,000 rpm.

The selection of the correct tractor size involves a considerable number of variables. The implements you plan to use will have a decisive influence on determining what tractor to buy. It's not the efficiency with which power is transmitted that is of greatest importance in the final analysis. The most important criterion is how much drawbar work the tractor can produce, and how much work needs to be done on your farm? To truly save money on machinery and fuel, the tractor should also be selected for the work to be done on your field.

The proper matching of implements to tractors improves field performance while reducing operating costs, repairs, fuel consumption, and (most important) initial capital outlays. The soil resistance, commonly referred to as implement draft, will affect field performance more than any other factor. Operating depth, speed of travel over the field, soil type, and moisture content all interact to determine the draft of an implement. Deep tillage implements, such as moldboard plows, will be markedly affected by these factors. Soil moisture can also affect draft. For example, a 1% increase in soil moisture can decrease the moldboard draft by more than 10%.

Thus, the tractor size selection comes back to sizing tillage implements. To be accurate, the usable power rating must be used rather than maximum PTO, engine, or other ratings. A PTO rating, for example, does not take into consideration the power lost in power trains and final drives. These are typically about 10%, but can be more than 25% in some situations. The horsepower requirements needed will be determined by the interaction of speed and total draft required.

The total draft is equal to the product of draft per foot of width times the width of the implement. Increasing the speed of the tractor will require a reduction in the draft, either by working shallower depths or narrower widths:

$$\text{DRAWBAR HORSEPOWER} = \frac{\text{TOTAL DRAFT (pounds) x SPEED (mph)}}{375}$$

Thus, to determine the maximum equipment width, the formula becomes

$$\text{WIDTH (ft)} = \frac{(\text{USABLE hp x 375})}{[\text{SPEED (mph) x DRAFT (pounds per foot)}]}$$

Assume you want to pull a heavy tandum disc harrow 5 mph with a 300 hp (engine) tractor. From the soil resistance table (Table 9), the average draft will require 325 pounds per foot of width. The 300 hp tractor has only 165 usable hp on firm soil, known as the drawbar horsepower. For most situations, a .86 factor can be used to convert engine hp to usable hp. Using these estimates, the tractor should be sized to a 38 foot disc. Operating at 6 mph, the width of the implement would have to be reduced to about 32 feet to maintain the same total draft.

Once you have decided on the proper power size for your needs, you then want to make some decisions about transmissions. Clutchless transmissions offer an infinite number of variable speeds, both forward and backward. These are most useful for mowing and landscaping operations. The standard shift transmission usually offers ten speeds forward and two reverse as a minimum. The easier it is to shift, the more likely you are to choose the most efficient gear for an operation. A differential lock puts the power of both rear wheels to work when you lose traction under one wheel.

The working attachments (depending on the type) may either be mounted on the tractor's three-point hitch (which enables tools to be raised and lowered by tractor's hydraulic system). Or they can be mounted in front, or connected to the tractor's drawbar and pulled behind the vehicle. If you plan to run your tractor on the road, the three-point hitch is needed to lift your implements clear of the ground. A front-end loader can also be one of the most important and versatile parts of your tractor: for moving manure, delivering feed, handling cordwood, building and repairing farm roads, pulling fence posts, and any number of tasks.

The final thing to look at in your tractor is the PTO. There are three basic types of PTOs: transmission, live, and independent. With transmission PTO, the shaft will stop any time the tractor's clutch is depressed. A live PTO enables you to stop the tractor's forward motion while the PTO continues to rotate. The independent PTO can be engaged and disengaged without clutching and without changing the tractor's ground speed or bringing the tractor to a stop.

Two-wheel-drive tractors have been standard since tractors replaced mules and horses on the farm. In the past, cheap fuel allowed farmers to be relatively unconcerned with traction efficiency. Four-wheel-drive tractors are more efficient but also very expensive. A new type of tractor has been developed to provide greater efficiency but at reduced cost. It is known as a front-wheel-assist (FWA), a unit for which the smaller front wheels are also powered. This improves drawbar horsepower more than 15% with the same engine, thus improving fuel costs. FWA type tractors are used extensively in Europe nowadays because they are more efficient. They convert a higher percentage of the engine horsepower to drawbar horsepower.

The economics of owning farm machinery can be deceiving. After buying the tractor, you must consider repair, insurance, taxes, and interest costs if a loan is required. As a rule of thumb, most small farmers can estimate the overhead costs of the tractor by first dividing the initial purchase price (including delivery) by eight (the life expectancy of a new tractor) to yield the average cost per year. This yearly cost is further divided by the average number of days, hours and acres to get respective overhead costs. For example, suppose you purchased a tractor for $1,500 and used it for 20 ten hour days for tillage and cultivation of 100 acres. The tractor, in this situation, would have an average overhead cost of $187.50 per year, $9.38 per day and $1.88 per acre. This does not include either labor or fuel costs, only the tractor's average overhead costs. For further examples, Table 14 (page 88) lists approximate cost summaries for a number of implements and power units.

TABLE 8

Soil Resistance or pounds of draft per foot of width for a number of farm operations

OPERATION	SOIL RESISTANCE POUNDS OF DRAFT FOOT OF WIDTH	OPERATION	SOIL RESISTANCE POUNDS OF DRAFT FOOT OF WIDTH
Plowing (8" depth)		*Field Cultivator*	
Gumbo	1,250	Heavy clay soils	650
Clay	1,050	Clay loam	450
Loam	950	Sandy loam	300
Sandy loam	700	Sand	150
Sand	350	*Spike Tooth Harrow*	
One-way Disc		Heavy draft	60
Heavy draft	400	Medium draft	40
Medium draft	300	Light draft	20
Light draft	200	*Land Plane*	
Chisel Plow (8")		Heavy draft	800
Hard, dry	800	Medium draft	550
Medium clay loam	500	Light draft	300
Sand, sandy loam	200	*Subsoiling*	
Tandem Disc (offset)		Sandy loam	70-110 #/in depth
Heavy draft	400	Medium clay loam	100-160 #/in depth
Medium draft	325	*Planting*	
Light draft	250	Corn, soybean, cotton	250-450
Tandem Disc Harrow		Grain drill	30-100
Heavy draft	300		
Medium draft	200		
Light draft	100		

From the American Society of Agricultural Engineers (ASAE) research.

Although the plow is one of the oldest agricultural implements, it has changed very little in shape and construction over the centuries. The only real change has been the plow tail, or handles.

The *coulter,* attached to the plow-beam, makes a vertical cut in the ground. The plowshare coming behind it determines the depth of the furrow. It cuts the soil horizontally and lifts it to the moldboard, which then turns it over. The slip heel provides bottom guidance and the landslide takes the side thrust. For completely turning the soil or for plowing-in straw or stubble, the plow is often equipped with a skim coulter. The plowshare and moldboard together are called the plow bottom.

The plow is attached to the tractor by means of securing pins to the towing control rods, which are usually hydraulically controlled. A two-way reversible plow has a right handed and left handed plow bottom. On reaching the end of a furrow, the farmer reverses the plow. He can thus plow in either direction and throw all the furrows in one direction. The ordinary moldboard plow can only be used in one direction. This means that the return journey to the starting end of the field must be made with the plowshares lifted out of the ground. A reversible plow reduces plowing costs on larger fields by eliminating these unproductive returns through the field. The option is plowing around the field, rather than back and forth, creating some problems when you finish the field at its center. The reversible plow eliminates uneven crops.

In order to create a good plow, the furrow should be turned to the proper angle and should be fairly straight. This requires a proportional or relationship between the depth of plowing and the width of the furrow. The best angles between the surface of the subsoil and the turned topsoil is 30 to 45 degrees. To obtain this angle, most farmers use the rule: *The depth of plowing should be one half the width of the furrow.* If plowing is too shallow (one third or less of the width), the furrow slice is inverted. Stubble and rubbish break contact with the subsoil and are poorly mixed with the soil.

When the furrow slice is set well on edge, water rising by capillary action from below and rainwater falling along the face of the furrows mix and break down the lower edge of the furrow slice. There is also better ventilation of plowed plants and roots so that the breakdown of organic and inorganic matter can proceed most efficiently. At the same time the upper angle of the inverted furrow slice can now be most easily pulverized by subsequent tillage operations to make good seedbeds. When heavy sod holds its form, heavy rolling and packing can be used to bring it in closer contact with the subsoil. You must always avoid intersoil spaces that are too large when you plow.

There are several important rules concerning the use of the moldboard plow:

1. The draft-per-foot cross-section of the furrow cut increases with the increased width. The draft is a measure of energy required to move a plow through the soil. Its units are usually expressed pounds per foot, (see Table 9).

THE SPADING MACHINE

A new development out of Europe is the spading machine. It operates off a PTO shaft from a tractor with primary reduction via a robust gearbox with machine cut gears. The machine more or less spades the soil, and therefore no plow effect is available to smear the soil or develop plowpan barriers. The machine's excellent mixing operation gives good soil structure. A major feature of this tillage system is the minimal tractor power requirement. Also, the machine is low maintenance. Although not readily available in North America, the spading machine is certain to achieve small farm application because of the many designs and working widths being manufactured.

Tools designed especially for small farms are surfacing around the world. The old attitude that machines must be too expensive for small farmers to own or compete against is fading as superfarms find their public policy support eroded.

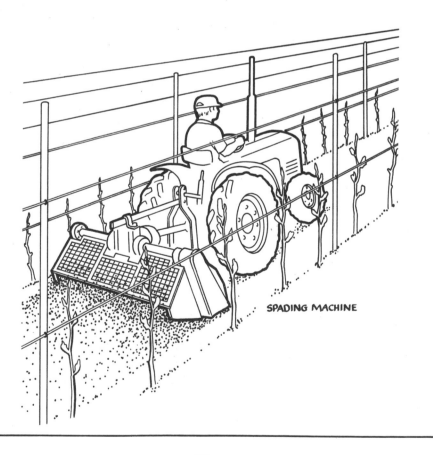

SPADING MACHINE

2. The draft-per-foot cross-section of the furrow cut decreases as the depth is increased.
3. The sharper the curve of the moldboard, the greater the draft of the plow. A fallow-ground moldboard pulls harder than the sod type of the same size. (See figure 1).
4. When the soil is either too wet or too dry, the draft is increased over that for the soil in good plowing condition.

There are chiefly two types of turning plow, the moldboard and the disc, although unique equipment is coming on-line in Europe. The disc is well suited to hard, dry soils and does fairly well where there is rubbish or vegetation which needs to be turned under. It does not work well on stony or sod soil types of land. It is more efficient than the moldboard plow on hard soils. If the soil is also stony, then the notched disc is used over a solid type disk.

To work the subsoil without turning it to the surface, a special plow is used. This is always done in the fall. Usually a solid type disc plow is employed. There are two discs, one behind and below the other. They are carried on a sulky frame, and with proper adjustments, can till 12 to 16 inches into the soil. They are used because the moldboard plow would throw subsoil to the top of your topsoil. Discs only partially throw subsoils. The right proportions of subsoil to the topsoil should be given special attention. These are what determine your seedbed characteristics and can vary widely from one crop to another. Wide sweep blades are less likely to become clogged, whereas moldboards clog all the time.

HARROWS

The farmer usually makes a distinction between harrows and cultivators. Harrows are used to prepare the seed bed, whereas cultivators are used to intertill growing crops and kill weeds. The two are interchangeable depending on crops and convenience. Their patterns differ markedly, but almost all are like harrows. The general practice now is to use cultivators carrying many shovels, so that the soil is kept level and stirred thoroughly at a constant shallow depth.

The harrow is a broad, many-toothed implement, usually without wheels and dragged behind the tractor. There are three basic types of harrows:
1. The spike-tooth harrow is light and well-suited to clean soils which are in generally good condition. The spikes are usually adjustable and consist of two to four sections, each adjustable by means of a lever. It is very effective in pulverizing, and to some extent, compacting land freshly plowed.
2. The spike-tooth harrow draws to the ground better than the spike-tooth harrow and works to greater depths. This tends to bring lumps and stones to the surface and is used to collect rootstock and vines, such as blackberries. It is more efficient in loosening soil and is usually used on

soils low in organic material or in poor physical condition. They are also used on newly cleared fields to loosen soil, break clods, expose root segments and loosen seedbeds that have compacted due to rain.

3. The disc harrow draws less draft than the other types of harrow. It is very effective in stirring, pulverizing, and compacting the soil, and ranks in importance to the plow in the preparation of the seedbed. There are several types of disc harrow: the solid disc, the cutaway disc, and the spading disc. The last two take hold of hard and stony soils better than the solid disc. The angle of the disc determines the extent to which it draws to the soil and the extent of pulverization and turning of the soil.

Rigid frameworks are used in loamy, non-rocky soils, while more flexible floating frameworks are necessary with stony ground. Both tandem and offset disc arrangements in the harrow now come in three-point hitch models and trailer types. The trailer type tandem disc harrow requires extra weights on the rear sections for even cutting effects. The trail offset unit needs adjustable transport wheels for depth control. Both rely for their penetration on the angled opposition of the gangs of discs and the cup of each individual disc.

Of all the soil stirring tools, the disc harrow is the most versatile. It is one of the most important tools for the small farmer. Discs were employed in the past for in-row weed control. Throwing soil in toward the row, the cultivator smothered the weeds.

COMPACTORS

The most common tool to pack the soil is the roller, originally just a large log dragged by several horses. The value of the roller depends mostly on its weight and diameter. They are used primarily to crush clods on heavier soils, to firm the soil in case of lighter soils (sand and sandy loam), and to smooth the surface soil. Subsurface compacters (corrugated and crusher types) are used in arid and semiarid regions to firm the soil beneath the surface. Moisture is then better distributed and conserved.

The smooth roller is used extensively, but is being replaced now by the culti-packer. This crushes the clods to a greater degree. The culti-packer is also effective in firming the soil and leaves the surface of the ground with a thin mulch instead of smooth, as does the smooth roller. The bar roller is said to be intermediate in effectiveness between the two. Plankers are excellent for crushing clods and leveling the ground, but they are not very efficient in compacting the soil. The treader is used to pack and pulverize the soil in stubble-mulch farming.

MOWERS

Most standing crops are harvested by mowing. The small farmer usually has two alternatives, the rotary swather and the side mount cutter bar. The swather is relatively new and works best for most specialty crops, large acreages, or where the crop does not want to be disturbed in its windrow. The fewer times a product must be handled, the more leaf is left on the harvested crop. They are, however, rather expensive and require some skill in driving them.

The most popular system, by far, is the cutter bar type mower. It cuts a 5 to 7 foot wide swath, and is mounted in front of the rear tire on the drawbar. It can also be dragged, but this type does not work nearly as well in uniform lines in harvesting your crop when trailed. The cutter bar type mower is PTO-driven and cuts by shearing the stems between reciprocating knife sections and stationary guards. The knives and bars are mounted on the bar that can be lifted (usually with hydraulics) to clear obstacles and for transport. It is hinged with a breakaway device that is designed to prevent damage to the pitman driving rod and mower gearbox.

There are disadvantages to the side mount bar cutters. The cutter bar is prone to tip-loading in heavy stands or crops that are wet. They do require less maintenance, however. Small farmers find that using a cutter bar effectively involves keeping tractor speeds down and knives sharpened, rather than increasing horsepower. Most mowers are designed to use one horsepower per foot of cutter bar length. Since most of these are geared to run up to about 900 rpm with a forward travel rate of 3 inches per stroke, this means they cut most effectively at speeds up to 5 mph.

Side-throw delivery rakes are then used to collect the crop cut in the swath and form a windrow. The same rake is also used to turn windrows when there is a need to control dry leaf-to-stem ratios. Conditioners can be used with a swather, but not a side mounted cutter bar. The conditioners break the stem in several places, allowing for sun cured products to dry uniformly. Since most

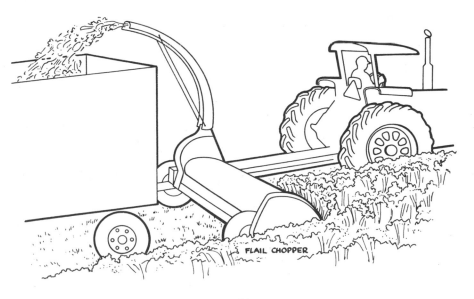

FLAIL CHOPPER

leaves dry before the stem, this conditioning allows stems to dry uniformly with the leaf. By turning the windrow several times, the stem will dry at the same rate as the leaf. This makes for a much more marketable product and is critically important to the small farmer.

GREEN CHOPPERS

Forage harvesters and flail choppers are recent additions to the list of tools used by the small farmer. These machines cut or chop standing forage crops and load them into wagons, or piggy-back systems. Although they are commonly used on row crops such as corn and hay type grasses for livestock, they have also been used for specialty crops that will be further processed by oil extraction or processing. The flail chopper, simplest of the two, involves a two-phase operation. A cutter bar or row crop cutting knives remove the crop from the field as the first phase of the operation. The crop is then force-fed with feed rolls into a second set of cutting knives. These knives cut with a shearing action against a stationary bar, similar to that of a lawnmower. A blower then delivers the processed crop to a wagon or piggyback system.

The flail chopper is based on a design similar to the hammermill type stalk shredders, and is best used on partially dried field crops. Cutting 2 to 10 inch lengths, its cut depends on the impact of its chisel-pointed, hook-shaped knives for both cutting functions and delivery operation. Although it is most often used for standing crops, it can be used on windrowed crops because of the suction pickup action of the whirling knives. Both the flail chopper and the forage harvester are PTO driven for tractors of 20 to 40 hp engines. They are quite versatile.

BALERS

The pickup baler is used to bale most crops directly from the windrow in the field. The crop is picked up by prongs and passed to the auger, which pushes it to the feed prongs. These deliver the crop to the bale chamber on each stroke of the compressing plunger. The latter compresses the crop into compact layers. Protruding stalks which sometimes cause jamming are cut off by knives. A number of these layers are then tied to form bales, whose length and density can be adjusted.

The baler is driven by an internal combustion engine mounted on the baler itself, or is driven by a PTO shaft from the tractor towing it. The flywheel equalizes the power thrusts of the compression plunger and carries the latter past its dead-center point. As a safeguard against damage from stones or wood pieces, the flywheel is driven by a shearing pin, mounted on the shaft. When overloaded, the pin shears through, allowing the flywheel to rotate. The new farmer must frequently replace this pin.

The compacted and finished bales are automatically tied with wire or string.

String is only used for bales with a weight of less than 65 pounds and with a storage life less than six months. Older type strings can rot when stored outside, albeit under cover. Wire costs more money, however, and sometimes there are shortages during critical harvest seasons. Most small farmers use wire whenever possible because it is stronger. This means the bales can be transported with minimal crop damage. Most truckers prefer to haul wired bales which weigh 90 to 120 pounds. If you plan to sell your crop from the field, 90 pound bales are best, all things considered.

COMBINES

The combine is a combination grain harvesting and threshing machine. The grain or flowerhead is cut, threshed and cleaned in one continuous operation. The combine is either self-propelled or towed by a tractor. The functional elements of the combine can be divided into five major sections: header, thresher, straw conveyers, cleaners, and bagging area.

The header section includes mowing and delivery machinery that brings down the straw and seed grains or flowerheads to the threshing cylinders. The threshing cylinder rubs the grain out of the heads against a "concave." The grains, chaff and short fragments of straw fall through the interstices between the bars of the concave and into the cleaning shoe. Some of the grain is carried along with the straw. This is stopped by checking flaps, and is shaken out of it on shaking screens on the straw rack of the machine. The straw drops out the back of the machine and is left in a windrow for later baling, or is scattered over the ground by a fan-like straw spreader.

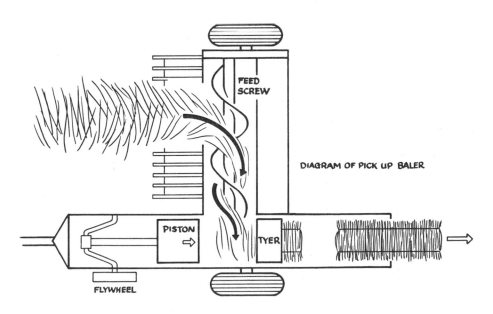

FEED SCREW

DIAGRAM OF PICK UP BALER

PISTON

TYER

FLYWHEEL

71

CARAWAY
(*Carum carvi* L.)
Umbelliferae family

As a biennial, caraway is among the best known and most widely used in almost every part of the world. Last year more than 3,400 metric tons of seed was imported into the United States alone from the Netherlands, Egypt, and Poland. This does not include caraway oil, another large market. Seeds are best sown at $^1/_2$ inch depths in either late summer or early spring. Germination is exceedingly slow, and special care must be taken to prevent weeds from taking over.

Caraway seems to prefer a fairly heavy soil on the dry side. It is often used to break up and aerate heavy soils. A spring planting will produce bushy green foliage about 8 inches high during the first summer. The foliage will retain most of its verdancy during the winter. The second summer 2 to 3 foot stalks will develop, topped with clusters of white flowers. Seeds form by mid-summer and ripen by fall. Harvest times can be shortened with seed sown as soon as they ripen in the fall for future crops.

Caraway should be harvested as soon as the seeds darken and ripen in the fall. Usually they can be separated from the umbel stems by threshing with a combine. The seed can be dried in the hot sun on racks, or a continuous-feed conveyor-tunnel system could be built cheaply. It would need propane heat and several fans for circulation. Look for insects among the seed, this is a common problem. If in doubt about their presence, pour boiling water over the seed sample in a strainer. Redry and seal in an air-tight jar. If any webs or musty smell develop it means weevils are present and the crop needs to be treated with the inert fumigant ethylene oxide.

The markets which use caraway seeds and oil are extensive. Not only is it a widely used domestic spice, it is also used in commercial food products such as baked goods (rye breads, etc.) and meat and meat products. The oil is used in all major categories of foods, including alcoholic and nonalcoholic beverages, frozen dairy desserts, candy, condiments and relishes. The list is endless. It is its enjoyable and distinctive licorice-flavored tang that has placed it in kitchens throughout the world.

It is used as an oil as a fragrance component in cosmetic preparations including toothpaste, mouthwash, soaps, creams, lotions, and perfumes. Caraway is also used in some carminative, stomachic, and laxative preparations. The oil has been used as a flavor in pharmaceuticals, with 6 pounds of seed yielding only 4 ounces of oil. Full sun increases oil yields.

The grain, or flowerheads, is shaken out of the straw and then delivered to the cleaning shoe. In the shoe, the grain, or flowerheads, is separated from the chaff and cleaned by sieves and a blast of air. The chaff and fragments of straw are thrown out from the back of the machine. The grain falls through the sieve and onto the clean-grain auger, or screw conveyor, which then conveys it to an elevator and into the storage tanks or bags. Any heads which fail to go through the sieves and are thrown backward by the air blast fall short and are dropped into a return auger to the threshing cylinder. Correct air flow is adjusted by throttling the intake of the fan and by altering the settings of baffles. This minimizes grain, (or flowerheads), losses drop out the back end of the combine.

These are the basic farm tools which will be needed for most small farm crops. There are a number of specialized devices for such things as lifting, blowing, pulling (wagons, etc.), and generally moving heavy, bulky items and crops in both the field and in a warehouse. PTO's are used to drive a number of other tools such as posthole diggers and any number of post-harvest devices. Since most of these are extremely specialized, the small farmer is advised to either lease them for specific jobs, or form a cooperative to buy them for use on a number of different farms.

The first step in equipping any small farm venture is to take stock of resources available in your neighborhood. This should include any surplus steel yards within 100 miles radius. I have found that the very best buys have been made at farm auctions and old "boneyards" carrying used farm machinery. You need to be cautious in buying lots of equipment too large or specialized for small farm needs. Seek alternative ways to do the job, or obtain access to equipment via custom farming methods and cooperatives. The objective of the small farmer is to make money, not spend it.

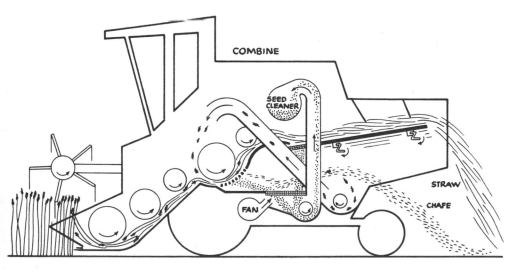

Catnip

CHAPTER 5

The Farm Plan,
With Specific Examples

A realm of intimate personal power is developing, the power of the individual to conduct his own education, find his own inspiration, shape his own environment.

Whole Earth Catalog

The typical family sized farm has the labor of the operator, several months of family labor, and some hired help at peak seasons. The total is equivalent to the work of about one-and-a-half to two men for the year. To make the most profitable use of this labor, it is desirable to have a definite and complete work schedule. This work schedule, or farm plan, should include work plans for the farm, storage, and eventual marketing of the harvested crop. It may also be desirable to have a work schedule for the use of machines that are used jointly by two or more families.

CONSIDERATION FOR THE WORK CALENDAR

Since the income from farming cannot be had without physical effort, the farmer who wants to make the greatest income must plan to keep both labor and equipment continuously busy. A work calendar will help achieve this objective because it enables the operator to plan ahead so that no person or item of equipment is idle, and to see that the most essential jobs are done first, and on time.

Farm plans are best when they are based on years of experience with a lot of common sense thrown in. Eventually routine jobs become standardized within reasonable limits, and schedules of past years become those of the future. It is then less necessary to put in writing many of the things that had to be worked out during the first few years of farming. The development of a work calendar, whether written in some prescribed form or not, is rather easy for some types of farming, but quite difficult for others.

The very fact that the time schedules must be changed in response to weather changes and other factors means that the calendar must be constantly modified. Although many might think of a calendar of farm work as applying to a single year, it necessarily must include things that affect the farm for many years running. Crop schedules help get the work done well and on time, and this results in a larger production of higher quality crops for a given amount of effort. Some of the things done in a single year without definite plans may place the farm under an operating handicap for many years to follow.

Plowing a field of sod at the wrong time, or planting a crop up and down instead of around the slope of a hill, or overworking a soft team of horses in the spring, may be the result of a faulty labor schedule. More often, however, the things that go undone count the most. Often a drainage job must be planned and scheduled in advance if it is ever to be completed. Sometimes the complete drainage schedule will extend over two or more years. The same holds true for extensive building repairs, new buildings, pasture improvement, orchard development, or any number of many other farm jobs that are part of farm development and maintenance.

A work schedule for the rainy day or cold weather is essential on any farm. These are the days when good licks can be gotten in that will save labor and expense on the days when the farmer should be in the field. These are the planning days when neighbors can be consulted and operating schedules worked out for cooperative use of labor and machinery. Rainy days are ideally suited for cleaning and whitewashing barns and hen houses, and for repairing doors, windows, floors, and gates. This is a good time also for indoor repair and maintenance of equipment and tools.

In cold weather, building materials and farm supplies can be moved. Manure can be hauled and spread in many sections. If a heated shop is available, harnesses can be oiled and repaired, machines and tools can be put into shape, and numerous other jobs completed. A well planned labor schedule finds plenty for everyone to do, and may actually result in less work overall.

A work calendar helps in scheduling time for work off the farm. This can be coordinated with neighbors when work is exchanged, but of just as much importance is the work plan for those who have time to spend away from the farm —at work, for pay. Of all the jobs a farmer does, work off the farm is often the most profitable when working with limited resources. Even farm operators of substantial means sometimes spend a great deal of time at other work. Important to the farming business is the buying and selling of crops, sometimes for immediate turnover, sometimes for feeding or finishing of livestock on the farm.

Once a work schedule and farm plan has been formulated, a statement of funds must be developed. This budgets how much money is needed at specific times during the farm year. This statement of funds should include labor, machinery needs, and any overhead costs, such as power and water ditch requirements. Storage and marketing should be also included in this summary. This gives a *pro forma* profit and loss picture for the next year or more, and projects necessary farm loans or support. Let's look at a specific example, as a model for any number of other herbs or spices.

CATNIP HERB AS A PRIME MINT EXAMPLE

With an inventory of 3,500 species on this planet, the mints represent roughly 1.5% of the flowering plant kingdom. When you look at a list of herbs, condiments and spices, you will find that close to 25% of the listed species are mints. Those currently imported into the United States and Canada in significant tonnages include anise-hyssop, apple mint, lemon balm, basil, bergamot, catnip, clary sage, horehound, hyssop, lavender, marjoram, oregano, rosemary, white sage, savory and thyme.

I think you get the idea. The potentials for "making a mint" in mint farming are great. The farming of catnip for commercial markets was chosen as representative of how most mint crops might be harvested for the spice and herb trade. As an alternative crop for the small farmer, it is ideal. It also is an excellent example of the opportunities available in herb and spice farming.

Before the use of tea from China became common, English peasants were in the habit of brewing catnip as a stimulant. The leaves and young shoots are still used in France as a seasoning, and is grown regularly for that purpose. Traditional uses for catnip include chewing the leaves to alleviate toothaches. It has been used by inhabitants of the Southern Appalachian regions as a cold remedy since the eighteenth century. Catnip oil, obtained from steam distillation, is used in small quantities as a scent in trapping bobcats and mountain lions even today.

The flowering tops of catnip yield up to 1.0% volatile oil, 78% being nepetalactone, the main attractant to cats. Also present in this oil are citronellal, geraniol, citral, carvacrol and pulegone, all excellent natural insecticides. Thymol, principally extracted from thyme, is also extracted from catnip as a fungicide. Thymol has beneficial antiseptic uses on the skin and in the nasal and pharyngeal passages. It can be found in most antiseptic solutions and aromatic sprays. Menthol, an alcohol found in most mints, can be prepared synthetically by the hydrogenation of thymol.

THE FARMING OF CATNIP FOR COMMERCIAL MARKETS

Catnip may be propagated from seed or by root division. The seed (3,500 per ounce) should be sown in rows late in the fall and covered lightly. Early spring seed should be germinated before sowing. This is done by soaking the seed in water for 24 hours to soften the casing, mixing in equal amounts of sand, and then storing the mixture in the refrigerator for ten days. The seed is much too small to drill with normal grain drills, so a spinner type broadcaster can be used. The seed should then be covered immediately with 1/4 inch soil and rolled with a cultipacker or roller. The recommended amount of seed is 10 pounds per acre.

Catnip needs liberal amounts of calcium, phosphorus and potassium. Manuring at the rate of 6 to 12 ton per acre is not uncommon, although manure is low in phosphorus. Calcium deficient soils need to be balanced with lime and brought to a pH of 6.5. If the soil is boron deficient, borax should be added at the rate of 20 to 40 pounds per acre. Borax can damage seed and should only be applied as a top dressing on established fields or worked into the soil at least one week before seeding. All of this soil preparation, needless to say, must be done on the basis of adequate soil testing and well before planting.

Usually sowing is not as satisfactory as planting rootstock. Shallow cultivation will favor a vigorous growth in most mints. Grasses remain a serious problem. Developing rootstock for spring or fall plantings will give the small farmer a tremendous advantage in control of orchard grass and other weeds. Sinbar, a pre-emergent herbicide often used for peppermint and spearmint, will work but is expensive and has a number of other drawbacks. For one thing it stays on forever. Also, once down, no other crop but a mint can be grown in that field for at least four or more years.

Initial rootstocks must be developed either by transplanting self-sown seedlings or by nursery cultivation. After the third year, a few fleshy, thick rooted catnip plants sprout several shoots from the top of their roots. Propagation can be carried out by slicing these roots in pieces, so that each has some of the fleshy root and a bud. These pieces are then buried just below the surface of the soil and kept well watered.

The best time to propagate by this method is in the spring, or as soon as new growth starts. Seedlings from nursery stock can be planted in the fall. This will give it a jump over weed growth. If leaf growth has become heavy, remove most of it before replanting, leaving only a small center leaf. Row cropping these new plants seems to give the best control of grasses through cultivation. Only after the rootstock has had three years of growth can the field be converted from rows into a general field crop.

Many mints which do well in full sun can also be grown in partial shade. Almost all will survive well in situations wherein they get only four to six hours of full midday sun. The higher the clay content of the soil, the more likely the mint will suffer from waterlogging or disease during excessively wet seasons. As a rule, the brighter and drier the habitat, the higher the oil content of mints. Disease can wipe out mint monocultures, especially those grown in heavy soils. With the high profits available to the small farmer from mint production, he can afford to rotate his rootstock often enough to avoid most of these problems.

Most mints prefer a 6 to 10 day irrigation schedule. This means that the crop receives 12 hours of irrigation water (usually from a side-roll system) every 6 to 10 days. Catnip prefers a slightly drier set of about 10 days, whereas such mints as lemon balm prefer 6 days. It is recommended that the water line be moved every 12 hours with most mints. Irrigation should be discontinued at least 10 days before harvest. This allows the oils to move further up into the plant while making the stem easier to dry at a more uniform rate with the leaf.

The flowering tops are harvested when the plants are in full bloom. The climate of most areas allows two cuttings a year, one in July and one in September. When grown on a commercial scale, catnip may be cut with a side-bar cutter mower set at a height of 10 inches. After one day of cutting, the crop needs to be turned into a windrow. This raking is usually done with a side-throw delivery rake in the same direction that the field was cut. To prevent leaf-shatter, subsequent rakings or teddings to fluff the crop (for more uniform drying) should be kept at a minimum. If catnip is cut with a rotary mower, with a good condition on the stem, it only requires two turns.

Gathering catnip, when the stem contains less than 15% moisture, can be done with a standard baler. Suitable dryness is easily determined when the crop is dry to the touch, and the stem cracks when bent. Most farmers leave the bales in the field approximately three days to further dry the stem, turning them in the field each day. If the herbage is to be used for oil distillation, it may be dried to only 60% moisture (usually two days of sun cure) and then be taken directly to the distillery via a flail-chopper, piggy-back system of wagons.

Yields of up to 3 ton per acre can be expected from good, irrigated fields after the third year of production. Each cut usually produces about 1.5 ton dry weight yields in bale form. Crude catnip, when sold in baled form, begins marketing at $800 per ton (40 cents per pound). With processing into a cut-and-sift (C/S) form, high quality catnip begins marketing at 85 cents per pound ($1,700 per ton). With further processing, catnip powders (80 plus mesh U.S.S.) can sell for $1.20 per pound, with 100 pound quantities of C/S selling for $1.80 per pound. For the same farm costs growing hay, a small farmer can realize a minimum of over $2,000 per acre gross incomes.

Most medium regional wholesalers use about 2,000 pounds annually in a C/S, with a gross national market somewhere around 800 tons. Most of this is imported now from Germany. These consumption figures do not account for the oil markets and their futures. Both markets will expand with availability. As an example, when one considers the fact that the oils in lemon balm are similar to those in lemon grass (a major imported tea flavoring), the actual potential in any of these mints become more significant.

The ratio of mint oils imported into the United States and Canada each year is more than ten times their export, with literally millions of dollars leaving both countries for crops that could easily be produced domestically. The dried leaf products are even higher, since these different mint spices are used in almost every form of manufacturing. These marketing perspectives only touch the tip of the iceberg. With a better understanding of the contents or physical chemistry of each plant, marketing becomes wide open for the small farmer.

A CATNIP FARM PLAN

The following tables present a series of schedules for operation and cost per acre which need to be compiled before beginning any small farm venture. They are critical to the success or failure of almost any project in agriculture. Even the alfalfa farmer should have costs squarely in front of him to remain in business. While data presented are only representative for a 40 acre field of catnip, *they can be used as a model for any number of other herbs or spices.* They are —

Table 9 is styled *Estimated Production Costs for Catnip During Establishment Year, Side-Roll Irrigation, (A).* This schedule outlines field operations by calendar month, sets down the type of machinery and labor used, and the hours used per acre and costs per hour, during the first year of production.

Table 10, *Estimated Production Costs for Catnip During Establishment Year, Side-Roll Irrigation, (B),* reveals costs which do not occur in (A), such as interest on operating capital, land costs and overhead (telephone, utilities, legal, accounting, etc.). This table presents on a yearly basis the total cost of establishing and producing catnip. Land costs ($100 per acre) are based on rental estimates, and neither table includes a charge for management.

Table 11 is identical to table 9 except that it is for the second and subsequent years of production.

Table 12 is also identical to table 10 except that it is for the second and following years of production.

The cost of field operations in table 9 and 11 are divided into two categories. The first is the cost of machinery ownership, or fixed costs. The second, or variable costs, is associated with operating machinery, hiring labor, and purchasing services and materials. Total cost is the sum of machinery fixed costs and selected variable costs.

Table 13, *Summary of Receipts, Costs, and Returns to Land and Management for Catnip Herb, with Side-Roll Irrigation,* summarizes the per acre returns to land and management for catnip herb production at prices received from a recent sale to a large pharmaceutical buyer on the East coast.

Table 14, *Hourly Cost Summaries for Implements and Power Units, (approxi-*

TABLE 9
Estimated Production Costs for Catnip During Establishment Year, Side-Roll Irrigation, (A)

OPERATION	TOOLING	MONTH	MACH. HOURS	LABOR HOURS	MACH. FIXED COST	VARIABLE COSTS FUEL, OIL REPAIRS	LUBE, LABOR	SERVICE	MATERIAL	TOTALS	TOTAL COST
					$	$	$	$	$	$	$
Irrigation (10x)	Sideroll Irr., 20 ac. in.	Apr-Oct	0.0	2.95	51.80	22.80	17.70	0.0	30.00	70.50	122.30
Disc (2x)	120hp, 12' Offset Disc	Nov	1.00	1.25	17.99	14.66	7.50	0.0	0.0	22.16	40.15
Plow	135hp, 4-Btm Plow	Nov	0.50	0.63	8.94	8.37	3.75	0.0	0.0	12.12	21.06
Fertilize	Custom Fert. App.	Mar	0.0	0.0	0.0	0.0	0.0	47.90	4.50	52.40	52.40
Roll-harrow (2x)	120hp, 12' Roller-Harrow	Mar	1.00	1.25	16.10	14.47	7.50	0.0	0.0	21.97	38.07
Float	120hp, 12' Float	Mar	0.50	0.62	6.93	7.07	3.75	0.0	0.0	10.82	17.75
Plant	Custom Plant	Mar	0.0	0.0	0.0	0.0	0.0	150.00	100.00	250.00	250.00
Rotary hoe	60hp, 10' Rotary Hoe	Mar	0.35	0.44	12.34	2.53	2.63	0.0	0.0	5.16	17.50
Harrow (2x)	60hp, 15' Drag Harrow	Apr	0.70	0.87	23.40	4.86	5.25	0.0	0.0	10.11	33.51
Apply herb.*	120hp, 27' Sprayer	Apr	0.06	0.08	0.77	0.94	0.47	27.38	0.0	28.79	29.56
Rotary hoe (2x)	60hp, 10' Rotary Hoe	May	0.70	0.88	24.68	5.07	5.25	0.0	0.0	10.32	35.00
Fertilize	Custom Aerial	June	0.20	0.25	1.69	2.75	1.50	32.00	7.50	43.75	45.44
Harvest & proc.	Custom Harv. & Proc.	Sept	0.0	0.0	0.0	0.0	0.0	0.0	60.00	60.00	60.00
Residue disp.	Custom Disposal	Sept	0.0	0.0	0.0	0.0	0.0	0.0	10.00	10.00	10.00
Misc use	3/4 Ton Pickup	Sept	1.00	1.25	5.87	7.50	0.0	0.0	0.0	15.98	21.85
TOTAL COST/ACRE			6.01	10.47	170.51	92.02	55.30	257.28	212.00	624.08	794.59

*Sinbar

81

TABLE 10
Estimated Production Costs for Catnip During
Establishment Year, Side-Roll Irrigation (B)

	UNIT	COST/UNIT	QUANTITY	COST
VARIABLE COSTS				
Preharvest				
Custom Fert.	Acre	4.50	1.00	4.50
Nitrogen	Pounds	0.32	200.00	64.00
Phosphate	Pounds	0.33	30.00	9.90
Zinc	Pounds	1.20	5.00	6.00
Custom Planting	Acre	100.00	1.00	100.00
Catnip Plants	Acre	150.00	1.00	150.00
Sinbar	Pounds	18.25	1.50	27.38
Custom Aerial	Acre	7.50	1.00	7.50
Irrig. Charge	Acre	30.00	1.00	30.00
Overhead Cost	Dollar	0.05	780.12	39.01
Machinery	Acre	10.88	1.00	10.88
Tractors	Acre	58.33	1.00	58.33
Irrig. Machinery	Acre	22.80	1.00	22.80
Labor (Tractor & Machinery)	Hour	6.00	7.52	45.09
Labor (Irrig.)	Hour	6.00	2.95	17.70
Interest on Op. Cap.	Dollar	0.14	266.32	37.28
Subtotal, Preharvest				$ 630.37
Harvest				
Custom Harvest & Proc.	Acre	60.00	1.00	60.00
Custom Residue Disposal	Acre	10.00	1.00	10.00
Subtotal, Harvest				$ 70.00
Total Variable Cost				$ 700.37
FIXED COSTS				
Machinery	Acre	33.94	1.00	33.94
Tractors	Acre	84.77	1.00	84.77
Irrigation Machinery	Acre	51.00	1.00	51.80
Taxes (Land)	Acre	22.00	1.00	22.00
Land (Net Rent)	Acre	100.00	1.00	100.00
Total Fixed Cost				$ 292.52
TOTAL COSTS				$ 992.89

mate), identifies the machine complement used to derive the budgets. It presents the type and number of machines used on the representative catnip farm, current purchase prices, annual hours of use, and estimated per hour fixed and variable costs.

Machinery fixed costs include depreciation and interest on investment, property taxes, and insurance costs that do not vary with the crop grown or the number of acres farmed. New purchase costs are used for all machinery and equipment. While this assumption may result in an overstatement of production costs currently experienced by producers, it provides an indication of the small farmer's ability to generate the earnings needed to replace depreciable assets.

Recent increases in the prices paid for new machinery and equipment mean that depreciation claimed on assets purchased prior to price advances understates the amount of capital currently required to replace assets. When a small farmer evaluates a long run viability, it is important to consider his ability to replace depreciable assets on a new cost basis. It should also be noted that interest on investment represents a 14% opportunity cost to the venture. These are earnings foregone by investing money in the machinery complement rather than in the next best alternative investment. This may also represent the interest paid on funds borrowed to finance capital purchases.

THE CROP ROTATION SCHEDULE

The typical small farm plan is not complete until a rotation plan is also developed. The purpose of crop rotation has many advantages. To begin with, it helps increase the overall fertility of the land, and keeps disease and insect problems from becoming established in your fields. Monocropped mints in clayey soils, for example, are quite prone to wilt, a consequence of a viral infection in the soil. By moving rootstock from one field to another approximately every fifth year, you can truly improve the resistance of the crop to these problems.

Table 17 represents a typical rotation plan for a two acre field split into six quarter acre plots. It can be used as a model for any number of other crops which you might want to consider. It also must be considered part of the farm plan, with each crop having a schedule of operations and selected costs per plot developed. Each crop should also have a gross receipts-from-production sheet included for an overall picture of your work schedule and production costs.

In review of this table, red clover could be grown instead of alfalfa. The red clover blossom could then be harvested for the cosmetic and dried-flower markets, rather than for hay, with its subsequent limitations. In this case, you have to reduce the amount of hay in the rotation because red clover will not produce a good yield of hay the second bearing year and should be plowed under.

With red clover, the rotation becomes dill, basil, beans, wheat, clover, and

TABLE 11
Estimated Production Costs for Catnip, Side-Roll Irrigation, (A)

OPERATION	TOOLING	MONTH	MACH. HOURS	LABOR HOURS	MACH. FIXED COST $	FUEL, OIL LUBE, REPAIRS $	OIL, LUBE, LABOR $	VARIABLE COSTS SERVICE $	MATERIAL $	TOTALS $	TOTAL COST $
Irrigation (12x)	Sideroll Irr., 24 ac. in.	Apr-Oct	0.0	3.50	52.08	23.52	21.00	30.00	0.0	74.52	126.60
Apply Herb.	Custom Spraying	Nov	0.0	0.0	0.0	0.0	0.0	5.25	27.38	32.63	32.63
Fertilize	Custom Fert. App.	Mar	0.0	0.0	0.0	0.0	0.0	4.50	82.70	87.20	87.20
Weeding	Hand Weeding	Apr	0.0	0.0	3.70	0.0	16.28	0.0	0.0	16.28	19.98
Apply Herb.	120hp, 27' Sprayer	Apr	0.06	0.08	0.77	0.94	0.47	0.0	15.00	16.41	17.18
Apply Insect. *	Custom Aerial	May	0.0	0.0	0.0	0.0	0.0	2.50	7.00	9.50	9.50
Harvest & Proc.	Custom Harv. & Proc.	July	0.0	0.0	0.0	0.0	0.0	60.00	0.0	60.00	60.00
Fertilize	Custom Fert. App.	July	0.0	0.0	0.0	0.0	0.0	4.50	43.75	48.25	48.25
Harvest & Proc.	Custom Harv. & Proc.	Sept	0.0	0.0	0.0	0.0	0.0	60.00	0.0	60.00	60.00
Residue Disp.	Custom Disposal	Oct	0.0	0.0	0.0	0.0	0.0	20.00	0.0	20.00	20.00
Misc Use	3/4 Ton Pickup		1.0	1.25	5.87	8.48	7.50	0.0	0.0	15.98	21.85
TOTAL COST/ACRE			1.06	4.83	62.42	32.94	45.25	186.75	175.83	440.77	503.19

*Insecticide applied once every three years.

84

TABLE 12
Estimated Production Costs for Catnip, Side-Roll Irrigation, (B)

	UNIT	COST/UNIT	QUANTITY	COST
VARIABLE COSTS				
Preharvest				
Custom Spraying	Acre	5.25	1.00	5.25
Sinbar	Pounds	18.25	1.50	27.38
Custom Fert.	Acre	4.50	2.00	9.00
Nitrogen	Pounds	0.32	200.00	64.00
Phosphate	Pounds	0.33	30.00	9.90
Zinc	Pounds	1.20	5.00	6.00
Sulfur	Pounds	0.07	40.00	2.80
Hand Hoeing	Hour	4.40	3.70	16.28
Herbicide	Acre	15.00	1.00	15.00
Custom Aerial*	Acre	2.50	0.33	2.50
Insecticide*	Acre	7.00	1.00	7.00
Overhead Cost	Dollar	0.05	729.50	36.47
Urea	Pounds	0.35	125.00	43.75
Irrig. Charge	Acre	30.00	1.00	30.00
Machinery	Acre	8.57	1.00	8.57
Tractors	Acre	0.86	1.00	0.86
Irrigation Machinery	Acre	23.52	1.00	23.52
Labor (Tractor & Machinery)	Hour	6.00	1.33	7.97
Labor (Irrigation)	Hour	6.00	3.50	21.00
Interest on Op. Cap.	Dollar	0.14	133.79	18.73
Subtotal, Preharvest				$ 355.98
Harvest				
Custom Harvest & Proc.	Acre	60.00	1.00	60.00
Custom Residue Disposal	Acre	10.00	2.00	40.00
Subtotal, Harvest				$ 100.00
Total Variable Cost				$ 455.98
FIXED COSTS				
Machinery	Acre	6.10	1.00	6.10
Tractors	Acre	0.53	1.00	0.53
Irrigation Machinery	Acre	52.08	1.00	52.08
Taxes (Land)	Acre	22.00	1.00	22.00
Prorated Estab. Cost	Acre	589.14	0.33	194.00
Land (Net Rent)	Acre	100.00	1.00	100.00
Total Fixed Cost				$ 374.71
TOTAL COSTS				$ 830.69

*Insecticide applied once every three years

TABLE 13
Summary of Receipts, Costs, and Returns to Land
and Management for Catnip Herb, with Side-Roll Irrigation

	UNIT	COST/ UNIT	QUANTITY	COST/ RECEIPTS
GROSS RECEIPTS FROM PRODUCTION				
Catnip Herb (July)	Pounds	0.65	3,000	$ 1,950.00
Catnip Herb (Sept)	Pounds	0.65	3,000	1,950.00
1. Total Receipts				$ 3,900.00
Less: Total Variable Cost				$ 455.98
2. Returns Over Variable Cost				$ 3,444.02
Less: Machinery Fixed Cost				$ 62.42
Prorated Estab. Cost				$ 294.00
Real Estate Taxes				$ 22.00
3. Returns to Land and Management				$ 3,065.60

then back to dill. In any given year, two plots will be in red clover, one in beans and heavily composted vegetables, and the other three in two spices and one grain. Three plots are adding more fertility than they are taking out, and three are taking more nutrients out of the soil than they are adding. Overall fertility can be increased by adding manure and small, economical doses of commercial fertilizers.

Because catnip is a perennial, this rotation plan must be modified. There are several ways you could do this. The first would be to consider this plan as one-half your land use, with the other planted in catnip. This rotation would switch fields every fourth or fifth year. Another method in modifying this rotation is by planting catnip rather than alfalfa or clover, moving from one section to the next every two or three years. Surplus rootstock from the rotations could be marketed as a byproduct of herbage. Use your imagination.

DRYLAND FIELDS — ROMAN CHAMOMILE (*ANTHEMIS NOBILIS*)

Marketing. Formerly cultivated as the source of Roman Chamomile oil, this herb is used throughout North America as a tea and home remedy. It ranks among the top five selling herbs in the United States, with the oil markets even larger than those for peppermint. The dried flowerheads serve chiefly as a flavoring for herb teas, with the oil used in cosmetics, liqueurs, and perfumes. Extracts are used as flavorings in bitters, Benedictine, vermouth, non-alcoholic beverages, baked goods, candies, frozen dairy desserts, gelatins, and puddings.

Extracts of Roman chamomile are also used in bath preparations, cosmetics,

DILL
(*Anethum graveolens* L.)
Umbelliferae family

Best grown along coastal areas, dill needs more irrigation than either caraway or fennel (also part of the Umbelliferae family). It is marketed in three forms, the dried foliage called dill weed, seed, and essential oil. It is started from seed by drilling 10 inches apart in rows. The seed is then covered with a light soil. Germination is 10 to 14 days at 60 F. Dill prefers a moderately rich, loose soil with full sun and good drainage.

When growing dill as a crude botanical, seeding is best done in early May. Plants left to mature grow to 3 feet in height and usually have only one stalk. Light soil cultivation to control weeds is about the only real demand during dill's growing season. The leafy plant is ready for harvest in about 8 weeks after seeding. It will need to be dehydrated when harvesting the plant as dill weed. For those who would like to form a cottage industry around this crop, a planned successive replanting April through mid-July could be implemented.

For high oil and fragrance the seed is harvested when light brown. Cut in early morning when the seed is less likely to be shaken loose accidentally, a combine can be used. The seed is easily dried on racks in the sun, or some form of continuous-feed conveyor-tunnel system using propane and forced hot air. The seed yields its oils to infusion of hot water or alcohols, bruising them first via a roller mill.

Dill weed oil is used as a fragrance component in cosmetics, including soaps, detergents, creams, lotions, and perfumes. Dill weed and its oils are used extensively in many food products such as baked goods, meat and meat products, condiments and relishes, fats and oils, and numerous snack foods. As a folk medicine the oil and seed are used as aromatic carminative and stimulant in the treatment of gas, especially in children.

For perspective, more than 800 metric ton of dill seed was imported into North America last year from such countries as India, Egypt, and Europe. Japan is also a potential large user of dill seed. This does not even include the oil or crude herb forms, used in pickling and other culinary uses. West Germany uses more than 200 ton of dill weed each year, as a further example of the world market potentials for dill.

TABLE 14

Hourly Cost Summaries for Implements and Power Units (Approximate)

MACHINE	HOURS OF ANNUAL USE	PURCHASE PRICE	DEPRECIA- TION PER HOUR	INTEREST PER HOUR	INSURANCE PER HOUR	TAXES PER HOUR	TOTAL FIXED COST PER HOUR	REPAIR COST PER HOUR	FUEL COST PER HOUR
Wheel Tractor, 120hp	800	41,623	3.252	4.553	0.195	0.468	8.468	3.64	8.80
Wheel Tractor, 135hp	800	46,638	3.644	5.101	0.219	0.525	9.488	4.08	11.00
Wheel Tractor, 60hp	100	19,885	12.428	17.400	0.746	1.790	32.363	0.50	5.50
Pickup, 3/4 Ton	300	8,500	3.015	2.489	0.107	0.255	5.866	1.01	6.50
V Ditcher	50	2,400	2.893	3.683	0.158	0.432	7.165	1.62	0.0
Slicker Ditcher, 12 ft.	300	1,200	0.539	0.371	0.016	0.036	0.963	0.28	0.0
Offset Disc 12 ft.	150	6,900	4.895	4.041	0.173	0.414	9.524	0.90	0.0
Plow, 4 BTM	150	5,593	5.327	2.610	0.112	0.336	8.384	0.0	0.0
Roller-Harrow, 12 ft.	150	5,433	4.137	3.044	0.130	0.326	7.637	0.71	0.0
Float, 12 ft.	75	2,715	2.275	2.679	0.115	0.326	5.395	0.37	0.0
Rotary Hoe, 10 ft.	150	2,100	1.490	1.230	0.053	0.126	2.898	0.42	0.0
Drag Harrow, 15 ft.	100	716	0.450	0.530	0.023	0.064	1.067	0.12	0.0
PTO Sprayer	250	4,600	1.958	1.617	0.069	0.166	3.809	1.34	0.0
Corrugator, 4 Row	200	4,500	2.394	1.977	0.085	0.202	4.658	1.13	0.0

Tables 9 to 14 have been adapted from the work of Herbert R. Hinman (Extension Economist, Cooperative Extension, Washington State University, Pullman) and James H. Griffin (Extension Area Agent, Yakima County) on Spearmint in Washington State.

hair dyes, formulas, mouthwashes, shampoos, and sunscreens. The essential oil is used in creams, detergents, lotions, perfumes and soaps. Pharmaceutical uses include antiseptic unguents and lotions to treat cracked nipples, inflammation, sore gums, and wounds.

All oils, extracts, and flowerheads from chamomile are imported at this time from Germany, Hungary, Egypt, Bulgaria, Yugoslavia, Turkey, Albania and Russia. The lowest import price (landed in New York) is $2.20 per pound, with regional wholesalers paying as much as $3.00 per pound. With these perspectives, realize that this herb is not grown commercially anywhere in North America. Further, it will grow easily on soil previously used for wheat!

Cultivation. All the chamomiles have a tiny chaffy scale between each two florets, a vital distinction between *A. nobilis* (Roman chamomile) and other species of *Anthemis.* Chamomile is a low growing hardy perennial, with the shape of its scales short and blunt. There are two forms of Roman chamomile, the single (or wild chamomile) with a single flowerhead, and the English chamomile with double flowerheads. The wild type prefers a dry, sandy soil. The best for commercial cultivation, however, is the English or double flowered variety. This type needs a richer soil and yields the biggest crop of flowers when grown in moist, stiffish black loam.

Starting seeds in either sphagnum moss or soil substitutes can permit great variation in both temperature and time. The plant seems to need cool conditions for germination, temperatures ranging from 55 to 65 F. Propagation may be accomplished with seed sown thinly in May in the open, seedlings then being transplanted when they are large enough to be moved to permanent locations. This technique usually allows only the single or wild variety to flourish.

The best technique for ensuring doubleflowers is propagation from sets, or runners from the older plants. Each plant normally can produce from 12 to 14 sets. With good black loam, some plants will give up to 25 or even 50 sets each. The old plants are divided up into sets in March. New planting is then done formed in well manured soil, in rows 2 1/2 feet apart and a distance of 18 inches between plants. Planting can be done as with strawberries, using a rootstock planter, after which plants are tread firmly into the ground. The harder the tread, the better the rootstock development.

In autumn, the sets may be more easily rooted by placing a ring of good light soil about two or three inches from the center of the old plant, pressing it down lightly. After the roots have grown into the new soil in the spring, the newer sets are then planted as above.

You will need to control insects in the flowerheads while flowering is underway. The flowerheads are the only commercially important part of this plant, other than the seed. While the head can be combined, like German chamomile *(Matricaria chamomilla),* more effort is required to combine *A. nobilis* because of its closeness to the ground. The flowerheads of both are easily dried in the sun. See Chapter 6 on dehydration for further details.

TABLE 15
Typical Rotation Plan for a 2 Acre Field Split Into 6 Quarter Acre Plots

FALL – Year 1

A	B	C	D	E	F
Second year alfalfa	First year alfalfa (planted previous fall)	Plant winter wheat Apply lime	Fall plow for Year 2 garden and soy bean	Fall plow for annual	Sod

SPRING – Year 2

A	B	C	D	E	F
Second year alfalfa	Apply potash in April	Broadcast clover (March) Apply rock phosphate (April)	Plant garden Plant soybean in late June	Manure Plant basil in early May	Plow down green manure Plant Dill in late May

SUMMER – Year 2

A	B	C	D	E	F
Make hay	Make hay	Harvest wheat, gather straw Clip clover seedlings	Plow beans for green manure in late August Harvest garden	Cultivate basil	Cultivate dill

FALL — Year 2

A	B	C	D	E	F
Make hay	Let late alfalfa grow	Let seedlings grow	Plow residue and mulch Plant winter wheat and lime	Harvest basil early	Harvest dill late

SPRING — Year 3

A	B	C	D	E	F
Plow alfalfa for green manure Plant dill in late May	Second year alfalfa	First year clover Apply potash in April	Broadcast clover (March) Apply rock phosphate to wheat greens	Plant garden and beans Mulch tomatoes and potatoes in June	Apply nitrogen Plant basil in early May

SUMMER — Year 3

A	B	C	D	E	F
Cultivate dill	Make hay	Harvest flower-heads (late May) Make hay	Harvest wheat, gather straw Clip clover seedlings	Plow beans for green manure in late August Harvest garden	Cultivate basil

The yield for *A. nobilis* flowerheads is in excess of 200 pounds per acre, measured on a dry-weight basis, on land suitable for wheat. A complete farm plan for Roman chamomile should look similar to one for strawberries, using a crop rotation of rootstock with wheat or peas about every fourth year.

IRRIGATED FIELDS — DALMATIAN WHITE SAGE
(*SALVIA OFFICINALIS* VAR DALMATIA)

Marketing. Sage is best known for its use as a spice for flavoring sausages, stuffings, soups and some canned vegetables. The fresh leaf is also used in cheeses, liqueurs, pickles and salad vinegars. The oil is used in perfumery, men's toilet lotions, mouthwashes and gargles. The ketone thujone is the active ingredient for making meats resistant to putrefaction. This curing agent is so important in many manufactured products, such as sausage, that the United States imported more than 3 million pounds of oil in 1979 at a total value of more than $3,000,000.

The major producers of white sages are Greece, Yugoslavia, Albania, Italy, Soviet Union, Turkey, and Mexico. The finest sages are those from the Dalmation regions of Greece. The average grade import price, landed in New York, ranges from $900 to $1,200 per ton for leaf product packaged as cut-leaf in burlap. Oil prices from the Dalmation coast of Greece begin at $2.80 per pound and leaf imports begins at 2,400 per ton. Regional spice companies will sell this high quality white sage for more than $3.50 per pound (or $7,000 per ton).

Cultivation. Sage can be grown from seed, but commercial cultivation is usually from cuttings. Seedling plants seem to have a tendency to produce narrow leaves. It is for this reason that the broadleaf varieties — which do not flower readily — are the most desired for cultivation. They also have larger yields per acre. Cuttings set early in spring, as weather conditions permit, produce the largest crops. In the North, the plants should be protected in winter with a mulch of manure. Sage may also be grown as a second crop after early vegetables.

The seed can be drilled at about 10 pounds per acre, spaced 8 inches apart. They are then thinned to 18 inches for perennial crops, using 18 inch furrows. Light cultivation is used to remove weeds. Attention to potash and phosphate fertilization is indicated. A low nitrogen soil produces the best oil percentages in the leaf. Fertilizer schedules — slated in terms of salt fertilizers — are best at 400 pounds per acre of 2-10-10, or 5-8-7, depending on soil analysis.

The tops of sage can be cut before the plant forms wood at the rootstock above the ground. This is done with a side-bar cutter. There should be no flowers or spikes when the sage is cut. Turn the crop once to give it a 50% sun-cure. Too much sun will drive the volatile oils out of the leaf, causing the product to brown and lose its "correct" appearance. The sage leaf is then picked up with a flail-chop, piggy-back system and taken to a dehydrator (see Chapter 6). An

TABLE 16

Abundant Life
Seed Foundation
P.O. Box 772
Port Townsend,
Washington 98368

Agway, Inc.
P.O. Box 4933
Syracuse, New York 13221

Apache Seed, Ltd.
10136 149th. Street
Edmonton, Alberta
Canada T5P 1L1

Applewood Seed Company
833 Parfet Street
Lakewood, Colorado 80215

Arco Seed Company
P.O. Box 9008
Brooks, Oregon 97305

Burgess Seed
& Plant Company
905 Four Seasons Road
Bloomington, Illinois 61701

W. Atlee Burpee Company
Riverside, California 92502

D. V. Burrell
Seed Growers Company
P.O. Box 150-T
Rocky Ford, Colorado 81067

Comstock, Ferre & Company
Box 125-T
Wethersfield,
Connecticut 06109

William Dam Seeds, Ltd.
P.O. Box 8400
Dundas, Ontario
Canada L9H 6M1

Dessert Seed Company
P.O. Box 181
El Centro, California 92244

J. A. Demonchaux Company
827 N. Kansas Avenue
Topeka, Kansas 66608

Glecklers Seedman
Metamora, Ohio 43540

Gurney Seed
& Nursery Company
Yankton,
South Dakota 57079

Hemlock Hill Herb Farm
Litchfield,
Connecticut 06759

Herbst Brothers
Seedmen, Inc.
Dept. 1051
Brewster, New York 10509

J. L. Hudson, Seedman
P.O. Box 1058-TB
Redwood City,
California 94064

Island Seed Company, Ltd.
P.O. Box 4278, Station A
Victoria, British Columbia
Canada V8X 3X8

Jackson & Perkins Company
11-A Rose Lane
Medford, Ohio 97501

Johnny's Selected Seeds
Albion, Maine 04910

J. W. Jung Seed Company
335 S. High Street
Randolph, Wisconsin 53956

Kilgore Seed Company
1400 W. First Street
Hanford, Florida 32771

Krider Nurseries
P.O. Box 109
Middlebury, Indiana 46540

McFayden Seed Company
P.O. Box 1600
Brandon, Manitoba
Canada R7A 6A6

Nichols Herbs & Rare Seeds
1190 N. Pacific Highway
Albany, Oregon 97321

Pike & Company, Ltd.
10552 114 Street
Edmonton, Alberta
Canada T5H 3J7

Redwood City Seed Company
P.O. Box 361
Redwood City,
California 94064

Sanctuary
2388 West 4th Avenue
Vancouver, B.C.
Canada V6K 1P1

Seed Savers Exchange
Kent Wheatly, RFD 2
Princeton, New Jersey 04073

T & T Seeds, Ltd.
Box 1710
Winnipeg, Manitoba
Canada R3C 3P6

Territorial Seed Company
P.O. Box 27
Lorane, Oregon 97451

Van Bourgondien Brothers
245 Farmingdale Road,
Route 109
Babylon, New York 11702

Wyatt-Quarles Seed Company
P.O. Box 2131
Raleigh, North Dakota 27602

unused wood kiln (used for plywood) or hop dryer can be a perfect "unused" resource in the community for this crop.

You will probably get two or even three cuttings during a season in the third year. The best way to continue the crop as a perennial is to plan cutting the rootstock every third or fourth year, or before the roots begin to form a bark. Raking this disced rootstock into other fields allows expansion of this important meat packing spice. First year yields are usually low, but second and third year yields can be more than two tons per acre, with two cuttings, presuming a 12% stem. This stem must not be woody, but cut when still in a green sapling stage. Grasses should not be present in the final product.

SOURCES FOR SEED

The commercial cultivation of most herbs and spices is a slow and laborious process involving rootstock development and hybridization of seeds for regional variations. Since most of these crops have been previously imported from Europe and other continents, there are limited sources of seed for commercial purposes. Almost all seed sources offer herbs and spices for the family garden, but at retail prices. A wholesale source for farm quantities of herb and spice seed might make a very profitable venture for new seed houses in the near future.

For most perennial herbs and spices, rootstock plantings in rows seem to be the best way to control grasses and weeds. This means that a nursery house might be an excellent way to begin any small farm venture. For most mints, approximately 10,000 plants per acre can be grown in such a house. Once a field is established and registered, another business can be developed: selling rootstock to other mint farmers. The need for quality rootstock, hybridized for a specific region of the continent will always exist.

While most small farm ventures involve 20 to 40 acre fields for a specific crop, I recommend that most new small farms begin with a 1/4 to 2 acre feasibility study. Learn how to grow the spice or herb first, developing a cultivation technique which controls the grasses and weeds best, and provides a good yield. With these details, and accurate cost of goods produced figures, you are in a better position to make a living from your farm venture.

The list of seed houses on page 93 may be of value in fulfilling seed needs.

COMFREY
(*Symphytum officinale*)
Boraginaceae family

Often called the "food of the future," comfrey has received much attention in recent years. Not only is it rich in vitamin B_{12} and several amino acids, it also has high concentrations of pyrrolizidine group alkaloids (oxalic acid-type plants). While initial reports vary, most animal studies show only positive response to its use as a supplement. It is very high in protein, and is also probably the highest bio-mass yields of any other herb.

It is primarily cultivated from rootstock. Roots from an older field are quartered and cut into 3 to 5 inch lengths (by hand). They are then planted 4 inches deep and one foot apart in rows, 17 to 20 inch furrows. Manure can be added as the taproot will grow to more than 6 feet in three years. Comfrey likes a heavy irrigation while it sets its root systems the first year, probably as much as a 5-day set. Some 6 to 10 inches of rootstock can be taken from an established field every fourth year with one acre reseeding five acres.

It should be cut before 10% of the crop goes to flower. It can not be dried in the sun because of the high mucilage. Even pellet milled comfrey will rot from the center. The best form of harvest is to cut it at 6 inches from the ground with a side-bar cutter, attempting not to bruise the leaf. Let it come to a 50% sun-cure and then pick it up with a flail-chop to be dehydrated. Such facilities as plywood kilns, tobacco dryers, and hop kilns work best. Care must be taken not to bruise and discolor the leaf.

Once comfrey is established in a field (four years), most parts of North America can expect up to four cuttings with dry-weight yields of 5 ton per acre. There is more than a 75 percent weight-loss in drying, so the actual wet weight per acre is quite high. Some studies indicate that it is probably the best futures crop for solar alcohol production in terms of yields-per-acre to cost-of-production. It certainly is easy enough to grow. The key to success is in dehydration.

The domestic markets for herb use went from 400 ton to 200 in one year when the first questions about toxicity occurred. However, recent studies indicate that a 60% comfrey/40% alfalfa pellet might have excellent export opportunities as a cattle food. This mixture of dehydrated comfrey and green alfalfa extruded into a pellet or cube constitutes a "whole food" for cattle. As availability increases and prices drop, the potential of this blend could become a major cash-crop for North America.

Comfrey in crude form begins marketing in the herb and spice trade at about 50 cents per pound. Since there is a limited market, prices can soar in winter months to more than $1.00 per pound (in tonnage). Since the small farm can yield more than 5 ton to the acre in four years, prices of $400 per ton (20 cents per pound) would allow new cattle feeds to be feasible. Those markets could be more than 10,000 ton per month as an export futures crop.

Basil

CHAPTER 6

Techniques for Bulk
Dehydration and Storage

The degree of simplification is a matter for each individual to settle
for himself.

Richard Gregg (on *Voluntary Simplicity*), 1936.

Drying is one of the most important processes in the production of crude
herbs and spices. Crude botanicals fall naturally into one of the following
classes:

Leaf. Consists either of the whole leaf or the leaf and small portions of the
upper end of the stalk, including some stem.

Herb. Consists of the portion of the plant above the ground, and may include
the flowers and fruit.

Root. Consists of the root of the plant, either whole or with the bark removed,
e.g., rubbed sassafras — "rossed".

Bark. Consists of the outer part of the plant or root section (also known as
rootbark).

Flower. Consists of the flowers of the herb or spice, often including some
parts of the stem and seed.

All of these parts of the plant must be dried correctly and to the percent moisture required for both storage and transport. After the crop is harvested, a

little care in drying will more than repay the farmer for the work and expense involved.

Drying consists of removing enough moisture from the crop that spoilage organisms, even though present and alive, are not able to grow and multiply in the crop. With proper dehydration, the crop will retain its color and fragrance, bringing higher prices to the farmer. Removing moisture from green crops and drug plants prevents not only molding, but also inhibits the action of intrinsic enzymes and other chemical reactions which reduce the value of the crop to end uses.

Drying has other advantages as well. Dried crude herbs and spices have the very great advantage that their weight is only one-fourth to one-ninth that of the fresh material, therefore the cost of storage and shipping is considerably less. Since transportation is the single greatest expense after labor in producing the crop, any economy in this area is of major importance to the grower. Quite simply, dehydration eliminates the hauling of water.

Preservation of food materials by drying is not particularly difficult or complex. But there are certain fundamental principles that must be considered. The objective of dehydration is not merely the removal of sufficient moisture to insure against spoilage, but the removal of moisture in such a way so as to prevent losses of volatile oils (natural flavors) and cosmetic integrity (color or appearance) of the crop. To obtain satisfactory results in drying spices and herbs, provisions must be made for the control of *air flow* and *temperature.*

AIR FLOW

Most failures in drying are due not so much to imperfections in the equipment used as to the failure of the farmer to understand a few fundamental principles. Moisture, to be removed from the plant tissue of green herbs and spices, must be converted into water vapor, which in turn must be taken up by the air. When in free circulation the air at the earth's surface rarely becomes entirely saturated with water vapor. Even in a heavy rain storm the atmosphere is capable of absorbing up to 60% of its moisture holding capacity. Beyond 60%, air will take up moisture only very slowly.

Consequently, any wet material exposed freely to the air will ultimately become dry, since the water will be converted into water vapor and taken up by the air in time. The rate at which this process occurs depends both upon the temperature of the air and the percentage of moisture present in it when brought in contact with the crop. If still air at a constant temperature surrounds the crop, the loss of water from the crop will be slow. This is because the air nearest the surface of the crop will soon become saturated and take up more water vapor only when that already in the air is lost by diffusion outward and upward into layers of drier air.

If the air is kept in constant motion, the drying will be greatly hastened. The incoming air displaces the blanket of moist air surrounding the material as rapidly as it is formed, and brings drier air to replace it. If the temperature and moisture content of air used are both constant, then the rate of drying increases proportionally as the rate of movement of the air is increased. Careful attention to the rate of air flow is important, particularly at the beginning of the drying operation.

There is a point, however, at which water can not pass from the interior to the surface of the crop as rapidly as the air is able to take it up. The moisture contained in the interior tissues of most spices and herbs reaches the surface rather slowly. If surface moisture is removed more rapidly than it can be replaced by interior moisture, the outer layers of cells will tend to dry out and become hard while the interior is still moist. When this point is passed, the crop will not dry correctly, or not at all in some cases like comfrey. This problem is more likely to occur when large volumes of hot air are circulated.

TEMPERATURE

At any specific temperature a given volume of air can hold only a specific quantity of water vapor. The raising or lowering of the temperature increases or decreases the amount of moisture that this volume of air can hold. As a rule of thumb, the amount of water vapor which a given volume of air can absorb doubles with every increase of 27 F. in temperature. In other words, if a quantity of air is warmed from 60 F. to 87 F., its moisture carrying capacity is doubled. If the heating is continued until a temperature of 114 F. is reached, the moisture carrying capacity is again doubled, becoming four times what it was at 60 F.. Further heating produces further increases until a point is reached at which water is vaporized at the surface more rapidly than it is replaced by movement outward from the interior of the crop material.

Air passing through a dryer system should never be allowed to exceed 60% of water vapor, all the moisture the air at that temperature can readily absorb. If it does become saturated, it will deposit some of that moisture on parts of the crop when reaching a lower temperature near the exhaust of the dryer system. Thus a part of the crop will become wetter rather than dry, causing discoloration and other serious problems. Keeping in mind this slower build-up of moisture beyond the 60% capacity, the air through your crop should contain no more moisture than this as it leaves the outlet of your dryer system.

As the herb or spice crop becomes drier, the air surrounding it will absorb less water. The end of the drying cycle is when no moisture is further evaporated from the crop. The upper range of temperature varies with individual crops, but it should never exceed 170 F. for barks, the temperature for peak absorption with most design configurations in dry systems. Better results are usually obtained by maintaining a temperature below 120 F., proceeding toward it only after the crop has dried for some time.

High temperatures at the beginning of the drying cycle bring about the same condition as the circulation of too great a volume of air, namely, the hardening of the surface tissues, and consequent retardation or stoppage of moisture from the interior of the plant to the surface. Integration of the temperature and air movement are the two main principles of drying. The objective should be to combine the two and force heated air over the material at such a rate that it will remove the moisture from the surface just as rapidly as it comes from the interior of the plant being dried.

Leaf and herb crops should be dried at moderate temperatures, somewhat below 100 F. in the beginning stages of dehydration. Flowers require even lower temperatures, as do spices where volatile oil losses become important. Barks can be dried in corn dryers with temperatures over 140 F., but these temperatures should only be used toward the end of the drying cycle. Roots also can be dried at higher temperatures, beginning somewhere around 120 F. Recommended lower-to-higher temperature limitations are given with other important drying data in table 20, toward the end of this chapter. You would be well advised to experiment with your own system to determine that it falls within the air movement/temperature ranges suggested.

VAPOR PRESSURE

Table 17 is a standard psychrometric chart, graphically showing the relationship of moisture in the air to the temperature for specific relative humidities. The condition of the air with respect to water vapor in it is called humidity. The absolute humidity refers to the actual amount of water vapor

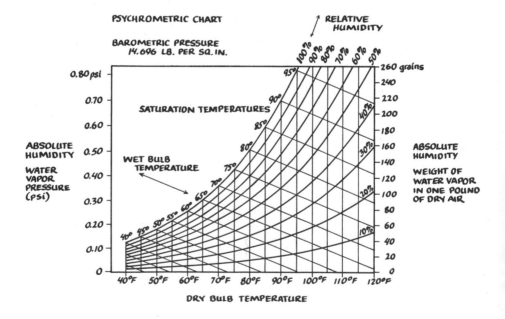

present in a given volume of air. Its units are usually measured in grains of moisture per cubic yard of air or pounds per square inch (psi). The relative humidity is the ratio of the amount that would be present if the air at that temperature were saturated.

It can be inferred from this table that when one increases the temperature for a specific water vapor pressure, the relative humidity decreases. This demonstrates the relationship that the crop can dry faster at higher temperatures. Another interesting aspect sometimes not seen from this graph, however, is the fact that if you could somehow lower the water vapor pressure in a given dryer system, the relative humidity will decrease also with a given temperature.

This is ultimately the principle of freeze-dried products. The partial pressure in a closed dehydration system is lowered quickly and to such a low pressure, the moisture is literally driven out of the material in a freezing process. While this is not practical for most herb and spice crops, it is possible to reduce the inside pressure with a squirrel cage fan of a small dryer system. This, in effect, allows higher temperatures to be used for a similar relative humidity. The overall effect is that your crop will dry faster without the disadvantages of hardening of the surface tissues.

SUN-CURE METHODS OF DRYING CROPS

Crude botanicals and spices can be dried either in the open or by artificial heat. When dried in the open, either sun-cure or shade-drying is used, depending upon the type of crop and appearance required for the finished product. Sun-cure methods should be employed only when quality or appearance is not unfavorably affected by the action of direct sunlight. It is the least expensive method for bulk production and should always be considered first, before other alternatives are considered.

The art of forming proper windrows uses all the principles discussed under air flow and temperature, in this case from the sun. The width and depth of the harvested crop depends primarily on the rate of leaf-to-stem drying. A looser pack will obviously dry more evenly between differing cell structures, because of air flow. Turning the windrow is another technique, but usually involves some leaf-loss and subsequent fragmentation from further handling.

A condition-bar on a rotary type mower crimps the stem in several places, allowing moisture to move to the surface more quickly. The amount of crimping is usually adjustable, as is the width — and thus depth — of a windrow. This width should be determined by weather forecasts as to available wind during drying stages. Spearmints, for example, with their larger leaf need to be cut twice in a season — in July and September. They need to lie on one side with a heavy condition for two days before turning and then subsequent baling two days later. Peppermint, on the other hand, is cut in September only. With a smaller leaf and less heat from the sun, it needs to be turned more often. Skill is required to maintain the very best oil contents and color of these products.

Roots and barks can also be dried in the sun. Barks are usually chipped for faster drying. Roots should also be split or chipped. Both are then spread out on tarps or racks to facilitate moving inside during periods of heavy dew or rain. Racks allow air flow through the screens, whereas tarp drying requires turning the crop at least once each day. The period of drying in this manner during normal summer months is only two or three days when left in the sun continuously. Most farmers have found that barks and roots can be stacked or piled up to 10 inches for drying, presuming that they are turned twice each day.

SHADE-DRYING METHODS

In shade-drying, the direct effect of the sun's rays is eliminated.

Long ultraviolet rays from the sun cause browning of the leaf, as do moisture from dew at night, or composting. Shade is used to protect the crops from the action of direct sunlight, which destroys the natural color or drives volatile oils off into the air. Certain spices, such as sages, cannot be sun cured for these very reasons. Peppermint, for example, is much better in both quality and appearance if dried in the shade, and without the use of artificial heat.

Such crops as thistle, and other high mucilage crops, are best dried next to a

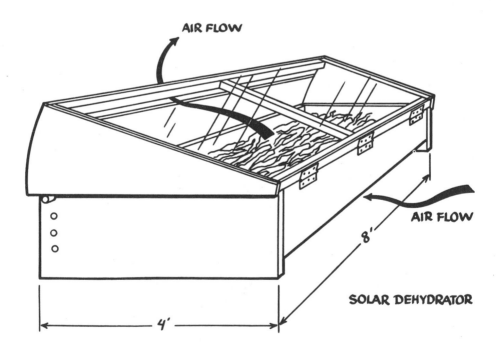

AIR FLOW

AIR FLOW

8'

4'

SOLAR DEHYDRATOR

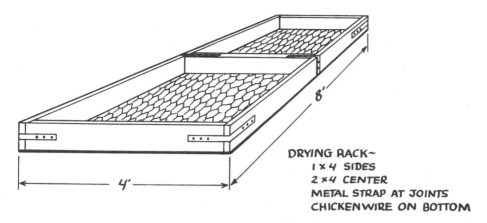

DRYING RACK~
1 x 4 SIDES
2 x 4 CENTER
METAL STRAP AT JOINTS
CHICKENWIRE ON BOTTOM

treeline, rather than in the hot sun. They not only give a better color when dried, they also dry slower and more uniformly that way. The key to good drying is to get the stem to dry at a rate similar to the leaf. The more uniform the drying, the better the product or crop is for marketing. Shade drying allows the crop to be dried more slowly, and more uniformly. Some crops can dry in partial sun. Thus the direction and method of harvest must be planned so that the product will lie in the sun (and shade) over the daylight hours.

Shade-drying (or field-drying of any sort) can prevent other problems. If the location of the farm is such that there are heavy dews in the morning, this extra moisture will cause browning of the crop. If the sun is too hot during the middle of the summer months, the crop will likely be "burned." The advantages of field drying far outweigh other options, however. Oftentimes, if a partial shade situation occurs in a field due to tree lines and other obstacles, the small farmer should consider this aspect in his overall approach to drying.

A SOLAR DRYER SYSTEM

Because of the broad range of plants and plant parts, and the variation in weather conditions over the long period of time in which these various herb and spice crops mature, it is best to build a drying apparatus in which some form of artificial heat can be employed when necessary. The simplest form is a solar type system in which the dryer is essentially a well ventilated box with an inclined glass top so located that the rays of the sun fall directly upon the glass for as many hours as possible every day. This system actually works well even in snow if the sun is out for some length of time, say 6 to 8 hours.

The box receives the heat from the sun's rays more rapidly than it is lost by radiation to the surrounding air. The result is that the internal temperature in bright sunlight rises decidedly above the outside air temperature. The capacity of the air to absorb moisture is increased as its temperature rises. Warm air

103

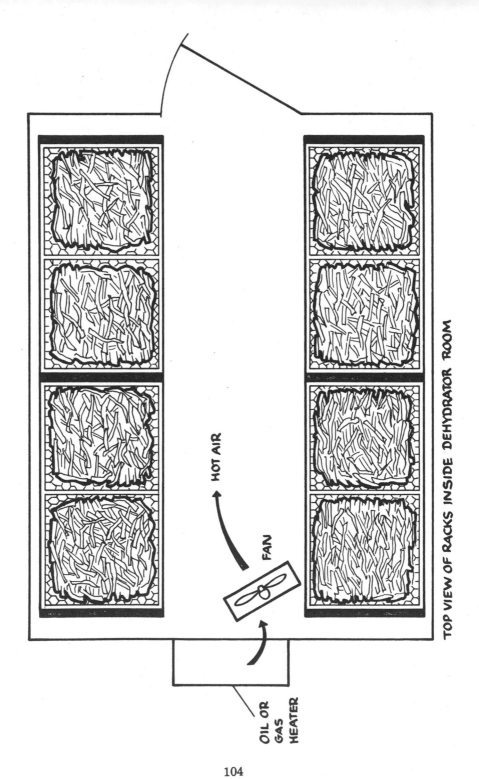

TOP VIEW OF RACKS INSIDE DEHYDRATOR ROOM

HOT AIR

FAN

OIL OR
GAS
HEATER

is lighter than cold air. With cold air inlets near the bottom, and an outlet at the top, a constant air current will enter at the bottom, rise as it begins to warm, and eventually escape at the top. If the air is forced to flower over the surface of wet crops in the course of this passage, it will take up moisture, and the material will dry much more quickly than if exposed to open air.

THE DRYING RACK

Rack drying has several advantages over sun-cure systems. Trays or racks are built to convenient sizes (usually 8 x 4) with wire mesh. The frames are built to be light and durable. Wire strap should be used to reinforce edges and corners which will take abuse and wear. Chicken wire can be used for most leaf and herb crops, cleaning easily when dumped. These racks are designed to stack at night if humidity during the night rises sufficiently to stop drying and result in condensation of moisture on the crop. The trays are then stacked with 2 inch to 4 inch boards between them to increase the width of the interval and promote better air circulation.

A 4 by 8 rack, when reinforced with steel strap and one middle cross-member, can hold up to 10 inches of wet produce. This amounts to approximately 35 pounds of wet leaf or more than 100 pounds of wet rootstock, sliced. These racks can be used in any number of ways, ranging from shade drying of roots and barks to the solar dryer system. They can also be used when transporting wet harvested products where possible composting might occur. By placing the crop on these individual racks with spaces between them during transportation, an air flow is created which helps begin the drying process, rather than inducing a composting process.

A SIMPLE DRYING SHED DESIGN

All things considered, drying by means of artificial heat is probably the most satisfactory method for most high oil spices and herbs, or when large quantities need to be dried in a relatively short period of time. A drying shed allows the crop to dry during rainy days, and in the winter. It is not advisable to construct a drying shed for solar heat alone. Rather, you should consider making one that can use artificial heat on cloudy days, or with crops of high oil volatility.

Dimensions for a simple drying shed need to be approximately 18 feet wide, 16 feet long, and at least 10 feet high. This means that the room will hold between 32 and 48 racks with a 4 feet x 8 feet dimension, each producing about 10 pounds dry weight leaf crop, or more than 40 pounds dry rootstock or bark per rack. It is important that the walls, floor, and door are made as nearly airtight as possible. Air should be allowed to enter the chamber only from the heat source.

The racks are stacked on frames made to hold them in two or three separate

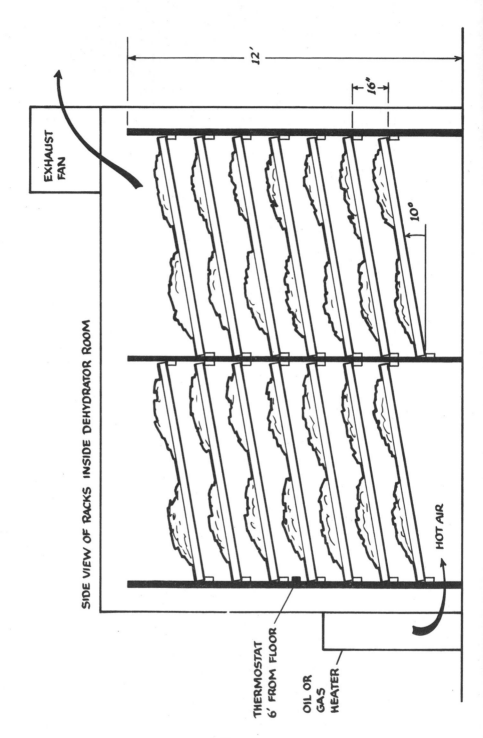

SIDE VIEW OF RACKS INSIDE DEHYDRATOR ROOM

EXHAUST FAN

12'

16"

10°

HOT AIR

THERMOSTAT 6' FROM FLOOR

OIL OR GAS HEATER

compartments, two or three deep. The additional 6 foot width is for moving racks in and out of the shed easily. With a castor wheeled rack holder, 8 racks high, an additional 16 racks can be added to the same space. This means that rather than loading the shed one rack at a time, you could wheel 8 racks in at one time via a rack holder.

The actual frames on which the racks slide and rest should be set at a 10 degree incline from the source of heat. This allows the air flow to break up, distributing it through a series of racks in such a fashion that drying occurs more uniformly throughout the rack arrangement. Every day the racks should be removed and the crop turned (via dumping it upside-down into a previously-emptied rack). The advantage of a castor wheeled rack holder is that the room will hold one third more racks with the same heat, and that of labor from moving one rack out at a time.

The heat source is either an oil burner stove with a floor level exhaust into the shed, or a wood heater below ground so that heat enters the shed from the lower front of the drying shed. A thermostat should be placed inside on the heat-side wall midway up around rack set number 5, 6 feet high from the source. A propane heater could be used as the heat source, being wheeled in after the shed is loaded. A large box fan should be put to one side to assist air circulation. A final squirrel-cage fan is placed on the rear top of the shed to exhaust the moist warm air.

Size the exhaust fan so that a partial pressure will exist inside the drying shed when the door is closed and the heat source is on. This means that more air is leaving the shed than entering it. This partial pressure changes everything. With this partial pressure, the exchange ratio of moisture from the wet crop to the air increases markedly. More importantly, it draws moisture from inside the wet stems. As the pressure decreases, the vapor pressure changes and the air can hold even more moisture, literally drawing it out from the interior of the plant.

When designed efficiently, a shed this size can produce as much as 500 pounds of dry leaf, or up to 1,500 pounds dry rootstock or bark for market within three days of continuous operation. Temperatures should never rise about 120 F. in this system, even with the vapor-pressure exhaust system. The temperature schedule should be 90 F. the first day, 105 F. the second, and 115 + F. on the final day of drying. The crop should be turned every four hours the first day, once on the second day, and once again at the beginning of the third day. When the product is turned, racks near the bottom should be rotated toward the top to insure more even and uniform drying in each rack.

Remember drying should be begun in the coolest temperatures and finish in the hotter temperatures. The inside box fan might not be used the first day, although the exhaust fan is *always used* during the drying cycle. The rate of heating necessary to dry any particular spice or herb is learned only through experience. *Never employ the highest temperatures at the beginning of drying cycles.* Gradually build up the heat level to the desired degree. Table 18 lists

107

low-to-high temperature variations for each herb and spice, along with other important drying and storage instructions. Start with these temperatures.

STORAGE OF HERBS AND SPICES

Drying should be continued until the crop is hard and inelastic, but must not result in loss of crispness, making the product brittle. When the herb or spice is removed from the drying shed, it should be allowed to remain for several days in the open, away from sunlight. During this period it will take up moisture from the atmosphere and become less brittle and easier to handle. Less brittleness means less fragmentation or loss from the crop turning to powder.

Crude herbs and spices can be packaged in burlap sacks, boxes, or fiber drum barrels. While most barks are still shipped in burlap potato sacks, fiber contamination problems which result are unacceptable for most high-oil botanicals. The latter are most often shipped in polypropylene feed sacks. These are available from most feed and grain stores for less than 15 cents per sack. Paper cartons are often used to hold baled herbs, especially those which tend to fragment. Large hydraulic compressors are sometimes used for hops and other light flower-type crops, and then wrapped in burlap as 200 pound bales. Almost all of the larger pharmaceutical houses require fiber drums for their storage.

The moisture content — when the material is stored — should not be more than 8 to 10%. Although most organisms are unable to grow or multiply when the moisture content of the crop is below 24%, there are the problems of spontaneous combustion and heat from localized moisture spots which could damage the product in both color and odor at this higher moisture content. The enzyme from milk, lysine, when properly applied to some farm crops will allow the moisture to be over 30% without heating the crop. However, lysine is generally not used in the herb and spice industry.

Farm products are stored to make them available the year around, to balance periods of plenty with periods of scarcity. Obviously, catnip prices at the time of harvest are much less than those during the winter months, when less is available. Technically, all products are in storage during the interval between harvest and consumption. Each crop has its own particular conditions under which it can be stored without much, if any, loss in quality. The requirements range from one extreme of no structural facility to large cold storage houses with elaborate equipment.

The typical farmer usually does not give much thought to the matter when he stores his products with a public warehouseman. Many times he does not know what will, or will not, happen to his crops in storage. Public warehousing is similar to banking in many ways. Products are stored in warehouses; money is placed in banks; in both, the depositor has a legal right to get back in kind and value the thing he deposited. Protection of depositors in public warehouses, however, has not kept pace with the protection given to depositors in banks.

It is best to own your own storage facility, one in which you have control of most of the unknowns. You need to examine your product frequently to see that it is not deteriorating. It is important to hold open the option of taking guard against infestation. Safe storage to a processor has a different meaning. He wants a reasonable quantity of the product stored at or near his mill, where it will be kept in good condition and available for use.

Heated buildings are best in that moisture is not deposited when lower temperatures arrive. Pallet loading is best for stacking bales, sack or whatever way the crop has been packaged. The pallets provide an air space between the floor and the crop, improving circulation and maintaining dryness. *There should always be an air layer between the ground and the crop,* even if it is packaged in a fiber drum. Keeping the moisture controlled is the primary focus of good storage practices.

Pallets are easy to load and unload for trucking when farm production is of five tons or more. As a rule, a single pallet can hold approximately 1,000 pounds of baled catnip, 500 pounds of a sacked sage, and more than 1,500 pounds of a sacked Oregon grape root when stacked properly. Stacking bales is an art. The best system for flatbeds or warehousing is called the locking bale technique. A pattern of running two bales in one direction, and the next two in the other, actually locks them together. When the crop emerges from a baler, one side of the bale is smooth, the other rough (from stalks). By using the rough side of the bale, two can essentially interlock with each other, forming a very stable unit for transport or extended storage on a pallet.

Once stacked in this manner, the bales have a tendency to hold their form, rather than sagging to one end. Further labor in loading them onto some form of transport is easily done with a hydraulic front-end loader system on your tractor. This cuts overhead and helps the receiving warehouse unload, a job taking minutes rather than hours. The cube of herbs and spices is what denotes their potential as a cash crop, the cube being the dollar value in one cubic foot of trailer space.

Trying to envision the space required to store a 5 ton crop in bale form requires some practice. A good rule of thumb is that a one half ton truck with a long bed can hold about 1 1/2 tons (28 bales per ton). To store 10 tons of baled product a space 20 feet long, 10 feet wide, and 8 feet high, is needed, which is equivalent to one tractor-trailer load. When moving spices or herbs as bales on a trailer, always cover the crop with a tarp. This not only protects the crop from browning by the sun, but also prevents wind-burn or extreme drying of the crop.

Hoppers and bins should be made for sack loading, using a bagging scale. The inside of the hopper needs to be lined with sheet metal so that loading and unloading is facilitated. Conveyors, belt and chain, work well in moving unpackaged crops around. A cleaning line where foreign matter is pulled from

TABLE 18

Dehydration and Storage Requirements for most Herbs and Spices

HERB/SPICE	PART USED	TEMP. VAR. LOW	HIGH	DRYING METHOD AND PROBLEMS	STORAGE	PACKAGING
Alfalfa (Medicago sativa)	Herb	90F	120F	Sun-cure, Leaf shatter	B	UW
Angelica (Angelica atropurpurea)	Root	100	140	Sun-cure, Split roots	S	HW
Anise (Pimpinella anisum)	Seed	85	120	Dryer, Turn continuously	FD	HW
Basil (Ocimum basilicum)	Herb	85	120	Dryer, Leaf browning	P	HW
Bay (Umbellularia californica)	Leaf	85	100	Dryer, Leaf must be whole	FD	HW
Bergamot (Monarda fistulosa)	Herb	85	115	Sun-cure, Loss of oil	B	HW
Blackberry (Rubus fruticosus)	Leaf	90	110	Dryer, Watch for cane	S	UW
Black Cohosh (Cimicifuga racemosa)	Root	100	140	Sun-cure, Split roots	S	UW
Blessed Thistle (Cnicus benedictus)	Herb	90	120	Sun-cure, "Condition" stalk	B	UW
Blue Cohosh (Caulophyllum thalicatroides)	Root	100	140	Sun-cure, Split roots	S	UW
Borage (Borago officinalis)	Herb	90	120	Shade, Stalk dries slowly	S	HW
Burdock (Arctium lappa)	Root	90	120	Sun-cure, Split roots	S	UW
Calamus (Acorus calamus)	Root	90	120	Dryer, Dry slowly	P	HW
Caraway (Carum carvi)	Seed	85	120	Dryer, Turn continuously	FD	HW
Cascara Segrada (Rhamnus purshiana)	Bark	90	140	Sun-cure, Remove moss	S	UW
Catnip (Nepeta cataria)	Herb	85	120	Sun-cure, "Condition" stem	B	HW
Chamomile (Anthemis nobilis)	Flower	85	110	Dryer, Turn continuously	FD	HW
Chapparal (Larrea mexicana)	Herb	90	120	Sun-cure, Stem dries slowly	B	HW
Chervil (Anthriscus cerefolium)	Herb	85	110	Shade, Color important	P	HW
Chickweed (Stellaria media)	Herb	90	120	Dryer, High water loss	P	HW
Chicory (Cichorium intybus)	Root	90	140	Sun-cure, Turn often	S	UW
Coltsfoot (Tussilago farfara)	Leaf	85	110	Dryer, Leaf tends to brown	P	HW
Comfrey (Symphytum officinale)	Leaf	85	120	Dryer, Most difficult to dry	P	HW
Coriander (Coriandrum sativum)	Seed	85	120	Dryer, Turn continuously	FD	HW

					FD	HW
Cumin (*Cuminum cyminum*)	Seed	85	120	Dryer, Turn continuously	S	UW
Dandelion (*Taraxacum officinale*)	Leaf/ Root	90	120	Sun-cure, Split roots	P	HW
Devil's Club (*Oplopanax horridum*)	Root	90	120	Dryer, Slice roots	P	HW
Dill (*Anethum graveolens*)	Leaf	85	110	Dryer, Loss of oils	FD	HW
Desert Tea (*Ephedra nevadensis*)	Herb	90	120	Sun-cure, Hard to package	B	HW
Echinacea (*Echinacea angustifolia*)	Root	85	110	Dryer, Dry slowly	P	HW
Elder (*Sambucus nigra*)	Flower	85	110	Sun-Cure, Turn often	FD	HW
Eucalyptus (*Eucalyptus globulus*)	Leaf	85	120	Dryer, Leaf tend to brown	P	HW
Fennel (*Foeniculum vulgare*)	Seed	85	110	Dryer, Turn continuously	FD	HW
Garlic (*Allium sativum*)	Bulb	85	110	Dryer, Dries slowly	FD	HW
Ginger (*Zingiber officinale*)	Root	85	100	Dryer, Loss of oil	P	HW
Ginseng (*Panax quinquefolium*)	Root	85	110	Dryer, Dry slowly	FD	HW
Goldenseal (*Hydrastis canadensis*)	Root	90	120	Sun-cure, Split roots	P	HW
Hop (*Humulus lupulus*)	Flower	85	120	Dryer, Dry slowly	B	RW
Horehound (*Marrubium vulgare*)	Herb	90	120	Sun-cure, Leaf tends to brown	B	HW
Horsetail (*Equisetum arvensa*)	Herb	85	120	Sun-cure, Tends to discolor	B	HW
Hyssop (*Hyssopus officinalis*)	Herb	90	120	Sun-cure, Loss of oil	B	HW
Kelp (*Fucus versiculosus*)	Plant	100	140	Dryer, Tends to "cake"	FD	HW
Kinikinnick (*Arctostaphylos uva-ursi*)	Leaf	90	120	Shade, Turn often	P	UW
Lavender (*Lavandula officinalis*)	Flower	85	100	Dryer, Loss of color	P	HW
Lemon Balm (*Melissa officinalis*)	Herb	90	120	Sun-cure, Loss of oil	B	HW
Lemon Verbena (*Lippia citriodora*)	Herb	90	120	Sun-cure, Loss of color	B	HW
Licorice (*Glycyrrhiza glabra*)	Root	85	120	Sun-cure, Dry slowly	P	HW
Lobelia (*Lobelia inflata*)	Herb	90	120	Shade, "Condition" stalk	B	HW
Lovage (*Levisticum officinale*)	Root	90	120	Sun-cure, Split roots	P	HW
Mandrake (*Podophyllum peltatum*)	Root	90	120	Shade, Split roots	P	UW
Marigold (*Calendula officinalis*)	Flower	85	110	Dryer, Tends to discolor	P	HW

TABLE 18

Dehydration and Storage Requirements for most Herbs and Spices

HERB/SPICE	PART USED	TEMP. VAR. LOW	TEMP. VAR. HIGH	DRYING METHOD AND PROBLEMS	STORAGE	PACKAGING
Marjoram (*Origanum majorana*)	Herb	85	110	Dryer, Leaf browning	P	HW
Marshmallow (*Althea officinalis*)	Root	90	120	Sun-cure, Split roots	P	HW
Mistletoe (*Phoradendron flavenscens*)	Herb	85	110	Dryer, Drys slowly	P	HW
Mugwort (*Artemisia vulgaris*)	Herb	90	120	Sun-cure, Leaf browning	B	HW
Mullein (*Verbascum thapsus*)	Herb	85	120	Sun-cure, "Condition" stalk	B	UW
Nettle (*Urtica urens*)	Herb	90	120	Sun-cure, Stalk is sapling	B	HW
Oatstraw (*Avena sativa*)	Herb	90	120	Sun-cure, Leaf shatter	B	UW
Onion (*Allium cepa*)	Bulb	85	110	Dryer, Dries slowly	FD	HW
Oregano (*Origanum vulgare*)	Leaf	85	110	Dryer, Loss of oil	P	HW
Oregon Grape (*Berberis aquifolium*)	Root	90	120	Sun-cure, Chip roots	P	UW
Parsley (*Petroselinum crispum*)	Herb	85	110	Dryer, Loss of color	FD	HW
Passion Flower (*Passiflora caerulea*)	Herb	90	120	Sun-cure, "Condition" stalk	B	HW
Pennyroyal (*Mentha pulegium*)	Herb	90	120	Sun-cure, Loss of oil	B	HW
Peppermint (*Menta piperita*)	Leaf	85	100	Sun-cure, Loss of oil	B	HW
Pippissawa (*Chimaphila umbellata*)	Herb	90	120	Sun-cure, Tends to brown	P	HW
Plantain (*Plantago major*)	Herb	90	120	Sun-cure, Tends to brown	P	HW
Poke (*Phytolacca americana*)	Root	90	120	Sun-cure, Split roots	S	UW
Queen-of-the-Meadow (*Eupatorium purpureum*)	Herb	90	120	Sun-cure, Tends to brown	B	HW
Raspberry (*Rubus idaeus*)	Leaf	90	110	Dryer, Watch for cane	S	UW
Red Clover (*Trifolium pratense*)	Flower	85	110	Dryer, Tends to discolor	B	HW
Rosehip (*Rosa canina*)	Buds	90	120	Shade, Loss of nutrients	P	UW
Rosemary (*Rosmarinus officinalis*)	Leaf	85	110	Dryer, Loss of oil	FD	HW
Rue (*Ruta graveolens*)	Herb	85	110	Dryer, Loss of oil	P	HW
Sage (*Salvia officinalis*)	Leaf	85	110	Dryer, Loss of oil/color	P	HW
St. John's Wort (*Hypericum perforatum*)	Herb	90	120	Sun-cure, Watch for insects	B	UW
Sarsaparilla (*Smilax regelii*)	Root	90	120	Sun-cure, Split roots	S	UW

112

Herb	Part			Processing	Packaging	Storage
Sassafras (*Sassafrass albidum*)	Root Bark	90	140	Sun-cure, Loss of oil	S	UW
Savory (*Satureia hortensis*)	Herb	85	110	Dryer, Loss of oil	FD	HW
Scullcap (*Scutellaria lateriflora*)	Herb	90	120	Sun-cure, Tends to brown	B	HW
Shepherd's Purse (*Capsella bursa-pastoris*)	Herb	90	120	Shade, Leaf shatter	B	HW
Slippery Elm (*Ulmus rubra*)	Bark	90	140	Sun-cure, Loss of oil	S	UW
Spearmint (*Mentha viridis*)	Leaf	85	110	Shade, Leaf shatter	B	HW
Strawberry (*Fragaria vesca*)	Leaf	85	110	Dryer, Leaf discolors	B	HW
Tansy (*Tanacetum vulgare*)	Herb	90	120	Sun-cure, Watch for insects	B	UW
Tarragon (*Artemsia dracunculus*)	Leaf	85	110	Dryer, Loss of oil	FD	HW
Thyme (*Thymus vulgaris*)	Herb	85	110	Dryer, Loss of oil	P	HW
Valerian (*Valeriana officinalis*)	Root	85	110	Sun-cure, Unpleasant odor	S	UW
Vervain (*Verbena hastata*)	Leaf	90	120	Shade, Leaf browning	P	HW
Walnut (*Juglans nigra*)	Hull	90	140	Dryer, Sticky mess	S	UW
White Oak (*Quercus alba*)	Bark	90	140	Sun-cure, Needs chipped	S	UW
Wild Cherry (*Prunus serotina*)	Bark	90	120	Sun-cure, Loss of color	S	UW
Wild Lettuce (*Lactuca scariola*)	Herb	90	120	Shade, Leaf shatter	B	UW
Wintergreen (*Gaultheria procumbens*)	Leaf	90	120	Shade, Loss of oil	B	HW
Witch Hazel (*Hamamelis virginiana*)	Bark	90	120	Sun-cure, Turn often	S	UW
Woodruff (*Asperula odorata*)	Herb	90	120	Shade, "Condition" stems	B	UW
Wormwood (*Artemisia absinthium*)	Leaf	90	120	Shade, Loss of color	B	HW
Yarrow (*Archillea millefolium*)	Flower	85	110	Dryer, Dry slowly	P	HW
Yellow Dock (*Rumex crispus*)	Root	90	140	Sun-cure, Split roots	S	UW
Yerba Mate' (*Ilex paraguaiensis*)	Leaf	85	120	Sun-cure, Tends to shatter	P	HW
Yerba Santa (*Eriodictyon californicum*)	Leaf	90	120	Sun-cure, Stem dries slow	P	UW

Storage Key: HW – Heated Warehouse, UW – Unheated Warehouse, RW – Refrigerated Warehouse, *Packaging Key:* B – Baled, S – Burlap Sack, P – Polypropylene Sack, FD – Fiber-Drum Barrel the crop improves marketing prices substantially for certain spices and flower crops. Roller conveyors are sometimes used when moving large quantities of sacks around a warehouse.

Several types of sacks are used when storing herbs and spices. Almost all high oil products and flavorings should be stored in polyproplylene sacks, a very light thermo-plastic resin used in the grain and seed industries. The bag can be sewn with an industrial grade sewing machine in seconds, and a label attached. Most barks are still packaged in burlap sacks because the fiber contamination is usually not a problem. Some roots are now shipped in polypropylene because it is stronger than burlap.

Fiber drums, when available, are the best containers for marketing a processed spice. They are often lined with a polyethylene liner. Although this does not keep air from entering the crop, it does prevent the oils from staining the barrel. A number of the major pharmaceutical houses can now receive powders of herbs and spices in fiber drums for their storage. The actual choice of packaging really depends, to a certain extent, on your market's storage facilities and the disposition of the product when it enters the warehouse. *Storage and marketing of crude botanicals is quite different from storage or marketing of a processed herb or spice.*

TAGS AND LABELS

All packaged herbs and spices must be labeled, whether being stored or shipped.

If a product is being shipped, the tag must carry the name of the producer, the destination of the product, and the net contents. Every bag, drum, or bale should be labeled. Oftentimes a crop will not be tagged until it is ready for shipment. There is no problem with this procedure as long as each is labeled when it is loaded on a truck. Although each sack — and there may be several thousand — should be numbered, this requirement is often ignored. This practice increases the work for the receiver when inventorying a received shipment into their warehouse. If they are numbered, then the warehousman can simply check each sack off a packing list as it is removed from the truck.

TRUCKING

Almost all herbs and spices are sold f.o.b. your warehouse or field. When shipping common carrier — a trucker with published rates — all herbs and spices are shipped *Class 70, Dried Herbs and Flowers.* This is the most expensive way to ship, and often is the limiting factor in making a sale. Back-haulers are truckers who are returning to some location with a partial load or an empty truck. Often special rates can be negotiated for loads over two tons. Rates can be less than half that of the common carrier.

Alternatives in trucking include full loads, wherein the rate might be "by

STORAGE RACK
FORKLIFT

115

MARIGOLD
(*Calendula officinalis*)
Compositae family

This well known garden plant is probably one of the most used herb flowers. It is valuable medicinally, yields a yellow dye, and is used in numerous cosmetic preparations and potpourri. Used in the Mediterranean region since ancient Greece, it was used by India and Arabic cultures even before the Greeks. It has a very long flowering period, hence its Latin name *calends* meaning "throughout the months."

As an annual, it is not found wild. It tolerates any soil in full sun, although preferring loam. Seed sown mid-spring usually establish quickly, and will self-sow itself for following years. The perennial marigold (*Tagetes lucida*) is a substitute for French tarragon in climates where the Artemisias do not winter well because of being too warm. It is not as tender as the larger flowering marigolds.

The flowerheads can be raked or separated from the plant using a device similar to a cranberry scoop. The flowers dry easily on tarps in partial sun, or on racks in a dryer. The *Calendula* variety yields larger flowers per acre, sometimes as much as 1,500 pounds per acre. Prices for the flowerhead to the potpourri and cosmetic markets can range from $1.00 to $2.00 per pound. In a typical year, Yugoslavia alone exports more than 400 ton dried flowerheads into the United States.

The *Tagetes* species is primarily cultivated for the oil, especially the Mexican marigold (*T. minuta*). Used extensively in both cosmetics and foods as a fragrance component and flavoring additive, the tagetes meal and tagetes extract are extensively used in chicken feed to give the characteristic yellow color to chicken skin and egg yolk. Both marigold are also used in folk medicines.

the mile" rather than weight. This is the cheapest form of shipping and should always be explored first. Just because the price on your crop is less than that of a competing product imported into the country from overseas does not mean that it is cheaper when landed, which includes the freight bill. In some situations, especially when negotiating large shipments, the farmer must provide a landed price for his crop to the dock of the buyer. This assures the buyer of his total costs for the crop. It is also a way the farmer might make some extra money from the sale of his crop.

Sage

118

CHAPTER 7

The Art of Processing

Art is a kind of innate drive that seizes a human being and makes him its instrument. The artist is not a person endowed with free will who seeks his own ends, but one who allows art to realize its purpose through him.

C. G. Jung

Processing is defined as "a series of changes by which something develops or is brought about." Changing crude herbs and spices from field harvest condition into usable products for consumption or further manufacture is critical to any successful marketing program. Processing also involves improving cosmetics or visual appearance of an herb or spice. The art of processing is the skill required to make field crops usable to the manufacturer, thus increasing their value to the grower.

Large pharmaceutical houses which tablet or capsulate herbs do not have facilities to process crude, raw botanicals. Neither do most herb companies which manufacture teas. Both usually buy their ingredients in specific intermediate, processed forms which are compatible with their packaging machinery. Many crude botanical imports are therefore processed before they enter the country. Wholesalers and importers who do have processing facilities usually set such processing businesses up as a separate entity, with separate balance sheets and profit and loss statements.

In any exchange of goods, the buyer and seller must agree on how much of a commodity is to be delivered. As soon as trade gets beyond simple barter, it has to depend on weights and measures. In addition, all trade beyond barter involves price. Price in practically all markets is the common denominator by which the customer expresses his desire not only for quantity but also for quality. Besides weights and measures, therefore, standards for the quality of goods have achieved trade practice status. Grading is a basic function in practically all transactions. The purpose is to establish a common language understood by both buyer and seller as a basis of judging the quality of a product in relation to its sales prices.

MILLING GRADES AND STANDARDS

Much like wheat, which has been processed into flour, the trade and the cosmetic industry both require specific forms and qualities that must be met when herbs and spices are received. Specific machinery utilized in these industries demand specific and exacting grades of processed botanicals. A tea bagging machine, for example, will not evenly load a tea bag if the density flow ratio of the herb is not precisely correct.

Therein lies the art form or skill of the miller. Taking a crude botanical from the field and somehow putting it into a form whereby it can be used directly by packaging manufacturers takes skill and experience. To take crude spices and make them attractive to the retail customer is an art form which enhances your total cash yields. Proper milling not only broadens the marketing potential, but also accounts for the actual price difference between crude farm product, and the cash returns from wholesalers who process these herbs. The difference can be more than a 100% markup on cost to the buyer.

Almost all spices and herbs are sold with the following "cut" labels:

Whole (whl). Most seeds and flowers are sold as "whl." Examples are caraway, poppy (as spices), and hops or rose petal (as flowers). Another group sold as "whl" has been cut to predetermined lengths for uniformity. Licorice root and cinnamon stick are good examples. Depending on the width, 10 to 20 roots of licorice are bundled with wire to hold them together, and are then cut with a bandsaw to 3 to 6 inch lengths and sold as "whl."

Chip, also known as "cut." Most barks and roots are "chipped" into two to six inch pieces (non-uniform) for ease in drying and eventual packaging for shipping by truck. This is a crude cut and is basically sizing an unmanageable root into a form that can eventually be used on a conveyor to feed further processing. This first step in sizing is necessary when further processing into a smaller cut product is desired. When chipping, powdering is not desired, so care must be taken to avoid these forms of losses.

Shredding. This form of processing essentially tears the product apart, much like a lawn mower, leaving a wide range of particle sizes. It is very rarely used and is only appropriate when further processing of the material to powder is required. It does nothing for physical appearance or cosmetics, and oftentimes results in loss of quality due to oil losses or nutrient damage. The only real advantage of shredding is to shorten the drying time requirement for one reason or another, when total particle sizes need to be small for feeding into further processing.

Chop. This form of cut is made with what is known as a bark mill. Bark mills consist of a series of knife-edges of a variety of designs in a large plate. A hydraulic punch then pushes the product through the screen, leaving it with specific pre-sized cuts. It is only used with specific spices such as garlic and onion, and is considered a specialized cut used primarily for the food industries. Onions and garlics, and other specialized spices, are marketed sliced and diced. This is done for cosmetic reasons in food preparation, and these cuts are sometimes made in such a way that these various products can blend with other ingredients. Examples would include soup manufacturers and other fabricators of prepared foods.

Cut and sift. This is the most familiar way in which herbs and spices are sold. There are varying particle sizes associated with C/S, based primarily on what the public has most generally become accustomed to buying. These C/S variations can range from about 1/2 inch to less than 1/8 inch. Sifting means that the product has been separated via sifting or seed cleaning devices so that there is uniformity in particle sizes. Most botanicals are sold in this form. The mill pre-sizes the botanical to the upper size, and the screen sifts the botanical to the lower sizes.

Tea bag cut (tbc). This form is used only by tea manufacturers who produce tea bags for the mass market. Product size is predicated on a flow density, or rate of fall, down a specific tea bagging machine's loader. Its rate of fall varies with the cut-sizes of the other ingredients. For example, orange peel is considerably more dense than black tea (as in orange spice tea blends). For this reason, orange peel needs to be a different size than the black tea so that the blend will not separate due to handling. Because of these factors, tbc requires the most care in milling.

Screen sizes for tbc vary from 1/8 inch to 1/16 inch, also known as 8 mesh (United States Standard) to 30 mesh U.S.S.. Anything smaller or larger than these sizes cannot be sold as tbc. The art in keeping these "losses" to a minimum, especially when one realizes that the requirements for alfalfa herb — for example — is usually 8 to 18 mesh U.S.S. for most tea bagging machines.

Granule (gran). This is a rare cut, usually from a square-cut punch mill, similar to those used for chop. It is used for some barks and roots, those which might be used for a beverage where roasting is involved. Examples are dandelion root and chicory root (both used as coffee substitutes). This milling process uses a large screen with a punch which essentially crushes the root or bark through the screen. Sometimes onion and garlic are sold as gran. Particle sizes range from one fourth inch to one sixteenth inch.

Ground (grn). This form of cut is used in the baking and food industry when texture in the ingredients is indicated. Nutmeg and other high-oil spices are usually cut to this size. Particle sizes range from 20 to 40 mesh USS. Ground products are produced from milling in two ways: either by sifting the product from a tbc milling process, or by a roller mill more commonly used to crush or fracture seeds, nuts, and some barks.

Powder (pwd). This is the backbone form in which most pharmaceutical houses like their products. *Tableting* requires a 40 to 60 mesh USS and *capsulating* requires even finer grades, usually as small as 80 to 120 mesh USS. Dusts this fine require special ventilation and capture systems for airborne particles to minimize losses. Milling products to this fineness generally requires special hammermills equipped with special hammers and screens. Milling some crops to this standard also requires processing at low temperatures (cryogenic) to prevent high volatile oil losses when fragmented. Powdering requires the most skill in milling.

PRE-MILLING PROCEDURES

Most crops contain a number of foreign materials, ranging from rocks and pieces of wood to unwanted weeds and diseased or insect infested materials. The purpose of pre-milling procedures is to catch these problems and to eliminate them, thus improving the value and quality of processed crop. Rocks and wood must be removed also to prevent damage to mill knives.

Weeds must be removed to assure the quality of the material sold. While milling does improve the cosmetic appearance of the crop, it also hides grass and other weed contaminants. Pharmaceutical houses normally run laboratory inspections to ferret out hidden contaminants. Certain crops have more latitude or leeway for contamination. Spices, as a rule, do not. Sale of diseased plant material will not only loose future sales, but often prompts rejection after a sale has been made. The seller then pays return freight costs.

Usually rocks and sticks are removed by hand as the material passes operators along a conveyor system. Dirt, gravel and other small particle contaminants are removed by shaking the conveyor carrying crude botanicals over a screen. Unwanted dirt particles fall through a screen. This technique is often used to remove valuable seeds from crops which have gone to seed as well. The flowerheads are often thrashed before loading them on the conveyor.

Insect infested materials are usually not salvageable, and are burned to prevent further contamination. There are some exceptions. Many seed crops contain either larvae or eggs of insects. These are not a problem during milling, but cause serious problems in storage when larvae and eggs hatch. They cannot only contaminate the seed, but can also spread to neighboring crops in the storage facility. Sterilization of infested seed crops is required by both the federal government and the American Spice Trade Association (ASTA) for all imported crops. This treatment is called "LoBac," meaning low bacteria. Essentially the botanical is gassed with an inert fumigant, usually ethylene oxide or carboxide, which kills most known bacteria, insects and their larvae and eggs. The standard procedure is to expose the seed in a closed room for 24 hours to an open cylinder of the fumigant. The room is then opened to the atmosphere for 12 hours before either seed or air in the room are safe. Sometimes fumigation is carried out in railroad cars as the seed is transported to its final destination.

The problem with fumigation is that while it does kill all unwanted organisms, and leaves the crude seeds and botanicals unchanged in terms of chemistry, it does not remove the insect fragments within the material. Most manufacturers have therefore established specific tolerance levels. You can count on them to run laboratory tests to detect insect fragment counts, especially if you are a new supplier.

TYPES OF MILLING MACHINERY

The hammer miller. This is the most commonly used mill on the small farm. Crude material enters the mill through some form of feed throat, is struck by blades, bounced off a chamber roof, and passed on a tangential path to a screen. The milled material is released from the mill only when it is reduced to a size that is smaller than the hole size of the screen. The resulting particle size is substantially affected by the type of feed throat, blade and screen utilized, plus the speed chosen for the rotor. The hammermill is used today chiefly to grind livestock and poultry feed. It grinds faster than most other mills, but takes more power and is more expensive. It usually employs rows of free swinging, steel flails whirling at high speeds with an action more or less like a leaf shredder. Hammermills will grind all manner of crops, even mixed grains, ear corn, and hay.

The selection of rotor speed and screen affects particle size. At higher speeds, the particle tends to approach the screen hole at a tangent, thus making a round hole appear as an ellipse. Therefore, a smaller particle is obtained from the same screen size opening if the rotor is run at higher speeds. Alternatively, a smaller particle size can be achieved by keeping the screen opening and speed constant, but changing to a heavier gauge screen. Conversely, when using heavier gauge screens for greater strength, it is usually necessary to increase the size of the opening if the same product size is required.

Three alternative screen perforations are: round perforated, herringbone slot, and cross-slot perforation. Of these, the *round perforated screen* is structurally stronger. It is used for most crops with a high fiber content. The *herringbone slot* consists of a series of slotted holes repeated across the surface of the screen at an angle of 45 degrees to the length of the screen. It is used primarily for grinding crystalline materials —such as gum resins and sugars — and seeds. The cross slot screen has the slots arranged across the screen at right angles to the length of the screen. Refer to the artwork for visual descriptions and differences.

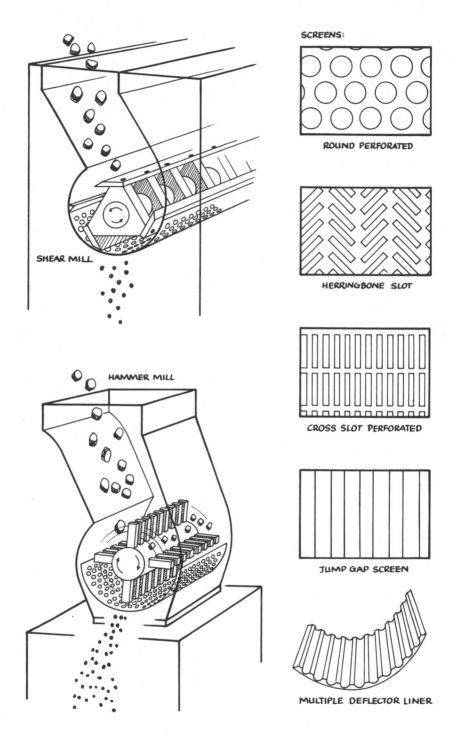

SHEAR MILL

HAMMER MILL

SCREENS:

ROUND PERFORATED

HERRINGBONE SLOT

CROSS SLOT PERFORATED

JUMP GAP SCREEN

MULTIPLE DEFLECTOR LINER

124

ASSORTED HAMMER MILL PARTS:

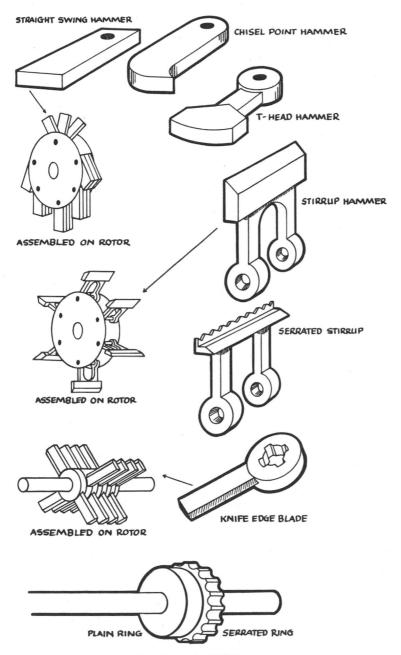

STRAIGHT SWING HAMMER

CHISEL POINT HAMMER

T-HEAD HAMMER

ASSEMBLED ON ROTOR

STIRRUP HAMMER

ASSEMBLED ON ROTOR

SERRATED STIRRUP

ASSEMBLED ON ROTOR

KNIFE EDGE BLADE

PLAIN RING   SERRATED RING

ASSEMBLED ON ROTOR

125

The cross slot screen provides the same fineness of grind as the round perforated one, but a grind slightly finer than the herringbone screen. This means that it is preferred when powdering is the primary function of the mill. The *jump gap screen* has a series of bars so arranged that the particle approaching the bar essentially approaches a ramp. The slope of this ramp deflects the particle into the air away from the gap in the screen. This type of screen is ideal for milling abrasive, or clogging types of material and for heavy duty service.

The selection of blades is also important. In general, a flat edged blade, known as an impact edge, is used for such things as pulverizing, emulsifying, and pureeing, when it is important that only the maximum size be controlled. Because the flat-edged blade essentially shatters the product, the size of particles range widely after a milling operation. Knife edged blades are used for granulating, chopping, and sizing. A knife edge should be used when "finds" are undesirable, fiber and tissues have to be severed, and a narrow range of particle size is desired. Please refer to the line drawings for detail.

Hammers range from 1/16 inch swinging bars to 100 pound bullhead (rigid) hammers. Other forms include the chisel point, "T"-head swing, plain ring, serrated ring, and stirrups (used primarily in powdering). Line drawings give some detail. Most are either case hardened or have tungsten-carbide inserts for longer life. The labyrinth pattern (see line drawing) in some mills provides a shearing action in addition to impacting, primarily for emulsion preparation (oil separations in water). Most hammermills also have a multiple deflector liner to provide a multiplicity of breaking edges for still further reduction of particle sizes. See the drawing for detail.

Selection of the feed throat also affects performance. The location of the inlet can be used to accentuate or to minimize finds. The horizontal inlet produces the finest grinding, since maximum metal surfaces are present for rebounding. The forward, vertical inlet is best for fragile materials when "finds" are undesirable, since the product is immediately exposed to the screen area and thereby has a minimum amount of solid surface for impacting. It tends to give a narrower range of mesh sizes.

Automatic feeding devices help achieve optimum production rate and product uniformity. Non-uniform feeding ("slugging") results in an erratic range of ground product since the alternatively crowding and starving the milling chamber allows some of the product to pass through the screen radially, when crowded, or tangentially, when starved. Also, when overfed, more "finds" are produced due to attrition among particles within the chamber. Irregular feeding results in a broad-spectrum of sizes which may not be acceptable to the manufacturer.

If the raw or crude size of the product varies, the final product from a hammermill will also be erratic since initial size is analogous to alternately overfeeding and starving the chamber. A pre-break milling operation is often used to make sizing more uniform. Adding a second mill in series reduces the larger pieces to the size of the smaller ones in the original product. This gradual reduction approach has the added advantage of reducing the temperature rise that occurs if the product is reduced in one pass. To powder, for example, you must really have several reductions in particle size before it enters a mill with screens set for particle sizes less than 1/16 inches.

The range of particle sizes can be broadened or narrowed for a given product by heating or cooling the product before milling. Dipping the crop in liquid CO_2 or liquid N_2 makes the material more brittle. Ultra-fine grinding of nutmeg and pepper, for example, is often done in this manner to prevent incurring temperatures that degrade or drive off essential oils. More than 17% weight loss can be incurred by cracking whole nutmegs into a granule for teas at room temperatures. Maximum cooling is critical when you realize that this 17% loss in volatile oil represents the marketable aspect of nutmeg. Today, this crop is milled at very low temperatures and mixed immediately with the other tea ingredients. As it approaches the ambient temperature, and the oils begin to evaporate, the other ingredients absorb much of the oil. Losses are kept at a minimum and higher profits are shown.

A number of good manufacturers make hammermills. Bear Cat makes a good product for reducing dehydrated alfalfa-like crops into 6 inch pieces at rates of 3 to 5 ton per hour. Crops requiring more precise milling are best worked with either Fitz or Bell Mills. Gruendler and Asplund both make an excellent mill for "hogging" (the chip procedure), while Mikro-Pulverizer is excellent for powdering.

The shear mill. This is the most widely used mill in the spice and herb processing industry. It can handle fairly large cut, unprocessed crops with very low "finds" or powdering. Also known as a "cutter mill," the rotor has three knife blades which shear against two die-edged surfaces, similar to the action of a hand mower (see artwork). The knives are usually high-chrome, high-carbon blades, with a steep angle one eighth inch land with a more or less scissor cutting action.

Larger throats allow crude botanicals to be fed without pre-cutting. The actual design requires variations of from 5 to 50 hp motors, allowing the processing capacity to excede 2,000 pounds per hour. These mills give a much better cosmetic cut to leaf and root products which are marketed as C/S or tbc. They reduce losses by cutting the product cleanly, rather than hammering the product apart —fragmentation. They are primarily used in the plastics and metal industries, where such things as engine blocks from cars are powdered for recycling.

The angle of the die edges and knives is important and is related to both the speed of the rotor and the crop fiber content. Most crops I have worked with respond best to an angle of about 10 degrees —or slightly less —with rotor speeds of 1,700 rpm. The dies usually have slots to move them back and forth. When you sharpen them, as you eventually must, these slots allow adjustment of the dies so that their cutting action is flush with the blade-knives. They must be case-hardened after each sharpening, as well. The screen requirements and feed systems are identical to those for the hammermill.

You won't have much luck finding a used shear mill in a farm community. Look to those industries surrounding large cities which cut scrap. The shear mill is used extensively in almost all plastics operations. The brand most used is the Cumberland, manufactured by that firm in Providence, Rhode Island.

The burr mill. This is the old time gristmill, used throughout the ages for flouring wheat, rye, oats, corn, and other grains. The principle of operation is to crush the grain between two heavy wheels, one stationary, the other revolving. These mills are well suited for grinding your own flour for the table. None of the whole grain is lost in the burrs. It gives a finer grind than most other types of mills, although steel burrs have to be replaced quite often. The burrs should never be run when the mill is empty. They will wear out fast enough as it is. There are very few occasions when this type of mill is used in herb and spice processing, although it works well for powdering seed.

The roller mill. These are primarily used for grains and seed which must be crushed into fine powders. Grain is mashed between two rollers running with the same kind of action as the old clothes wringer. The roller surface is often serrated, or cogged, so that the teeth on one roller fit the space between the teeth of the other. Grain can be merely hulled, cracked, or even ground quite fine with this design. They account for loss of some germ from grains, but that value can be saved and run back through for further powdering. They are the least expensive of the mills, but again, they are rarely used in the spice and herb industry, except to powder some spice seeds.

The ball mill. This form of milling uses the principles of centripetal force, with roughened inside surfaces. As it turns, gravity forces the product to wear when it falls onto the lower surface. At faster speeds, a moment of inertia is created where products can wear into balls. This occurs when the heavier part of the product is thrown outward and wears on the abrasive surface. Ball mills are useful in cleaning outer bark off roots, or for cleaning dirt off products in general. They may even be constructed from 55 gallon drums for general work with roots and barks.

SEPARATION AND CLEANING

Once the crude botanical or spice has been milled, it needs to be separated and further cleaned. Particle fragments can range from the largest screen size to powder. Most manufacturers and retailers want and need a uniform cut and appearance for their product. When the milled product is separated and cleaned, the different sized products can then be sold to different markets. The more uniform product appearance commands higher prices. Large off-sized products can be re-milled. Seed cleaners can be found in almost every community. At farm sales they can always be found for around $50, with new ones from Nasco or Sears selling for about $150 and up. These cleaners shake seeds across a series of screens wherein anything larger or smaller, lighter or heavier, is sifted or winnowed out. There are many principles used for the diverse seed cleaning operation. Almost all are suitable for the diverse separation requirements for most herbs and spices. The following drawings show several different forms of seed separators.

Standard equipment used by most of the larger herb companies is known as "shaker boxes," like those made by Sweco. A series of three to eight different particle sizes are separated by screens using a rotating vibration system, usually with a variable speed control. As the milled botanical falls onto the screen, this rolling action causes the product to be separated and roll down the screen. If the product is smaller than the screen, it falls through. If it is larger, than it rolls down to one end, and is collected in a different barrel.

By placing the different trays at opposite angles, the milled herb or spice particle falls through the appropriate screen or screens and is then collected by gravity flow. Most systems employ only 4 or 5 screens at one time. Powdered materials are usually re-milled into even finer particle sizes. Sifting powders requires a plastic hood and fan arrangement over the shaker box, coupled with faster vibrator action and less angle on the screens.

The variable speed and the angle of the screen determine how a particle falls through a given screen. It is important that these two variables be adjustable for any system used for a diversity of processed products. The final product should have less than 10%, by weight dust sized particles in a C/S product, or it will not be marketable at that grade of cut. Because additional dusts are created by fragmentation conducting during separations, care must be taken to clean the final product when packaging and taking inventory.

Keep a product record sheet on all milling and sifting operations. This record should include the crude weight entering the milling operation, the resultant weights of the various sifts, what screens were used in milling and sifting, how much time was required to complete the process, and losses due to airborne powders and spillage not recovered. This record will give the farmer a complete picture of cost of goods produced. Table 21 provides a complete list of herbs and spices, with information on screen sizes usually used, and milling problems specific to each.

Manufacturers usually find that a complete program usually costs from 25 cents per pound for most C/S processing, to as much as 75 cents per pound for elaborate powdering. When you consider that nutmeg normally costs about $4.50 per pound, a 17% loss represents more than 75 per pound. Therefore elaborate cryogenic installations are well worth the effort in terms of profits and cost of goods produced figures. If grades are not as critical, then overall costs can be as little as 5 cents per pound, including labor and machinery depreciation.

When one compares the differences between raw farm prices and those from a wholesaler (table 29, 30, *Price Variations, Bulk Wholesale through Retail Sales, for some Herbs and Spices),* it becomes obvious that milling should be considered by all before just selling a crop in crude form. Milling not only

TABLE 19
Standard Processing Specifications for some Herbs and Spices, with Milling Problems

HERB/SPICE	PART USED	USE	Whl	C/S	Pwd	MILLING PROBLEMS
Alfalfa (*Medicago sativa*)	Herb	T		3/8	1/16	Needs pre-sizing
Angelica (*Angelica atropurpurea*)	Root	T		3/8		Look for dirt
Anise (*Pimpinella anisum*)	Seed	C		1/4	1/16	Needs "dewiskered"
Basil (*Ocimum basilicum*)	Herb	C		1/4		Avoid powdering
Bay (*Umbellularia californica*)	Leaf	C	X			Wholeness desired
Bergamot (*Monarda fistulosa*)	Herb	T,C		1/4		Sift for stem
Blackberry (*Rubus fruticosus*)	Leaf	T		1/4		Remove cane
Black Cohosh (*Cimicifuga racemosa*)	Root	M		3/8		Look for dirt
Blessed Thistle (*Cnicus benedictus*)	Herb	T		1/4		Remove "furry" seed
Blue Cohosh (*Caulophyllum thalicatroides*)	Root	M		3/8		Look for dirt
Borage (*Borago officinalis*)	Herb	M,T		1/4	1/16	Watch for insects
Burdock (*Arctium lappa*)	Root	M		3/8		Split the rootstock
Calamus (*Acorus calamus*)	Root	M,T,P		1/2		Hallucinogen
Caraway (*Carum carvi*)	Seed	C	X			Look for bugs
Cascara Segrada (*Rhamnus purshiana*)	Bark	M,T		1/2	1/16	Needs to age one year
Catnip (*Nepeta cataria*)	Herb	T		1/4		Pull excess stem
Chamomile (*Anthemis nobilis*)	Flower	M,T	X			Remove foreign matter
Chapparal (*Larrea mexicana*)	Herb	M,T		1/4		Often dusty
Chervil (*Anthriscus cerefolium*)	Herb	C		1/4	1/8	Remove discolored leaf
Chickweed (*Stellaria media*)	Herb	T		1/4	1/16	Tends to fragment
Chicory (*Cichorium intybus*)	Root	C		1/4	1/8	Roast after cutting
Coltsfoot (*Tussilago farfara*)	Leaf	T		1/4		Tobacco ingredient
Comfrey (*Symphytum officinale*)	Leaf/Root	M,T		3/8	1/8	Tends to "blacken"

Herb/Spice	Part	Use		Screen 1	Screen 2	Notes
Coriander (*Coriandrum sativum*)	Seed	C	X		1/16	Clogs milling screen
Cumin (*Cuminum cyminum*)	Seed	C	X			Look for insects
Dandelion (*Taraxacum officinale*)	Leaf/Root	T		3/8		Look for dirt
Devil's Club (*Oplopanax horridum*)	Root	M		1/4	1/16	Needs pre-sizing
Dill (*Anethum graveolens*)	Seed/Leaf	C	X	1/4	1/8	Remove excess stem
Desert Tea (*Ephedra nevadensis*)	Herb	M,T		1/4	1/4	Tends to shred
Echinacea (*Echinacea angustifolia*)	Root	M,T		1/2		Look for dirt
Elder (*Sambucus nigra*)	Flower	T	X			Look for stem
Eucalyptus (*Eucalyptus globulus*)	Leaf	M,T	X	5/8		Sift for dust
Fennel (*Foeniculum vulgare*)	Seed	C	X		1/16	Needs re-cleaning
Garlic (*Allium sativum*)	Bulb	C	X	1/4	1/16	Anti-caking agent needed
Ginger (*Zingiber officinale*)	Root	C		3/8		Clogs screen
Ginseng (*Panax quinquefolium*)	Root	M	X	1/2	1/8	Needs pre-sizing
Goldenseal (*Hydrastis canadensis*)	Root	M		1/2	1/16	Hard to powder
Hop (*Humulus lupulus*)	Flower	M,T	X	5/8		Creates dust
Horehound (*Marrubium vulgare*)	Herb	M,T		1/4		Remove excess stem
Horsetail (*Equisetum arvensa*)	Herb	T		1/4		Quite fiberish
Hyssop (*Hyssopus officinalis*)	Herb	M		1/4		Tends to powder
Kelp (*Fucus versiculosus*)	Plant	M,C			1/16	Use high speeds
Kinikinnick (*Arctostaphylos uva-ursi*)	Leaf	T		1/4	1/8	Remove extra stem
Lavender (*Lavandula officinalis*)	Flower	P	X			Remove discolored flowers
Lemon Balm (*Melissa officinalis*)	Herb	T,P		1/2		Remove excess stem
Lemon Verbena (*Lippia citriodora*)	Herb	T,P		1/2		Remove excess stem
Licorice (*Glycyrrhiza glabra*)	Root	M,T	X	3/8		Tends to shred

Use of Herb/Spice: T – Tea; C – Culinary; M – Medicinal; P – Potpourri; LH – Drug Plant.

HERB/SPICE	PART USED	USE	FORM & SCREEN			MILLING PROBLEMS
			Whl	C/S	Pwd	
Lobelia (*Lobelia inflata*)	Herb	MTLH		1/4		Don't breath dust
Lovage (*Levisticum officinale*)	Root	M,T		3/8		Look for dirt
Mandrake (*Podophyllum peltatum*)	Root	M,LH		3/8	1/16	Hallucinogen
Marigold (*Calendula officinalis*)	Flower	M,P	X			Remove brown flowers
Marjoram (*Origanum majorana*)	Herb	C		1/4		Remove excess stem
Marshmallow (*Althea officinalis*)	Root	M,T		3/8	1/8	Look for dirt
Mistletoe (*Phoradendron flavenscens*)	Leaf	M,T		3/8	1/16	Don't breath dust
Mugwort (*Artemisia vulgaris*)	Herb	P		1/2		Allergen, irritant
Mullein (*Verbascum thapsus*)	Herb	T		1/2	1/4	Don't breath dust
Nettle (*Urtica urens*)	Leaf	P		3/8	1/16	"Stinging" nettle
Oatstraw (*Avena sativa*)	Herb	T		3/8	1/16	Needs pre-sizing
Onion (*Allium cepa*)	Bulb	C		1/4	1/16	Anti-caking agent needed
Oregano (*Origanum vulgare*)	Leaf	C		3/8	1/8	Remove excess stem
Oregon Grape (*Berberis aquifolium*)	Root	T,M		5/8	1/16	Look for dirt
Parsley (*Petroselinum crispum*)	Herb	T,C	X		1/16	Tends to "yellow"
Passion Flower (*Passiflora caerulea*)	Herb	LH		1/2		Remove excess stem
Pennyroyal (*Mentha pulegium*)	Herb	T,M		1/4	1/16	Don't breath dust
Peppermint (*Menta piperita*)	Leaf	T,C		3/8	1/16	Loss of volatile oils
Pippissawa (*Chimaphila umbellata*)	Herb	T,M		1/4	1/8	Tends to fragment
Plantain (*Plantago major*)	Herb	M,T		1/2		Watch for roots
Poke (*Phytolacca americana*)	Root	M,T		3/8		Split larger roots
Queen-of-the-Meadow (*Eupatorium purpureum*)	Herb	T		3/8		Clean roots
Raspberry (*Rubus idaeus*)	Leaf	T		1/4		Tends to ball together
Red Clover (*Trifolium pratense*)	Flower	T	X			Remove discolored flowers
Rosehip (*Rosa canina*)	Buds	T	X			Remove seeds
Rosemary (*Rosmarinus officinalis*)	Leaf	C		1/4		Stemmy
Rue (*Ruta graveolens*)	Herb	M		1/4		Remove foreign matter

Name	Part	Use				Notes
Sage (*Salvia officinalis*)	Leaf	M,T,P			1/4	Remove any "bark"
St. John's Wort (*Hypericum perforatum*)	Herb	M			1/4	Avoid breathing dust
Sarsaparilla (*Smilax regelii*)	Root	T			3/8	Split rootstock
Sassafras (*Sassafrass albidum*)	Root					
	Bark	T		1/16	1/2	Hard woody surfaces
Savory (*Satureia hortensis*)	Herb	C			1/4	Stemmy
Scullcap (*Scutellaria lateriflora*)	Herb	M,LH		1/16	1/4	Sedative, depressant
Shepherd's Purse (*Capsella bursa-pastoris*)	Herb	M,T			1/4	Tends to dust
Slippery Elm (*Ulmus rubra*)	Bark	M,T		1/16		High loss in dust
Spearmint (*Mentha viridis*)	Leaf	T,C	X	1/16	3/8	Loss of volatile oils
Strawberry (*Fragaria vesca*)	Leaf	T		1/16	1/4	Look for runners
Tansy (*Tanacetum vulgare*)	Herb	T			3/8	Don't breath dust
Tarragon (*Artemisia dracunculus*)	Leaf	C		1/8	1/4	Loss of volatile oils
Thyme (*Thymus vulgaris*)	Herb	C	X	1/16		Stemmy
Valerian (*Valeriana officinalis*)	Root	M,LH		1/16	1/4	Disagreeable odor
Vervain (*Verbena hastata*)	Leaf	M			1/4	Look for dirt
Walnut (*Juglans nigra*)	Hull	M			1/2	Remove dust
White Oak (*Quercus alba*)	Bark	T			1/2	Tends to dust
Wild Cherry (*Prunus serotina*)	Bark	M,T		1/16	1/2	Tends to fragment
Wild Lettuce (*Lactuca scariola*)	Herb	LH		1/4	5/8	Narcotic
Wintergreen (*Gaultheria procumbens*)	Leaf	M,T,P			5/8	Stemmy
Witch Hazel (*Hamamelis virginiana*)	Bark	M			3/8	Watch for dirt
Woodruff (*Asperula odorata*)	Herb	M,P			1/4	Tends to fragment
Wormwood (*Artemisia absinthium*)	Leaf	M		1/16	3/8	Don't breath dust
Yarrow (*Archillea millefolium*)	Flower	M,T	X		1/2	Remove all stalk
Yellow Dock (*Rumex crispus*)	Root	T			1/2	Clean dirt off roots
Yerba Mate' (*Ilex paraguaiensis*)	Leaf	T			1/4	Tends to fragment
Yerba Santa (*Eriodictyon californicum*)	Leaf	M,T			1/4	Tends to powder

Use of Herb/Spice: T – Tea; C – Culinary; M – Medicinal; P – Potpourri; LH – Drug Plant.

increases your prospective markets, it also allows increased profit margins of as much as 300%. Milling should be considered as a separate business by small farmers. Separate accounting books should be kept for the farming and milling operations.

LAYOUT CONSIDERATIONS FOR THE MILLING ROOM

Mills should be enclosed in a special room equipped with good ventilation because dusts created are quite extensive and potentially explosive. If the room is cleaned before operations, and is sealed during the operation, then airborne losses can be "found" by sweeping the room after milling is completed. The milling room also must have some form of ventilation with a trap to catch airborne dusts. Ventilation reduces the possibility of dust explosions resulting from the heat of milling or machinery sparks. Simple ventilation systems can be made by locating a squirrel-cage fan above the mill, venting to the outside. In more primitive systems it is just a box fan next to the mill, blowing dust out an open door.

Since dust from some herbs and spices is toxic, a miller must wear protective coveralls to protect his body, and a respirator to protect his lungs. Enclosed protective glasses should be used to protect the eyes. Gloves are required for most work. A simple dust mask may be used in short simple operations, but more elaborate respiration devices, with filter systems and good fitting masks, are required for extensive milling operations. Even if milling is conducted outside, respirators should be worn routinely.

Most milling machinery is fastened to feed tables on the second level of barn of storage facility, separated from the rest of the structure to hold dust levels down elsewhere. Raw material is conveyored into the room by the same type of elevators used for handling alfalfa. As it is milled, the product falls onto shaker boxes for separation and cleaning. These sifted products are either bagged on the spot or conveyed to hoppers for bagging. Mills and related equipment is sited high so that products need not be handled excessively between operations. If gravity fall designs are feasible, this not only cuts labor, but also the cost of goods produced.

Ribbon blenders are sometimes used to mix ingredients such as tea blends or formula preparations. Roller conveyors are used to stitch bags and move them individually from one end of the warehouse to another. Eventually they are then loaded onto pallets for shipping and storage. Warehouses and milling rooms should be kept free of insects and rodents and all materials which are not properly part of the operation. If you don't, the Food and Drug and NAWGA will. The warehouse should also be thoroughly disinfected and sprayed with mild disinfectants on a regular basis to minimize bacteria and molds. The milling room and all machinery used to process and clean products should be thoroughly cleaned immediately after use.

Surprise visitors and their first impressions of your operations are often critical for effective marketing. If the warehouse and milling rooms are spotless, your reputation for a quality product is markedly increased. Word gets around when one keeps a pig pen processing facility. Remember that contamination includes materials from previous milling schedules.

STANDARD PROCESSING SPECIFICATIONS FOR SOME HERBS AND SPICES, INCLUDING MILLING PROBLEMS

The table on pages 130 to 133 gives the recommended screen sizes and standards for some of the more important herbs and spices. This table includes milling problems which will be encountered with these crops. The table on specific use can also be used as a first identifier for marketing.

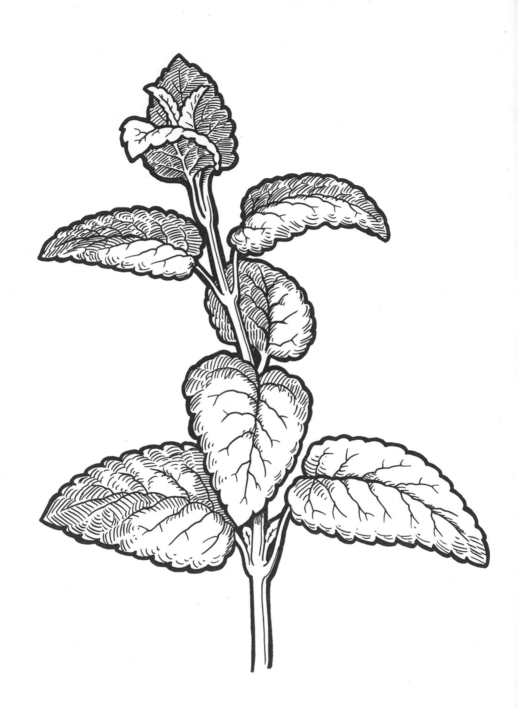

Lemon Balm

CHAPTER 8

Direct (Retail) Marketing

The work of our communities is to lay the foundation, the ground-
work . . . to develop the models, designs, and archetypes of a new
civilization.

The Northwest Provender Alliance

Direct farm marketing has been adopted as a business alternative by most of
the current small farms and practitioners of eco-agriculture. Last year, more
than 65% of all small farmers sold their crops by this method. This type of
marketing is defined as the sale of agricultural products to the consumer primarily through the efforts of the producer. More specifically, direct marketing
is the sale of agricultural commodities at any marketplace established and
maintained for the purpose of enabling farmers to *sell their agricultural commodities directly to individual consumers,* otherwise known as retail sales.

Justification for establishing a direct farmer-to-consumer marketing outlet
is based primarily on producer desire for increased financial returns from production. This results from reduced marketing costs attributed to middlemen,
and a consumer desire to buy riper, fresher produce. Moreover, direct marketing may provide outlets for products which do not attract commercial buyers.
These markets include gourmet markets, where consumers desire products
which vary from commercial standards in size, maturity, appearance, volume,
and grade. In addition, restaurants and restaurant supply houses represent

potential direct markets. Direct marketing can also turn vine ripened, or field run produce, normally considered lost produce, into additional income. Direct marketing also reduces the risk of relying on a single market channel.

There is another side to the *why* of direct marketing, and this relates to consumer demand. The primary consumer attraction to direct marketing outlets is the opportunity to purchase fresh, ripe, flavorful products at their source. This demand seems to be coupled with the popularity of automobile travel, more leisure time, and a basic curiosity. Buying direct from farms, especially pick-your-own operations, also offers an opportunity for family recreation and learning.

SOME BASIC QUESTIONS

There are a series of basic marketing questions which you need to ask yourself before beginning any venture of this type:

Start with a preliminary evaluation.

1. What are the marketing needs (consumer use, packaging, etc.) for your crops?
2. Is your focus on profit, a way of life, or some other value?
3. What are your expectations from direct marketing?
4. What are the alternatives?
5. Is direct marketing feasible with your crops?

Any individual evaluation will need to rely on answers to the following questions.

1. Do you have a personality which lends itself to direct marketing?
2. Are you friendly and outgoing?
3. Do you enjoy meeting people and having them visit your farm?
4. Do you have the knowledge and experience to sell direct?
5. Can you produce what the public wants?
6. Is direct marketing in line with your personal goals and future operational plans?

A business evaluation, similarly, must consider the following.

1. Will direct marketing fit your existing operation?
2. Is the necessary capital available?
3. Can you produce sufficient volumes of the crop?
4. Can your family supply sufficient labor?
5. Is labor available locally?
6. Is there adequate space and access for direct marketing?

Finally, a market evaluation —

1. Is there a demand for your product?
2. Is there an advantage for you to sell direct?
3. Is your direct market location satisfactory?
4. Is there competition, making your business marginal?

Personality is important in direct marketing. The need to meet and welcome customers is critical for any successful venture. Knowledge of retailing methods and techniques is also necessary. Retail sales knowledge is vital to the successful operation of a direct market outlet. The plans of direct market producers can have substantial impact upon the viability of direct operations and should be considered in the initial decision to sell directly to the consumer.

DIRECT MARKETING FOR THE SMALL FARMER

There are a variety of direct marketing options available to the small farmer. Selecting a method depends on the individual, the farm location, the volume of products to sell, and other factors.

THE ROADSIDE STAND

The roadside stand is usually located on the farm. The operation is seasonal and corresponds to farm harvests. Occasionally, products produced by neighbors are sold to provide a broader product variety. A successful roadside stand requires a suitable location with adequate access, parking, and knowledgeable sales personnel.

The advantages for producers include the opportunity of allowing operators to perform on-farm chores during slack periods, and lower product transportation costs. They also allow producers to expand with consumer demand. Facilities usually begin very simply and many expand as success and volume warrant. They allow considerable flexibility with respect to size, season, and method of operation.

Roadside signs are the first indication potential customers will have about your farm. Signs seem to be the deciding factor on how many customers actually take the time to stop and examine your roadside stand. It is important that this sign be attractive, easily read and informative. Color combinations vary in their visibility and legibility at a distance. The most easily read color combinations are black on yellow, black on orange, bottle green on white, and scarlet red on white. Letter size and number of words also affect the legibility of signs. The speed of the motorist must also be considered as a major factor. Table 20 is a relationship between the visibility of a sign's content and the speed of a potential customer.

Where a sign is posted in relation to the farm entrance and your roadside stand depends on the average speed of traffic going by the farm. Table 21 can help determine the most effective placement of the sign.

Before you begin designing your sign, be sure to check applicable regulations. The state highway department restricts signs along state and federal highways, and county zoning laws affect signs along some rural roads. The number of signs needed will depend on the farm location and what is trying to be accomplished with the signs. If your farm is off the beaten path, directional signs near key intersections will be appreciated by potential customers.

139

THE U-PICK OPERATION

This form of marketing is operated on either a planned or salvage basis, and relies on the customer to harvest that which is purchased. The distinction is that the planned operation is managed strictly for U-picking, whereas the salvage operator allows customers to clean up the fields and/or orchards after the commercial harvest is completed. The advantages for pick-your-own sales are numerous. It requires far less on-farm harvest labor, handling, packaging, shipping, and storage than other marketing alternatives. The U-pick method of sales provides an immediate payment upon harvest with no deductions for shipping, handling, spoilage, or risk of price change. Disadvantages include providing a large parking area and lavatory facilities, tolerating inexperienced pickers, getting enough pickers to harvest the entire crop, reduced crop harvest due to pickers' carelessness and increased risk of accidents and liability.

THE ROADSIDE MARKET

In this form of direct marketing, the owner grows a portion of the produce sold and buys additional products for resale. These markets often operate year-round and rely heavily upon wholesalers for produce during winter season. They may retail products other than produce, but the operation is generally identified by its rural atmosphere and sale of "home-grown" products. These markets are usually located on the producer's property which identifies its direct association with the farm.

The primary advantage of the roadside market is the on-farm location and the diversity of products made possible by purchasing from wholesalers. Year-round employment is provided and additional income may eliminate the need for off-farm employment. The major limiting factors are the need for a good location and substantial capital requirements for facilities and inventory. A successful operation requires retailing background and experience.

THE FARMERS' MARKET

This is a place where several growers come together to display and sell their products. It involves renting a stall or space. These markets are usually owned and operated by an individual, corporation, municipality or growers' cooperative. Most function under a formal set of rules, guidelines, or by-laws agreed to by the seller.

For the producer, collective selling attracts more customers because of the variety of products offered for sale. Other advantages might include the opportunity to attract customers to a declining business district within a community and to improve farmer-consumer understanding through this direct contact. Centrally located markets may provide a buying opportunity for low income families and older citizens who have limited mobility.

Disadvantages of a farmers' market should be considered, also. Selling through a farmers' market requires producers to absorb the cost of transportation and the cost of selling their products. Time spent selling means time away from the farm and limited productivity when business at the market is slow. Farmers also find that limited market days may not provide a large enough sales volume to cover the additional marketing costs or provide the movement of sufficient quantities of produce.

Most of these types of markets are not open year round, and thus the owners of the market space may find that other options would be more profitable with that space. A final disadvantage is the difficulty in finding good market managers at an affordable salary level.

There are some more important points to consider when pricing your products for a farmers' market. Price is only one factor consumers consider in deciding whether to buy or not to buy. More important is product quality — freshness, flavor, and bright, attractive colors. Try to produce the best possible quality and then harvest and handle it so that it looks as good as possible for display. Offering small samples of the product always is a good policy for closing sales.

Consumers generally prefer to have prices posted — one price for all seems fairer to most, but some want to haggle. Be prepared. Will you dicker? If you do it for one, others will want to test you. You lose time dealing with this form of sale, often losing other customers willing to pay the full price. And always

TABLE 20
Visibility, Letter Size and Content of Roadside Market Signs

DISTANCE FROM WHICH SIGN MUST BE VISIBLE TO BE FULLY READ	MINIMUM LETTER HEIGHT	NUMBER OF WORDS WHICH CAN BE READ BY THE AVERAGE MOTORIST TRAVELING AT VARIOUS SPEEDS			
Feet	Inches	30 mph	40 mph	50 mph	60 mph
50	1.75	4	2	1	0
100	3.50	8	5	4	3
200	7	15	11	8	6
300	11	22	16	13	10
400	14	30	22	17	14
500	17.5	38	28	22	18

From *Small Farm Newsletter* (April, 1983), King County Extension Service, Seattle, Washington.

remember the first rule in sales: it's easier to lower prices than to raise them. Don't start too low. There are two sure signs that your prices are too low: no complaints and you sell out too early.

Abundant displays offer greater selection for the customer, and may suggest that your display is more likely to have what they want than your less abundantly stocked neighbors. Restock after each surge of customers to keep display areas well filled. Use color contrasts to enhance eye appeal. A display at an elbow to eye level lets customers see, feel, and evaluate the product better than lower levels. Those displayed at ground level are more likely to be contaminated with dust, insects and rodents.

People like to do business at a busy stand. There are always things that need to be done. Don't just sit on the tailgate of your truck and wait. You're not only killing time, you're killing opportunities. Don't expect to do a land office business the first day. It takes time for customers to get to know you, and for other vendors to know you and begin to refer customers to you. If you ever have the choice, it helps to be next to an experienced seller. Not only do they attract larger crowds, you can learn how to sell your own crops more efficiently.

PEDDLING AND OTHER DIRECT MARKETING ALTERNATIVES

This set of direct marketing alternatives include rent-a-tree operations, "self-serve selling," gift baskets, and mail order sales. These selling options are often combined with other marketing alternatives to increase sales. A good example of peddling is a farmer selling his crop as produce to specific restaurants, basil to Italian restaurants or oregano to pizza manufacturers, for instance. Advantages to peddling include low overhead, easy entry into the peddling business when a product surplus exists, and easy exit from business when product supply is short. The disadvantages are legal restrictions and required licensing.

Gift basket, mail order methods are popular options with products that can be packaged attractively and have limited perishability. Such products include herbs, spices, and dried flower arrangements. Gift baskets and mail order sales offer opportunities to increase sales, but success is limited to specialty products and is usually seasonal.

Of the five basic methods of direct farm marketing, most of these operations are usually located in rural settings, but within an approximate 10 mile radius from major population centers. Of those currently in operation (1985), nearly 70% will generate less than $10,000 in gross dollar sales, with most above $500 that same year. Although this is the primary way most small farm production is marketed in North America today, these levels of sale only represent partial incomes, and none of the farmers participating in the statistical analysis found this form of marketing viable in supporting land payments or growth.

The average purchase per customer is also quite low, usually less than $5.00 per customer. With average customer contacts limited by parking and location, the farmer is severely limited in what he can expect from this form of marketing. Price determination is a key to better profits. Promotion is also an important factor. Most farmers spend less than $200 per year for promotion. Only 65% use newspapers, and the rest rely on such direct market promotions as maps, signs and logos. Operations in the lower gross sale categories have a tendency to spend less on advertising, whereas those in higher gross sales categories have a tendency to spend more. There seems to be a direct relationship between the size of the operation and the amount spent on advertising.

SOME FURTHER DIRECT MARKETING
ALTERNATIVES FOR THE SMALL FARMER

Several of these following markets appear potentially much larger and more certain for the small farmer growing herbs and spices than market channels

TABLE 21
Sign Locations for Various Speed Zones

SPEED LIMIT (mph)	DISTANCE OF SIGN FROM ENTRANCE
30	1,050 feet
40	1,320 feet
50	1,740 feet
60	2,100 feet

Based, in part, on details from *Sportsmanlike Driving*, 3rd Edition, American Automobile Association, Washington, D.C.

such as roadside stands and U-pick operations. The latter are more commonly associated with vegetables and fruits used in substantial quantities. Those who are growing thyme, sage, savory, mints, and other herbs and spices will find that families use these products in fairly limited quantities, resulting in low gross sales per customer. Other direct selling methods are needed to effectively market herbs and spices.

THE LOCAL STORE

There are tremendous opportunities available for the small herb and spice grower at the local level. These retail outlets include grocery, health food, gourmet, gift, and other neighborhood stores, where the grower sells directly to the retailing outlet, not in bulk to a wholesale distributor. While the grower does not realize full retail prices, he will get more than from sales to a wholesaler.

Cottage industries (Chapter 10) is another form of marketing your same crops to the same stores by packaging them differently. This means that rather than selling crude or semi-processed products to the neighborhood store, you take the time to manufacture something with them first. These forms of marketing can add to the local store's offerings of your product. Herb pillows, sachets, bath perfumes, and air fresheners are typical examples. When choosing a crop, byproduct marketing should always be part of the plan.

Even now, the largest mass market food chains, such as Safeway, are moving toward bulk food operations. Many now also offer bulk herbs and spices, with specially designed compartment dispensers for easy shelf loading and customer packaging. These forms of marketing require processing (see Chapter 7) for entry. Also, the larger mass market grocery chains buy either from their own warehouse or from a regional wholesaler. This is not often the case, however, for the local health food, gourmet, gift, and grocery store in a community.

A SUCCESSFUL HERB & SPICE SECTION
FOR THE NATURAL FOODS STORE

Recent years have seen a growing number of well managed natural foods stores opening successful Herb & Spice sections, often in response to customer requests. The supermarket is usually a wasteland for someone looking for good quality herbs and spices. Indeed, supermarket teas are always limited to a wide range of similarly mediocre tea bag blends which are very rarely fresh in either color or flavor. When developed correctly, Herb & Spice sections are not only quite profitable, they also enhance sales in other sections of the store.

A typical Herb & Spice section should include —
- *Flavoring herbs,* such as orange peel or spearmint.
- *Medicinal herbs,* such as golden seal or cascara.
- *Spices,* such as clove or allspice.

- *Black teas,* such as Formosa or Oolong.
- *Blended herbal and spiced-black teas,* such as orange spice tea.
- *Potpourries and sachet,* including such things as bath oil mixtures.
- *Herbal mixtures and blends,* such as herbal tobaccos and formulas.

The blended herbal and spiced black teas, and other herbal mixtures and formulas, can be made directly from the store's own inventory. The odors from these different blends act as a draw to customers in the store. They stimulate a sense other than vision, which helps in marketing.

The Herb & Spice section usually goes next to the highest income section in the store. In the case of a Health Foods Store, this is the vitamins and minerals section. Higher traffic is generated in this part of the store by these special odors, generating larger cash flows in both sections. Larger stores have found that by increasing the buying consciousness of the public, they can stimulate sales for other herbal products, often in the vitamin section. Some of the more successful Herb & Spice sections include appliances, gift items, and other related high-ticket products with good markup. They all include books, of course.

There are several ways herbs and spices can be sold, each having advantages and disadvantages. Coffee houses, delis, and the neighborhood cooperatives sell them from one-gallon glass jars. This is labor intensive, and the customers should not be serving themselves for a number of reasons. While color attracts the buyer via glass jars, light is devastating to the quality and oil content of most spices and botanicals. Direct contact with the customer, however, always increases sales, and stimulates public awareness toward future purchases. Larger natural foods stores have found this to be an impractical way of marketing for the larger volume of sales.

Herbs and spices can be delivered to individual stores by the farmer and marketed similar to the bulk sections on nuts and grains. Most herbs and spices are harvested only once each year. Most stores would like to find a regular supplier with fresh crops, meaning those less than one year old. Their option is usually a regional wholesaler, who may or may not have clean shelves — shelf inventory of less than one year old crops. The other major advantage to the farmer is that his products are "locally grown."

Prepackaged herbs, spices, and blended herbal teas can be as old as two or even three years when bought from a distributor or warehouse. There are a growing number of customers who prefer to buy a better quality product, one nearly as good as home-dried botanicals from the garden. It is the store buyer's responsibility to find herbs and spices with the correct price-quality ratio for the customers to whom the store caters. This can vary widely from one neighborhood to another, as can the quality and cut of a given spice. Store layout and displays seem to be the key to having a successful center. Herbal tobaccos, potpourries, and other blends can be made directly from inventories. Everything should always be packaged in glassine-lined bags which are opaque. These are available from coffee suppliers. Smaller samples can be displayed in glass for customer inspection, and are simply changed when they begin to discolor or fragment. Emphasize your own personal blends of herbs, spices, and teas by offering a special each week, with samples of the tea blends brewing in an automatic coffee maker. Creating a good orange spice tea is an art form, and making it in-house from your physical inventory gives a whole new perspective to blending teas. Custom herb blends add character to the store's line of products.

A good inventory should include table 22 (spices), table 23 (herbs), and table 24 (black teas). The farmer or gardener should simply order small quantities of those items he does not produce. These initial cash outlays are very small in comparison to what can be offered to local stores when put in combination with crops. The imported spices which can not be grown in a given region are needed to balance offerings in any case. These, in combination with products that can be grown locally only, broaden the full market potential available in a community.

From these lists (100 of the most commonly used herbs, spices and black teas), an additional ten blended herbal teas and five black spiced teas can be created, plus a variety of other herbal products. Some stores like to market essential oils in this section, allowing other herbal products to be manufactured, such as herbal salves and lip balms. With a good display including books on "how-to" in creating herbal compounds, cosmetic sections in a store can also have increased sales. It all comes back to educating the buyer. The customers all really want a better quality product in their kitchen: that's why they shop in natural foods stores in the first place.

You needn't look far to answer the question of "why" to consider the Herb &

TABLE 22
List of Most Popular Spices, and their Cut

Allspice, grnd.	Coriander Seed, whl.	Paprika (100ASTA), pwd.
Anise Seed, whl.	Cumin Seed, whl.	Parsley Flakes, whl.
Arrowroot, pwd.	Curry, pwd.	Pepper (Black), whl.
Basil, C/S	Dill Weed, C/S	Pepper (Black), grnd.
Bay Leaf, whl.	Fennel Seed, whl.	Poppy Seed (Blue), whl.
Caraway Seed, whl.	Fenugreek Seed, whl.	Rosemary, C/S
Cardamom Seed, whl.	Garlic, gran.	Sage (Greek), C/S
Carob (Roast), pwd.	Garlic, pwd.	Savory, C/S
Cayenne (Hot), pwd.	Ginger Root, pwd.	Tarragon (French), C/S
Celery Seed, whl.	Marjoram, C/S	Thyme, C/S
Chili, pwd.	Mustard Seed, pwd.	Tumeric, pwd.
Cinnamon, stick	Nutmeg, pwd.	Vanilla Bean, whl.
Cinnamon, pwd.	Onion, chop	
Clove, whl.	Onion, pwd.	
Clove, pwd.	Oregano, C/S	

Spice section addition to your neighborhood store. Profit margins on all repackaged herbs, spices, and blends are still competitive with cooperative prices, even with a 100% minimum markup (see table 28). And the quality and price is far better than prepackaged spices, including those sold as bulk in mass supermarkets. Buying bulk herbs and spice, compared to those prepackaged, for the quality, is much like buying fresh ground coffee compared to institutional grades from a can. There is no comparison! As with instant coffees, there is always a market and need for tea bag products. Such companies as Celestial Seasonings and Select Tea Company do a better than average job, and their teas can market quite well next to your own blends.

If your inventory is purchased correctly, initial costs can be less than $400, and will turn a minimum of 12 times in one year. A newly created Herb & Spice section should only inventory one to three pounds of each item listed in tables 22, 23 and 24 per store in which you have your section inventoried. Reordering can occur once each week with these quantities, giving you a better perspective on how and when to order. Profit margins will improve with experience. Sources of supply are listed in table 30 on small wholesale buyers (500 pound minimum). Be sure to consider the cost of freight and minimum order costs when considering the cash requirements in opening these type of sections in a neighborhood store. (See page 171.)

The customer will also appreciate these services for a number of reasons. While herbs, roots, and barks are an alternative to vitamins and minerals, offering them juxtaposed to each other is very much like placing one restaurant across the street from another. The two do not take business away from each other. They only increase the number of persons who frequent the area. Purchase and consumption of the products increase directly with customer awareness. It is critical that this factor be taken into consideration when designing a successful Herb & Spice section. The store should also plan to carry at least three other prepackaged products. The larger the selection, the broader the market, and the larger the cash flow.

With your own prepackaged herb or spice, be sure to include the grade of the spice and botanical, its country of origin, and the quality of cut of the product. The freshest botanicals are a gourmet item, and might even be marked slightly higher than those with some previous shelf life. Use tables 25, 26 and 27 as a guide for creative inspiration in the content and depth of your marketing. By mixing these different products together into other products, you can now sell more of your base stocks.

Adding the Herb & Spice section to the neighborhood grocery, health food, deli, or other retail sales is like taking ginseng: *it sets a "tone" to the store and gives it more body.*

SPECIALTY MANUFACTURERS

The specialty manufacturer is yet another excellent outlet for direct marketing, particularly for such local and small manufacturers of such items as mus-

TABLE 23
List of Most Popular Herbs, and their Cut

Alfalfa, C/S	Hibiscus Flower, whl.	Passion Flower, C/S
Cascara Segrada, C/S	Hop Flower, whl.	Peppermint Leaf, C/S
Catnip Herb, C/S	Kola Nut, pwd.	Red Raspberry Leaf, C/S
Chamomile Flower, whl.	Lavender Flower, whl.	Red Clover Tops, whl.
Chicory (Roast), gran.	Lemon Balm, C/S	Rosehip, C/S
Chickweed Herb, C/S	Lemon Grass, C/S	Scullcap Herb, C/S
Coltsfoot Herb, C/S	Lemon Peel, C/S	Shave Grass Herb, C/S
Comfrey Leaf, C/S	Licorice Root, C/S	Slippery Elm Bark, pwd.
Comfrey Root, C/S	Marigold Flower, whl.	Spearmint Leaf, C/S
Damiana Leaf, C/S	Marshmallow Root, C/S	Strawberry Leaf, C/S
Dandelion Root, gran.	Mullein Herb, C/S	Uva Ursi, C/S
Devil's Club Root, C/S	Nettle Herb, C/S	Valerian Root, C/S
Elder Flower, whl.	Oatstraw, C/S	Wild Cherry Bark, C/S
Eucalyptus Leaf, C/S	Orange Peel, C/S	Yerba Mate', C/S
Golden Seal Root, pwd.	Oregon Grape Root, C/S	Yarrow Flower, whl.
Gotu Kola Herb, C/S	Orris Root, pwd.	*Prince Ginseng, pwd.

tard, salad dressings, sauces, relishes, pickles, spices and herb packers. The list goes on and on, and is quite accessible through such sources as the yellow pages of a telephone directory and the Chamber of Commerce. Let your imagination soar, start reading labels in various stores. As you become "tuned" to the real uses of these crops, you will be first overwhelmed with the fact that most of these businesses currently buy most of their products from import houses. Then you begin to see the possibilities.

When the grower sells directly to the manufacturer, the price received is still lower than retail. The depth of use in local markets can, however, more than make up for this disadvantage. There's room for hundreds of new markets. For example, consider the Italian food markets and the need for a fresh year round supply of basil, for the pasta industries. Why couldn't a small farmer, growing this crop as an annual, mix his basil with a good quality olive oil and several other important ingredients, and market it as "frozen *pesto*" in the one pound cardboard ice cream containers?

Besides the standard herb vinegars, jellies, and other food items, consider such diverse food concepts as herb candies for breath fresheners. Making herb scented stationery and herbal air fresheners are other ways in which a local manufacture might start a new line of products. These are just a few directions of specialty manufacture which the grower might approach. *Chapter 10,* on cottage industries, gives more examples. I'm quite sure you probably have other ideas not even covered in this book. Many are worth further thought for direct marketing.

RESTAURANTS

All small, medium, and large cities have specialty restaurants. These include Chinese, Italian, French, and Mexican establishments. They all use spices and herbs. Their standard way of buying is on a weekly or biweekly basis, usually in one to five pound containers. Their source of supply is usually a regional wholesaler who is also marketing coffees and rental brewers. A delivery route is set and a truck, holding some inventory from the regional distributor, fills orders right on the spot with the cook or manager-owner. All the products are dried and processed, albeit grown in other countries.

The more exclusive restaurants, and those that take the time to truly prepare foods for repeat business, would much rather buy their crops from domestic sources that can also supply fresh-cut produce. Imagine a classic Italian restaurant serving home made pastas without fresh basil? They simply can not do that. Other markets would be manufacturers of sausages. They cannot make their products without sage. The potentials of domestic markets is quite open when attended by the right organization and delivery schedules.

These types of markets are always available to the small farmer, even when his major market plan is to dehydrate most of his crop for wholesale markets. The differences in cash yields to the farmer are well worth exploring before ignoring them as marketing outlets. These markets for the grower of thyme, sage, savory, mints, and other flavoring and cooking spices can be dicey. The best policy is to actually visit their kitchens and processing facilities. Learn what their needs and schedules are. This will help you determine whether these markets have any potentials for you as direct markets.

MERCHANDISING CONSIDERATIONS FOR THE NATURAL FOOD STORE

Supermarkets always have full shelves, with every inch of shelf space paying for itself. In the supermarket, when a new item goes *in,* and the old item must

TABLE 24
List of Most Popular Black Teas

China Black	Keemun	English Breakfast
Darjeeling	Lapsang Souchong	Irish Breakfast
Formosa	Oolong (green tea)	
Jasmine Flower	Earl Gray	

TABLE 25
Formula for Jasmine Spice Tea, Typical Blend from List of Herbs and Spices

Jasmine Tea	4	Clove	1/8
Orange Peel	1	Nutmeg	1/4
Cinnamon	1/2	Cardamom	1/8

TABLE 26
Formula for a Typical Seasoning Salt

Mix one part each of the following ingredients:
Monosodium Glutamate (MSG), pwd.⎤
Salt, rock ——————————————⎬ or Dried Mushroom, pwd.
Celery Seed, whole
Garlic, gran.
Sugar, gran.
Calcium Stearate, pwd.
Paprika, pwd.
Coloring (Yellow Lake #6)

go *out.* They let the buyer be the manager of their stock by simply counting purchases, and respond accordingly. You can take advantage of a supermarket weakness: buying practices give no consideration to product quality, except those imposed by legal restrictions, product effectiveness, or the integrity of the manufacturer. They also make little effort to educate the customer. They just stock the shelves and track the results.

Today, the small store is in a good position to use the same marketing tools and techniques as the supermarkets, and beat them at their own game by offering additional personal services, education, and selective in-depth stocking. You need to provide the same kind of item by item tracking that can put your store back on an equal basis with the giants. Some of the larger wholesalers will offer this service to your purchases for the last three months, but you should always be the one doing your own accounting.

The keys to merchandising are *turnover, cash flow,* and *profit.* Profit is not generated by margins or by depth of stock. Healthy margins and huge inventories are useless if the stock just sits there and does not sell. Profit is generated by one thing: *sales.* Turnover is the critical factor. To increase your turnover, you will have to pay very careful attention to the buying trends of *your* customers. Again, every inch of shelf space must pay for itself.

The average health food store should turn over its stock about eight times

TABLE 27
Typical Herbal Salve Recipe

Sunflower Oil	2 gallons (a little extra)
Bees Wax	2 pounds
Comfrey Root	2 pounds
Comfrey Leaf	2 pounds
Golden Seal Root	3 pounds
Marigold Flower	1/2 pound
Elder Flower	1/2 pound
Flavoring Oil	1/4 - 1 ounce (optional)

each year. You should strive for 12 turnovers a year. Why? Because, as a rule of thumb, you can expect to lose about 3% of your profit for every week an item sits on the shelf. After four months of sitting there, even a 50% item is a dead loss. To avoid this problem, there are several strategies available for the small retail seller:

1. Look over your report to find any items that have not moved in three months. These become *specials,* and are put on sale.
2. Determine what items are moving well in the store. Invest the working capital you're not spending on the slow movers in your fast moving items. Don't overstock, but order up to your measured sales velocity and just a little extra.
3. Check to see which items might be replaced with higher margin items, or those that are higher priced. This will give you a higher profit per sale.

TABLE 28

Merchandising Analysis Worksheet

CATEGORY	1/MARK-UP (A)	OS/SS (B)	$/FOOT (C)	SHELF SPACE (D)	BREAK-EVEN (E)
Vitamins	2.0	6.41	12.82	360	$4,615
Herbs	2.0	6.41	12.82	210	2,692
Cosmetics	2.5	6.41	16.03	75	1,202
Books	2.8	6.41	17.95	24	431
Groceries	2.8	6.41	17.95	395	7,090
Appliances	2.9	6.41	18.59	36	682

Monthly Overhead	$ 1,500
Monthly Labor	$ 3,500
Other Monthly Cost	$ 2,050
Overhead Sum (OS)	$ 7,050

Total Shelf Space in Linear Feet (SS)   1,100 feet

To determine your monthly break-even dollars per foot, divide the Overhead Sum (OS) by the total Shelf Space (SS);

OS/SS = 7,050/1,100 = $ 6.41 break-even per foot.

Next, measure the number of feet of shelf space in each product category, and enter that as column D. Then enter the break-even dollars (OS/SS) in column B.

Now determine the markup in each product category and divide the number 1 by each markup. For example: if the markup is 40%, divide 1 by 0.40. The result is 2.5.

The rest is fairly straight forward. *First,* multiply column A times column B, and enter as column C. *Second,* multiply column C times column D, and enter as column E. Column E show you how many dollars you must take in monthly in each category in order to break even.

4. Look for those items that show a definite upward trend, but are not now a part of your current core stock. *Core* stock is your steady, long term movers, and should make up the bulk of your inventory. Set aside a percentage of your cash flow for *"explore"* stock — focusing on those items showing an upward trend.

When cutting dead wood from your inventory, two kinds of stock must be considered. You must be sensitive to your customers special needs, often ignored by mass marketing, and you may want to retain some stock that does not sell at high velocity. The general rule of sales shown by most reports indicated that —

1. 10% of the items in a given category will account for 50% of all sales in that category.
2. 20% of the items in a given category will account for 80% of all sales in that category.

Consider which product categories you are most comfortable selling and which product categories your customers are buying most, and then stock those items in depth. This is your *specialty stock.* Supermarkets cannot justify using their shelf space that way, and your customers will come back for the in-depth selection, information and service you offer.

The other category of stock to be sensitive to is your *service stock.* Service stock consists of those items which sell only a few each month, but are kept there because of special requests, or because of their importance to the industry as a whole. Some books and appliances may fall into this category. In all cases, these items must pay their way. This means that your store is now organized into one of four categories: core stock, service stock, specialty stock, and explore stock. Group your product list into major categories such as vitamins, herbs, cosmetics, groceries, books and appliances.

With these lists, now measure the shelf space devoted to each category, and then use the Merchandising Analysis Worksheet to determine if every inch of your shelf space pays for itself. If your actual sales in any category are less than the amount shown on the worksheet, your shelf space in that category is not paying for itself. It would be time, in that case, for you to start thinking about your best way to alter your business plan for the store.

PRICE DETERMINATION

The most important aspect about of marketing is determining of price. How much are you going to ask for your crop? Over 50% of all small growers set their prices based on their competitors' prices. Other marketers set prices based on grocery store prices, and another 10% set prices based on cannery and wholesale offerings.

About one-fourth use a cost-plus method to determine their prices, whereas about 10% actually set prices based on what "sounds good." Two examples of cost plus method (cost being either production costs or costs in purchasing the product) are the *markup* and the *margin.*

Mark-up method. selling price = (per unit cost × percent markup) + per unit cost. If your product cost .50 cents and you wish a 50% markup, then (.50 × .50) + 50 = 75 cents sale price, however,

Margin method. selling price = $\dfrac{\text{per unit cost}}{1 - \text{desired percent of margin of sale}}$

If your product cost 50 cents and you wish a 50% margin, then,

$$\frac{50 \text{ cents}}{1 - 50 \text{ cents}} = \$1.00 \text{ sale price.}$$

These methods assume that the direct marketer can produce or obtain the goods at competitive costs.

While the direct marketing method is the primary form of marketing for most small farmers in biological agriculture, this trend is changing. I think that the future will be toward bulk marketing since most communities need to export at least part of their crops. There usually is not enough money in a given community to support more than a dozen families marketing their produce and crops direct. Where will the additional 90 families in a given valley market their crops? The future for the small farmer in marketing lies in bulk marketing to wholesalers.

Cottage industries can add some support in marketing to those who choose to export. Manufactured items, using ingredients from local producers, provide a typical example. In this case, direct marketing might mean selling manufactured goods to regional wholesalers and warehouses. Again, transportation becomes a significant factor. But the limiting factor in these examples is usually access to packaging and package manufacturers.

Chamomile

154

CHAPTER 9

Bulk Marketing

. . . like all great ends, singleness of mind is not an end but a beginning . . . A countryman has it who, being himself very old and without hope of the event, goes upon his knees to plant an acorn in the ground.

Charles Morgan

The marketing of agricultural products plays a dominate role in all of our lives, often requiring a wide variety of skills from the small farmer. The continual change of processes used to manufacture food products is a good indicator of the skills required in finding better ways to satisfy the varied demands of the consumer. In addition, the buying habits of North America are changing, both in demographics and attitude. These affect the buying behavior and consumption habits of the public.

Unfortunately, too often the farmer's production plans are formulated without an appropriate *market plan*. As with the lack of a farm plan, the consequences of marketing decisions without a market plan generally leads to disappointments, and possible failure in an otherwise successful farm venture. Historically, farmers have thought of the production process as *tangibles*, and marketing problems are *intangibles*. This attitude must change if the small farmer is to survive. Some conceptual perspectives are needed before a market plan can be developed.

WHAT IS MARKETING?

The American Marketing Association (AMA) defines *marketing* as "the performance of business activities that direct the flow of goods and services from producer to consumer or industrial user." While definitions vary from one system of marketing to another, there are some fundamental considerations which must be included in the scope of any market plan. They are —

1. *Ascertaining the needs and wants of the markets.* What does the consumer want and need? This is called market research.

2. *Planning product availability.* Overproduction can limit market options. How much should you grow, how much should you sell in bulk, and how much should you inventory (for future shortages)? This involves pricing, transportation, storage, and commodities speculation.

3. *Effective transfer in ownership of products.* How does the field crop finally end up in the consumer's home? This can involve such important considerations as processing, packaging, advertising, and transportation.

4. *Providing for product distribution.* What system or systems of marketing should you use with your crop? Storage, transportation, and processing are only part of this important aspect of marketing.

5. *Providing for the appropriate functions to facilitate the entire marketing system.* Is credit available? These are functions which usually are not part of the actual product, but necessary for any successful market venture.

These five aspects of marketing must always be considered as part of what makes up any successful plan. As an academic discipline, marketing is closely related to the social sciences of economics, sociology, psychology, and even anthropology. It is as old as civilization. As we expand our ability to produce, the need to understand marketing principles also increases. It is the small farmer's only real hope for survival.

Marketing is important to the small farmer in part because it stimulates demands, thus creating income and employment, helps introduce new products, and helps keep the public informed about changes in old products. Its value is indicated to some extent by the fact that 50 to 60 cents of every consumer dollar spent goes to cover marketing costs.

It would be inaccurate to say that marketing is more important than production, or vice versa. The effective performance of both functions is necessary to a prosperous economy. However, sound marketing means the small farmer must put the consumer first in all facets of his planning and operations. This is the first key to the successful operation of a business.

Marketing can be studied from a variety of approaches —commodity, functional, institutional, conceptual, managerial, and eclectic. Herbs and spices are best seen as commodities, although conceptual approaches in such markets as cosmetics have often led to very lucrative business.

THE IMPORTANCE OF THE WHOLESALER

One of the oldest and most persistent criticisms of marketing is that "there are too many middlemen." Those who take this position reason that a reduction in the number of middlemen would mean lower prices for consumers and larger returns for farm efforts. This assumption is wrong, however. The wholesaler is the middle link in the distribution chain, providing such functions as transportation, warehousing, storage, buying and selling activities, credit, marketing research, and management advice.

It should be remembered that while it is possible to eliminate a wholesale middleman, it is not possible to eliminate the functions he performs. A drug manufacturer, for example, may choose to bypass wholesalers and sell directly to retailers. But in order to do so, he must assume the work and function of the wholesaler. That is, he must assemble, warehouse, sell, and deliver the product, provide credit, and otherwise service retail customers.

In a competitive business environment, businesses that do not perform needed economic services eventually disappear. Patterns of wholesale distribution are dynamic. Of course manufacturers will bypass wholesalers when it is to their advantage to do so, and retailers will buy directly from manufacturers if it increases their profits.

Intermediate sorting activities of accumulation and allocation are often performed by wholesalers in the distribution process. Through accumulation, wholesalers develop a cluster of products that are related, either by production or by consumer demand. Allocation is the process of matching products to consumer demand. Assortments are collections of products that are related functionally. Most wholesalers furnish warehousing, because one of their primary functions is to break up the large shipments of an item into smaller orders for delivery to retailers.

One role of the wholesaler is to maintain a rapid flow of merchandise through his warehouse to retail and institutional accounts. He attempts to do so by furnishing a wide selection of merchandise, competitively priced. He often furnishes advice to help the retailer sell more goods as well. The role of the wholesaler is important to the small farmer for the following reasons —

1. *Buying for customers.* Even a small health food store carries several thousand different items. Imagine how many employees it would need just to contact the manufacturers of each product. Or how time-consuming it would be for the manager of such a store to listen to the hundreds of presentations by manufacturers' salesmen, accepting hundreds of deliveries, writing hundreds of checks, and keeping the books each month.

2. *Selling for suppliers.* You will find it more economical with most 20 to 40 acre crops to sell in relatively larger quantities to service wholesalers than to call on thousands of small retailers or industrial users. Because they sell the crops from a number of different farms, this lowers the per unit expense.

3. *Assembly and division.* Wholesalers assemble merchandise in large

157

quantities from many manufacturers or growers and then divide it into small quantities. This is called breaking bulk. Being able to buy in truckload lots reduces the manufacturer's or wholesaler's per unit transportation and handling costs. Small shipments cost much more per unit than large shipments. The retailer benefits by being able to purchase goods in relatively small quantities, thus avoiding overbuying and inventory problems.

4. *Delivery.* Most service wholesalers make deliveries on a regular basis, usually much more quickly and more economically than a farmer or even a manufacturer. This means that a retailer or industrial user need not keep as large an inventory as would be required if deliveries were made directly from the farm. This in turn results in less capital being tied up in inventory and the risks of product deterioration is reduced.

5. *Warehousing.* Wholesalers are specialists in storage and can often perform this function much more efficiently than either manufacturers, retailers, or even growers. This allows the small retailer to devote portions of his total physical space to displaying the items he carries.

6. *Credit extension.* Service wholesalers commonly grand credit to their accounts. Retail customers are offered a discount if they buy on a cash basis or pay within a certain period of time. The bookkeeping costs alone make credit extension prohibitive to manufacturers and retail accounts selling in small quantities to thousands of customers.

7. *Assumption of risk.* Once the wholesaler takes possession of and has paid for the crop, the farmer need no longer worry that it will become overabundant in the market (like Alfalfa) or deteriorate physically before it is sold. The wholesaler also assumes the risk that the retailer or industrial user may not pay for the product sold on credit.

8. *Information and advice.* Because the wholesaler services hundreds, sometimes thousands of retail accounts, he learns a great deal about what it takes for his accounts to succeed in business. Accordingly, wholesalers are often able to give advice on sales and merchandise trends, not only to their retail accounts but their suppliers as well.

THE HERB AND SPICE MARKETS

The herb and spice industry in North America is a young and rapidly expanding business, with most of the more successful companies in the field starting since 1970. The market is divided into several main categories. They are —

1. *Foods.* These include flavorings, additives, and condiments which are used by the food, spice and natural food manufacturers. There is, at present, a large and growing demand from the food manufacturers and spice companies, with the major food retailers now entering the marketplace to sell these products. These retailers operate more than 45,000 stores, representing a yearly wholesale business of more than $25 billion.

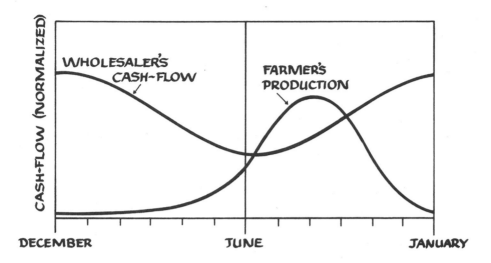

2. *Pharmaceuticals.* The drug and pharmaceutical manufacturers have all found that, whenever possible, the use of natural ingredients is much more cost effective than those made synthetically. Since botanicals are the original source of most of our traditional medicines, more and more mainstream doctors are prescribing these medicinal herbs over synthetic alternatives. The market is quite broad. For example, the bioflavonoid markets currently use more than 2,000 ton per month of rose hip in the manufacture of vitamin C.

3. *Cosmetics.* Almost all major manufacturers of cosmetics now use a variety of herbs, and some spices, in their formula preparations. These include facials and creams, hair rinses and shampoos, salves and lip balms, and many more applications. The perfume industries would be lost without these ingredients and fixatives. Some of the cosmetic products might overlap with medicinal uses, but a distinction is usually made between these markets.

4. *Florals.* The dried flower markets have always been part not only of the herb and spice market but the florist markets as well. Such things as baby's breath and mosses are quite important to the florist. Seed-cones and other wild seed also fall into this category of marketing. While the wild seed market is more limited than the other three, more people in North American currently earn their living from this market than the others.

The present problem with all four of these markets is that there are no companies with a supply base large enough to handle even token orders from those diverse outlets. In fact, a major blended herb tea company, which did over $12 million in wholesale business last year, was unable to accept new accounts. The newness of the industry in North America has created a significant supply problem. Only in Europe, the Middle East and Asia, where the herb business is hundreds, even thousands of years old is there the agricultural knowledge to support production of many of these key herbs.

159

Within the broad framework of the herb and spice markets, there are three distinct forms of wholesale buyer. They are —

1. *The 500 pound minimum buyer.* These are usually the regional wholesalers and cooperatives. Each state or province will have several dozen of this type of wholesale buyer. They include some of the chain food stores, small manufacturer or local marketers, and buying clubs and cooperatives. They each may need more than 500 pounds of a given herb or spice over a year period, but are usually not in a position to inventory larger quantities. The standard method of purchase is either spot buying on specials or on contract, where the farmer-supplier ships on a previously agreed monthly or bi-monthly basis.

2. *5,000 pound minimum buyer.* This category includes regional wholesalers who include processing as part of their services to other manufacturers. Some of the larger manufacturers also use these wholesalers to process their products for interfacing with specialized manufacturing machinery such as tea bagging machinery. While most of the larger manufacturers and wholesalers use more than 20 to 50 ton of a given product, they most often prefer to buy in 5,000 to 10,000 pound quantities on a monthly or bimonthly basis to stabilize cash-flow and manufacturing requirements.

3. *Import-export houses.* These are the large wholesale houses in each country — often oriented toward trade agreements — involved in both the import and export of natural resources. Most are located in cities which are major ports of entry. Crops are bought by the truckload. A typical wholesale house in this category might buy more than 200 ton of a given crop, although they will buy smaller quantities when opening new markets.

With these perspectives, the small farmer who grows herbs and spices has a number of alternative markets from which to choose. Regardless of the marketing method available to the small farmer, other factors, such as management considerations, may be the overriding factor in determining which alternatives a producer can actually use. Marketing is the critical factor, particularly to those farmers having limited land, capital and management experience. Farmers with these kinds of limitations are operating with large risks. An adequate job of marketing can help reduce or eliminate those risks.

Producer management and the ability to develop a working knowledge of marketing alternatives is a problem. This problem oftentimes causes the producer to become a price taker-risk assumer, and therefore, a less than efficient operator. For many, time, money and some educational support will take care of their problems. For others, however, the limitations of land, labor capital and management become an overriding concern and controlling forces in their operations. For these producers, marketing is important, but not the determining factor. It will take much perseverance and very understandable lenders to bail them out of their problems. The problem perpetuates itself, but a well drawn marketing plan can help reduce the limitations of these factors.

There are a number of different source directories which can help get most small farmers started with their marketing. These are usually divided or organized by commodity or crop. An excellent example is the annual *Whole Foods Source Directory* (P.O. Box 2068, Berkeley, California 94702). This source not only lists a number of different wholesalers, retailers and manufacturers for each herb and spice, it also lists manufacturers by items they make, and sources for warehousing and transportation.

The *OPD Chemical Buyers Directory* is another excellent source directory for the herb and spice markets. The *OPD* not only has a yearly *Buyers Directory*, but also issues a bi-monthly magazine and a weekly paper. This paper, *Chemical Marketing Reporter*, contains all important information on which spice company in the United States brought in what spice, quantity, and cost. It also advises where the herb or spice is being warehoused and what ship brought it in. The paper features stories on spice and herb fluctuations in price and availability, and critical information for any would-be domestic competitor. You really need to know your competition, and this source is one of the best first-places to start in keeping track of the markets and why they are changing. For more information and subscriptions, write directly to Schnell Publishing Company, 100 Church Street, New York, New York 10007.

In doing any market analysis and determining the market size, trends, competition, and so forth, full use should be made of the many available sources of market data. The librarian at the local business or university library should be able to guide you to the diverse data sources. To give you a headstart in finding market data, some of the primary, available sources of information are —

1. *Trade associations and journals.* Almost every industry has a trade association and a journal. This is one of the best sources of data about a specific industry. Trade journals print, on a regular basis, market surveys and forecasts. Moreover, advertisements provide an excellent source of information about competitors and their products. Attendance at trade association meetings is another good way of assessing the competition. The trade associations and journals or various industries can be found in *Encyclopedia of Associations,* (Volume 1, *National Organizations of U. S.),* Gale Research Company, Book Tower, Detroit, Michigan 48224 also, *Ayer Director of Newspapers, Magazines and Trade Publications,* Ayer Press, West Washington Square, Philadelphia, Pennsylvania 19106.

2. *General marketing data sources.* In addition to trade journals, data on market size and trends in a great many industries can be found in *Predicasts-Quarterly Reports,* Predicast, Inc., 200 University Circle Research Center, 11001 Cedar Avenue, Cleveland, Ohio 44106. Also *United States Industrial Outlook,* United States Department of Commerce, Government Printing Office, Washington, District of Columbia 20013.

FRENCH TARRAGON
(*Artemisia dracunculus* var. sativa)
Compositae family

Tarragon is a perennial herb used extensively as a seasoning throughout the world. The European variety, commonly called French or German tarragon, is the most desirable in the market. This variety is usually sterile, rarely producing fertile flowers that go to seed. It is for this reason the plant is usually propagated by cuttings and root division.

Second year plants may be lifted early in the spring, when new leaves begin to appear (less than 4 inches high). The mass of roots are shaken carefully to remove soil and taken apart into bunches. Each section which contains a stem from last year's growth will become a new plant. This should be done every 3 years to prevent deterioration.

It will take almost 1,000 stalks per acre to plant tarragon. The bunches should be planted in 12 to 15 inch rows spaced 18 inches apart. The planting should take place from April to mid-July. A planting remains in the same place for 5 to 6 years on the average. It is also necessary to have a three year interval before again planting tarragon in the same soil. The herb is hardy if it has good drainage, but will not winter in soils that are soggy during periods of prolonged cold or excessive humidity.

The entire herb can be cut and partially dried in the shade. It should be dehydrated and is easy to dry on racks. During the first year there should only be one cutting, averaging about 1.0 to 1.5 tons per acre of fresh plants. Beginning with the second year there will be two cuttings, one at the end of May and the other at the end of August. These yields range from 5 to 6 ton of fresh plants per acre. 20% of the dry plant contains 30 percent of pure leaves (on an average).

Other than the fresh herbs for pickling, and the dried herb for use as a seasoning, the principle oil extracted from tarragon is estragon. This oil is used in cosmetics as a fragrance and a number of food products, including a number of liqueurs. More than 2 million pounds of crude herbs were imported into North America last year at $9.00 per pound. Similar markets exist in both West Germany and Belgium. While some domestic cultivation now exists in the United States, there are still domestic and world shortages.

The Standard Industrial Classification Manual classifies establishments by type of activity. It can help facilitate the collection, tabulation, presentation and analysis of data.

The Thomas Register assists in identification of competition within a given market. It provides a capsule view of industries and includes the assets, capital and geographical location of firms in the industry.

The Commercial Atlas and Marketing Guide provides retail sales distribution maps, ranks major metropolitan areas by various sales factors, and provides some base statistical information for geographical regions.

In addition to these broad coverage data sources, market studies of particular industries are available from a number of sources, including —

Frost and Sullivan, Inc.,
106 Fulton Street
New York, New York 10038

Arthur D. Little
25 Acron Park
Cambridge, Massachusetts 02140

Business Communications
471 Glenbrook Road
Stamford, Connecticut 06904

Morton Research Corporation,
1745 Merrick Avenue
Merrick, New York 11566

3. *Consumer Expenditure.* Data on consumer expenditures can be found in —

Editor and Publisher Market Guide
Editor and Publisher Company,
850 Third Avenue,
New York, New York 10022

U. S. Census Report
Superintendent of Documents
Washington, D.C. 20013

Survey of Buying Power
Sales Management, Inc.
630 Third Avenue
New York, New York 10017

4. *Financial ratios.* Information on the financial ratios for various industries that can be useful in evaluating competitive operating practices can be found in —

Annual Statement Studies
Robert Morris Associates
Philadelphia Bank Building
Philadelphia, Pennsylvania 19107

Key Business Ratios
Industrial Studies Department
Dun and Bradstreet, Inc.
New York, New York 10007

5. *Guide to market data.* For an overall guide to sources of data on consumer and industrial markets, contact —

Data Source for Business and Market Analysis
Scarecrow Press, Inc.,
52 Liberty Street, Box 656,
Metuchen, New Jersey 08840

6. *Guide to journal articles.* Journals and periodicals are a large and excellent source of data on products, industries and markets. The title of an article can be a good clue to what it is about. Some useful directories of articles are —

Readers Guide to Periodical Literature.
Business Periodicals Index.
Applied Science and Technology Index.
Wall Street Journal Index.

There are a number of other sources of information for the small farmer to assist him in marketing. They include —

Agricultural Marketing Project
2606 Westwood Drive
Nashville, Tennessee 37204

This is one of the most active nationally known organizations addressing small farmers' marketing problems. They are primarily oriented toward how to organize and operate direct marketing through food fairs and farmers' markets.

Department of Agricultural Economics
University of Missouri, Columbia
200 Mumford Hall
Columbia, Missouri 65211

They publish *Economic and Marketing Information,* edited by nationally respected agricultural economist, Dr. Harold Breimyer. Excellent in-depth analysis of agricultural issues.

Organic Farms, Inc.
10714 Hanna Street
Beltsville, Maryland 20705

An organic food marketing service supplying the Eastern seaboard. This group is interested in making contact with organic growers nationwide.

PRICE VARIATIONS FOR SOME HERBS AND SPICES

Once a market or set of markets is identified, the next major step for the small farmer is *how much to charge for his crop.* There are a number of variables in determining these figures. Oftentimes you may be limited to which markets you can enter by your cost-of-goods produced and your required profit-margin. The following table 29 is a list of some herbs and spices and their current price variations, ranging from 2-ton wholesale quantities through retail when sold by the ounce.

The difference in price variation reflects not only the wholesaler's margins, transportation costs, and warehousing, but also such things as processing. The larger wholesalers that buy 5,000 pound minimums usually buy these crops in a bulk, unprocessed form. When they are resold in 500 pound (or less) quantities, most all of these crops have been milled into a form for retail markets.

HOW TO MARKET BULK HERBS AND SPICES

There are a number of ways the small farmer can notify wholesalers that bulk herbs and spices are available. They include —

1. *Bulk price sheet mailer.* This is the most successful way in which bulk herbs and spices are sold to major wholesalers. A one page flier is sent to a number of prospective wholesalers, indicating products available, price variations with quantity, and terms of sale. Most farmers will find that once they have begun to supply several firms, most of his crops will be under contract and the need for further mailings is limited. If the small farmer has chosen to hold some of his crop, waiting for shortages during the winter and spring months, a bulk price sheet can be very profitable.

2. *Magazine ads.* A well designed advertisement in a specific journal, magazine or even newspaper will often more than pay for the costs. Not only will the ad generate potential sales, many times it also brings in new opportunities. Examples would be prospective customers inquiring about other crops which they would like you to consider producing. Being listed in the *OPD* as a source of supply for a given crop is just one example.

3. *Source directories.* Not only is this a good place to advertise your crop, often those already listed as sources of supply might also be potential buyers. For example, almost all listings in the *OPD* as sources for dill oil are wholesalers, not farmers. This could be expanded into other directories such as those for restaurants: *Guide to Natural Food Restaurants* (Daystar Publishing Company, P. O. Box 598, Nicasio, California 94946).

4. *Telephone sales.* The fastest and surest way to determine a given wholesaler's needs are to talk to him. A conversation conveys a large amount of information and it takes only minutes rather than weeks to get a response. When there are only two to five wholesaler-customers for a particular product, phoning is the most cost-effective method of gaining sales. The best policy for most farmers is to call a potential customer after getting a response to an initial contact, usually a bulk price sheet offering.

5. *Personal letters.* This form of contact is always required in that *you should always get commitments and intent in writing.* A personal letter is also appropriate when the wholesaler has requested samples. You must always send a representative sample from your harvest. Oftentimes major wholesalers will hold these samples as a test on what you eventually deliver as your farm crop. You better be sure that the two are identical.

6. *Regional buyer shows.* Shows present an opportunity to make contacts

TABLE 29

Price Variations for Some Herbs & Spices, 2 Ton Quantities Through Retail

HERB/SPICE	2 TON	500 LB.	100 LB.	1 LB.	RETAIL $/LB.	RETAIL $/OZ.
Alfalfa (Medicago sativa)	0.16	0.80	1.60	2.55	8.00	0.50
*Angelica (Angelica atropurpurea)	2.40	4.80	5.60	6.25	13.60	0.85
Anise (Pimpinella anisum)	0.90	1.80	2.40	2.95	9.60	0.60
Basil (Ocimum basilicum)	1.60	2.50	2.80	3.50	8.00	0.50
*Bay (Umbellularia californica)	1.50	2.40	2.90	3.50	15.20	0.95
*Bergamot (Monarda fistulosa)	1.20	2.00	2.80	4.00	14.40	0.90
*Blackberry (Rubus fruiticosus)	0.60	1.60	1.85	2.50	12.80	0.80
*Black Cohosh (Cimicifugo racemosa)	1.20	2.80	4.00	6.30	10.40	0.65
*Blessed Thistle (Cnicus benedictus)	1.10	1.85	2.30	3.35	16.00	1.00
*Blue Cohosh (Caulophyllum thalicatroides)	1.00	2.50	3.75	8.00	12.80	0.80
*Borage (Borago officinalis)	3.20	4.00	4.60	8.00	19.20	1.20
*Burdock (Borago officinalis)	1.40	1.85	2.40	4.80	13.60	0.85
*Calamus (Acorus calamus)	0.90	1.60	2.20	4.40	14.40	0.90
Caraway (Carum carvi)	0.95	1.20	1.60	2.20	12.80	0.80
*Cascara segrada (Cascara segrada)	1.25	1.40	2.00	4.05	22.40	1.40
*Catnip (Nepeta catara)	0.85	1.40	1.90	3.55	11.20	0.70
Chamomile (Anthemis nobilis)	3.50	3.70	4.00	4.55	12.80	0.80
*Chapparal (Larrea mexicana)	0.90	1.70	2.20	3.35	14.40	0.90
Chervil (Anthiscus cerfoloum)	3.40	4.80	5.30	6.80	16.00	1.00
*Chickweed (Stellaria media)	1.80	2.50	3.20	4.50	13.60	0.85
*Chicory (Cichorium intybus)	0.90	1.40	1.90	2.80	10.40	0.65
*Coltsfoot (Tussilago farafara)	0.80	1.20	1.80	2.75	22.40	1.40
Comfrey (Symphytum officinale)	1.80	2.60	4.20	7.20	28.80	1.80

Coriander (Coriandrum sativum)	0.65	0.90	1.40	2.25	12.00	0.75
Cumin (Cuminum cyminum)	1.25	1.80	2.20	2.75	25.60	1.60
*Dandelion (Taraxacum officinale)	2.70	3.20	4.00	5.25	16.00	1.00
*Devil's Club (Oplopanax horridum)	1.80	2.20	2.60	3.00	25.60	1.60
Dill (Anethum graveolens)	1.00	1.80	2.40	4.00	12.80	0.80
*Desert Tea (Ephedra nevadensis)	1.10	1.90	2.20	3.50	28.80	1.80
*Echinacea (Echinacea angustifolia)	9.00	16.00	19.50	26.35	56.00	3.50
*Elder (Sambucus nigra)	2.40	3.20	4.30	8.95	22.40	1.40
*Eucalyptus (Eucalyptus globulus)	0.95	1.40	2.00	3.90	32.00	2.00
Fennel (Foeniculum vulgare)	0.85	1.40	1.85	2.55	12.80	0.80
Garlic (Allium sativum)	1.20	1.85	2.20	3.85	19.20	1.20
Ginger (Zingiber officinale)	0.85	1.35	1.85	3.25	13.60	0.85
*Ginseng (Panax quinquefolium)	180.00	220.00	270.00	340.00	1440.00	90.00
*Goldenseal (Hydrastis canadensis)	24.00	32.00	40.00	69.50	128.00	8.00
Hop (Humulus lupulus)	0.85	1.60	2.20	4.75	12.80	0.80
*Horehound (Marrubium vulgare)	0.80	1.45	1.80	2.40	14.40	0.90
*Horsetail (Equisetum arvensa)	0.75	1.20	1.55	1.85	16.00	1.00
Hyssop (Hyssopus officinalis)	0.65	1.05	1.80	3.55	12.80	0.80
*Kelp (Fucus versiculosus)	0.60	0.85	1.05	2.20	9.60	0.60
*Kinikinnick (Arctostaphylos uva-ursi)	0.75	1.00	1.60	2.35	14.40	0.90
Lavendar (Lavandula officinalis)	3.50	4.50	5.00	9.50	24.00	1.50
Lemon Balm (Melissa officinalis)	1.80	2.40	2.85	4.95	13.60	0.85
Lemon Verbena (Lippia citriodora)	2.20	3.20	3.65	4.80	19.20	1.20
*Licorice (Glycyrrhiza glabra)	0.80	1.60	1.90	4.05	16.00	1.00
*Lobelia (Lobelia inflata)	2.20	2.50	2.90	4.40	19.20	1.20
*Lovage (Levisticum officinale)	1.45	2.00	2.80	5.20	14.40	0.90
*Mandrake (Podophyllum peltatum)	0.95	1.65	2.00	3.80	24.00	1.50
Marigold (Calendula officinalis)	0.40	0.90	1.40	2.45	11.20	0.70

TABLE 29

Price Variations for Some Herbs & Spices, 2 Ton Quantities Through Retail

HERB/SPICE	2 TON	500 LB.	100 LB.	1 LB.	RETAIL $/LB.	RETAIL $/OZ.
Marjoram (Origanum majorana)	0.85	1.45	1.80	2.50	9.60	0.60
*Marshmallow (Althea officinalis)	2.20	2.80	3.20	4.60	25.60	1.60
*Mistletoe (Phoradendron flavenscens)	0.55	0.95	1.60	3.50	12.80	0.80
*Mugwort (Artemisia vulgaris)	1.00	1.60	2.20	3.65	14.40	0.90
*Mullein (Verbascum thapsus)	0.85	1.20	1.80	3.85	10.40	0.65
Nettle (Urtica urens)	1.10	1.80	2.40	4.20	9.60	0.60
Oatstraw (Avena sativa)	0.32	0.90	1.20	2.80	8.00	0.50
Onion (Allium cepa)	0.85	1.40	1.80	3.40	9.60	0.60
Oregano (Origanum vulgare)	0.80	1.60	1.90	3.75	14.40	0.90
*Oregon Grape (Berberis aquifolium)	2.00	2.80	3.50	4.80	16.00	1.00
Parsley (Petroselinum crispum)	2.00	2.65	2.90	4.80	13.60	0.85
Passion Flower (Passiflora caerulea)	0.85	1.60	1.95	5.25	12.80	0.80
*Pennyroyal (Mentha pulegium)	0.95	1.90	2.40	3.95	10.40	0.65
Peppermint (Mentha piperita)	1.20	1.80	2.40	2.75	16.00	1.00
*Pippissawa (Chimaphila umbellata)	2.20	2.65	3.40	5.45	24.00	1.50
*Plantain (Plantago major)	0.80	1.25	1.70	4.00	9.60	0.60
*Poke (Phytolacca americana)	1.40	2.00	2.60	3.20	8.00	0.50
*Queen-of-the-Meadow (Eupatorium purpureum)	1.90	2.40	2.65	4.80	24.00	1.50
Raspberry (Rubus idaeus)	0.85	1.30	1.60	3.35	14.40	0.90
Red Clover (Trifolium pratense)	2.00	3.50	4.80	8.95	16.00	1.00
*Rosehip (Rosa canina)	0.45	0.90	1.40	2.95	8.00	0.50
Rosemary (Rosemarinus officinalis)	0.45	0.90	1.35	2.30	8.00	0.50
Rue (Ruta graveolens)	1.60	2.60	2.90	3.80	24.00	1.50

Sage (*Salvia officinalis*)	0.95	1.40	1.85	3.70	12.80	0.80
*St. John's Wort (Hypericum perforatum)	0.90	1.80	2.45	4.95	16.00	1.00
*Sarsaparila (Smilax regelii)	0.95	2.00	2.60	4.60	14.40	0.90
*Sassafras (Sassafrass albidum)	2.60	3.50	4.20	10.95	19.20	1.20
Savory (*Satureia hortensis*)	1.20	1.90	2.20	3.10	9.60	0.60
*Scullcap (Scutellaria hortensis)	3.50	4.50	6.00	9.50	17.60	1.10
Shepherd's Purse (*Capsella bursa-pastoris*)	0.90	1.20	1.80	3.60	11.20	0.70
*Slippery Elm (Ulmus rubra)	3.20	4.00	4.80	9.40	8.00	0.50
Spearmint (*Mentha viridis*)	0.95	1.40	1.80	2.55	14.40	0.90
Strawberry (*Fragaria vesca*)	0.85	1.25	1.65	4.50	12.80	0.80
*Tansy (Tanacetum vulgaris)	0.85	1.00	1.65	3.20	8.00	0.50
Tarragon (*Artemesia dracunculus*)	4.80	6.00	8.00	12.95	32.00	2.00
Thyme (*Thymus vulgare*)	1.60	2.20	2.90	3.90	16.00	1.00
*Valerian (Valeriana officinalis)	0.85	1.20	2.00	5.25	14.40	0.90
*Vervain (Verbena hastatin)	0.85	1.40	1.90	3.20	16.00	1.00
*Walnut (Juglans nigra)	0.15	0.40	0.80	1.80	9.60	0.60
*White Oak (Quercus alba)	0.40	0.95	1.40	2.60	14.40	0.90
*Wild Cherry (Prunus serotina)	0.80	1.35	1.70	3.85	22.40	1.40
*Wild Lettuce (Lactuca scariola)	0.80	1.60	1.90	2.80	12.80	0.80
*Wintergreen (Gaultheria procumbens)	1.20	1.90	2.40	4.25	22.40	1.40
*Witch Hazel (Hamamelis virginiana)	1.40	2.20	2.80	4.60	12.80	0.80
*Woodruff (Asperula odorata)	1.00	1.80	2.40	4.20	12.80	0.80
*Wormwood (Artemisia absinthium)	0.85	1.40	1.90	4.65	12.80	0.80
*Yarrow (Archillea millefolium)	0.65	1.00	1.40	2.30	16.00	1.00
*Yellow Dock (Rumex crispus)	0.90	1.70	2.20	3.45	11.20	0.70
*Yerma Mate' (Ilex paraguaiensis)	0.60	0.95	1.40	3.35	14.40	0.90
*Yerba Santa (Eriodictyon californicum)	0.95	1.80	2.40	3.90	16.00	1.00

*Foraged or has good forage potential.

with wholesalers or manufacturers who might use your crops as ingredients in their process production. It also gives you some further perspectives as to how your crops might be marketed. Within a major city, there will usually be regional buyer shows once each quarter. These are only open to retail stores, but you can be "creative" and gain admission. You will probably only need a tax number or a letterhead.

7. *Brokers, jobbers, distributors, warehousing.* This system of marketing is primarily responsible for bringing buyers and sellers together for the purpose of negotiating sales. They differ from other forms of wholesaling in that they often do not take title to your crop, and perform fewer functions than the wholesaler. They do, however, reach a much larger market than you might be able to contact on your own. For example, if your crop is stored in a mass market warehouse, it will be sold in more than 200 retail stores. Because these operations act as middlemen to service wholesalers, you must also sell your crop for less. These systems are best for manufactured and processed products rather than when the crop is "raw" and not packaged for individual consumer buying.

Such things as magazine, television, radio, and yellow pages advertising are not usually as effective as the bulk price sheet mailer. This is because most markets are not the public, but specific wholesalers, such as pharmaceutical houses and food processors. These companies are the ones that buy raw materials from direct sources of supply, the domestic farmer or import houses. It is always wise to physically meet most of your customers whenever possible, and then keep in close touch via telephone and letters. Trips of this nature are expensive and use up a large amount of the marketing budget.

Therefore, developing and maintaining a bulk mailing list is extremely important. The following tables 30, 31 and 32 are only partial lists for you to begin one of your own. Using these and the other references should get most bulk marketing ventures off to a good start. The need to continually update these lists cannot be overemphasized.

BULK MAILING LISTS OF WHOLESALE BUYERS

Each of these lists should be set up for a Xerox label sheet if a small computer is not available. The Xerox sheets hold 33 addresses and usually cost about 25 cents per page. The labels can be peeled off the Xerox backing (or computer tape) and put directly into an envelope or self mailer. This saves enormous times in addressing. As individual companies indicate no interest in your product, their names and addresses can be removed from the master, with new potentially interested customers added in their place. Most bulk mailing lists can be made current within three mailings.

Your first inquiry might ask what the company plans to buy next year, including annual quantity needs, delivered price, quality-content requirements and shipping-packaging. Most crude or bulk botanicals and spices are

TABLE 30
Small Bulk Wholesale Domestic Buyers (500 Pound Minimum)

Aphodisia Products
62 Kent Street
Brooklyn, NY   11222

Area Shopper
1000 Main Street
Conneautville, PA 16406

Avatar's World
9106 Hurd Road
Edgerton, WI 53534

BDL
244 Walker Street
Watsonville, CA 95076

Bear Creek Operations
2518 S. Pacific Hwy
Medford, OR 97501

Biaggi's Wholesale
770 Wall Street
Los Angeles, CA 90014

Blue Ridge Botanicals
978 Laurel Branch Road
Vilas, NC   28692

Cap Seals, Inc.
12607 NE 95th. Street, Suite A-107
Vancouver, WA 98682

Crestwood International
3945 Myrtle Street
Burnaby, BC   V5C 4G3
Canada

Daisy Pickers
1690 Deliah Street
Corona, CA 91719-1866

Dee Cee Laboratories
304 Dee Cee Court
P.O.Box 383
White House, TN   37188

DMS Treasures
151 Essex Street
Haverhill, MA 01830

Environmental Systems, Inc.
3125 Nolt Road
Lancaster, PA 17601

F.C. Taylor Fur Co.
227 E. Market Street
Louisville, KY 40202

Flora Beverage Co. Ltd.
Bay F, 2828 54th. Avenue, SE
Calgary, AB T2C 0A7
Canada

Fmali, Inc.
831 Almav Avenue
Santa Cruz, CA 95060

Giadone Farms, Inc.
743 Lane Road, #24
Pueblo, CO 81006

Herbarium
11016 152nd. Ave.
Kenosha, WI 53140

Herbs Etc.
317 Aztec
Santa Fe, NM 87501

Historical Remedies
112 S. Wabasha Street
St. Paul, MN 55107

Homestead Gardens
Pumpkin Hill Road
Warner, NH 03278

G. Reising & Co.
2226 Bush Street
San Francisco, CA 94115

Jarrow Formulas
1824 S. Robertson Blvd.
Los Angeles, CA   90035

J&D Labs
2640 Progress Street
Vista, CA   92083

TABLE 30
Small Bulk Wholesale Domestic Buyers (500 Pound Minimum)

J&T Imports
P.O. Box 642
Solano Beach, CA 92075

Lam Enterprises
P.O.Box 2832
Union City, CA 94587

Lebermuth Co.
14000 McKinley Highway, Route 20
Mishawaka, IN 46545

Linderman's Naturals
2817 W. Locus Avenue
Fresno, CA 93711

McCreighty Wholesale Florist
1783 Prospect Road
Washington Boro, PA 17582

Native Scents
212 Camino de la Merced
Taos, NM 87571

Natures Supply
6909 Mark Terrace Drive
Edina, MN 55439

Nicole Leight Enterprises
6 Heartstone Drive
Manalapin, NJ 07726

Now Natural Foods, Inc.
550 Mitchel
Glendale Heights, IL 60139

Olfactory Corp. Inc.
1965 S. Factory Avenue
Yuma, AZ 85365

Organic Marketing
11270 Clayton Creek Road
Lower Lake, CA 95457

Oregon Exchange, Inc..
1758 Lincoln Street, #1
Eugene, OR 97401

Pro Health
1187 Coast Village Road, #1280
Santa Barbara, CA 903108

Rasi Laboratories, Inc.
1300 Airport Road, Suite A
North Brunswick, NJ 08902

R.B. Howell Co.
630 NW 10th Avenue
Portland, OR 97209

RJS Sceintific, Inc.
45 Seaview Boulevard
Port Washington, NY 11050

San Francisco Herb Co.
250 14th. Street
San Franciscol, CA 94103

SCI
540 New York Avenue
Lyndhurst, NJ 07071

Sportx Nutrition
P.O. Box 111
Fall City, OR 97344

Starwest Botanicals
11253 Trade Center Drive
Rancho Cordova, CA 95670

Strictly Vermont
P.O. Box 443
Island Pond, VT 05846

Tropical Gardens Wholesale Florists
7716 104th. Street
Edmonton, AB T6E 4C5
Canada

Vintage Market
P.O. Box 396
Spring Hill, TN 37174

Vitatech Inc
2832 Dow Ave.
Tustin, CA 92680

TABLE 31
Large Bulk Wholesale Domestic Buyers (5,000 Pound Minimums)

Abrey Organics, Inc.
4419 N. Manhatten Avenue
Tampa, FL 33614

Active Organics
7715 Densmore Avenue
Van Nuys, CA 91406

American Indian Art & Craft
P.O. Box 1358
Gallup, NM 87301

American Ingredients, Inc.
2929 E. White Star Avenue
Anaheim, CA 92806

American Merchantile Corp.
1310 Farmville Road
Memphis, TN 38122

American Oak Preserving
601 Mulberry Street
North Judson, IN 46366

Aromatic Industries
13201 Dahlia Street, Suite A
Fontana, CA 92335

Arrowhead Mills
100 E Street, Suite 214
Santa Rosa, CA 95404

Balsam Fir
P.O. Box 123
West Paris, MA 04289

Celestial Seasonings
4600 Sleepy Time Drive
Boulder, CO 80301

Crabtree & Evelyn, Ltd.
1010 Adelaide Street
South London, ON N6E 1R6
Canada

Flavor Specialties
790 E. Harrison Street
Corona, CA 91719

Flora Manufacturing & Dist., Ltd.
7400 Fraser Park Drive
Burnaby, BC V5J 5B9
Canada

Herbarium, Inc,.
11016 152nd Avenue
Kenosha, WI 53142

Hiawatha, Inc.
P.O. Box 297
Shelton, WA 98584

MacAndrew Forbes Co.
3rd Street and Jefferson
Camden, NJ 08104

M.F. Neal Co.
4400 Williamsburg Avenue
Richmond, VA 23223

Nature's Sunshine Co., Inc.
1655 N. Main St.
Spanish Fork, UT 84660

Nutriceuticles — Makers of KAL
104 Country Hills Drive, Suite 300
Ogden, UT 84403

San Francisco Herb & Natural Food Co.
1010 46th. Street
Emeryville, CA 94608

Sheldrick's Inc.
9206 Dickerson Road
Mt. Hope, ON L0R 1W0
Canada

Whole Herb Co
19800 8th. Street East
Sonoma, CA 95476

Wilcox Natural Products
755 George Wilson Road
Boone, NC 28607

TABLE 32
Bulk Wholesale Import/Export Houses

Abbott Laboratories
1401 Sheridan Road
North Chicago, IL   60064

Abco Laboratories, Inc.
2377 Stanwell Drive
Concord, CA   94520

Active Organics
7715 Densmore Avenue
Van Nuys, CA   91406

Aditiva
Rua 25 de Abril, 1
Rio De Mouro 2735 Cacem
Portugal

All-Tech, Inc.
3031 Catnip Hill Pike
Nicolasville, KY 40356

American Biorganics, Inc.
2236 Liberty Drive
Niagara Falls, NY   14304

Bell Aromatics, Inc.
500 Academy Drive
Northbrook, IL   60062

Berje Chemical Products, Inc.
5 Lawrence Street
Bloomfield, NJ   07003

William Bernstein Co., Inc.
15 Park Row
New York, NY 10038

Berje Chemical Products, Inc.
5 Lawrence St.
Bloomfield, NJ 07003

Bertram Laboratories
72 Readington Road
Somerville, NJ   08876

Best Formulations
522 South Allen Avenue
Pasadena, CA 91106

Bio-Botanica, Inc.
75 Commerce Drive
Hauppauge, NY   11788

Wm. Blythe & Co., Ltd.
Bridge Street
Church, Accrington   BB5 4PD
England

Botanicals International, Inc.
2550 El Presidio Street
Long Beach, CA   90810

Charabot & Co., Inc.
83 Cedar Lane
Englewood, NJ   07631

Chart Corp
787 East 27th. Street
Paterson, NJ   07504

Classic Flavors and Fragrances
125 W. 23rd Street, Suite 400
New York, NY   10010

Crown Imports Corp.
5813 N. 7th. Street
Phoenix, AZ 85014

Erie Foods International, Inc.
1201 South Main Street
Rochelle, IL   61068

Falcon Trading
1047-A South Road
East Fairfield, VT   05448

Florascense by Endar Corp.
43085-A Business Park Drive
Temecula, CA 92590

Florasynth, Inc.
410 E. 62nd. Street
New York, NY 21237

FMG/Tsumura International
1000 Valley Park Road
Shakopee, MN 55379

General Nutrition Corp.
921 Penn Avenue
Pittsburgh, PA 15222

Heartland Foods, Ltd.
400 25 Alexander Street
Vancouver, BC V6A 1B2
Canada

Importaciones Idel., S.A. de C.V.
Academia No. 44, 1er Piso
Col. Centro, D.F. 06060
Mexico

Intercontinental Fragrances, Inc.
800 Victoria Drive
Houston, TX 77022

Int'l. Commodities Export Corp.
2975 Westchester Avenue
Purchase, NY 10577

International Specialty Products, Inc.
1361 Alps Road
Wayne, NJ 07470

Jun Jin Enterprises, Inc.
150 W. 31 Street
New York, NY 10001

Knud Nielson Co., Inc.
P.O. Box 746
Evergreen, AL 36401

McAuley's, Inc.
1814 S. 3rd. Street
Memphis, TN 38109

Meer Corp.
9500 Railroad Ave.
North Bergen, NJ 07047

Paul Muggenburg GmbH & Co.
Bahnhofstr. 2
D-2081 Alveslohe
Germany

Natual Oils International
12350 Montague St., Suite C
Pacoima, CA 91331

Oilseeds International, Ltd.
P.O. Box 2799
San Francisco, CA 94126

Omega Nutrition
8564 Fraser Street
Vancouver, BC V5X 3Y3
Canada

Penick Corp.
158 Mt. Olivet Avenue
Newark, NJ 07114

Pharmachem Labs
130 Wesoley Street
S. Hackensack, NJ 07606

Plantation Botanicals, Inc.
P.O. Box 128
Felda, FL 33930

Point Vert
7236 Salisbury Avenue
Burnaby, BC V5E 3A2
Canada

Pure Foods of Europe, Inc.
Amfitritis 17
GR 16673 Voula, Athens
Greece

Quimdis S.A.
85 Rue Edouard Vaillant
F 92307 Levallois Per,
France

Reactana Gmbh
Justus-Von-Liebig Strasse 3
D-6083 Biebeshgeim
Germany

Robertet, Inc.
125 Bauer Drive
Oakland, NJ 07436

E.L. Scott & Co., Inc.
1 World Trade Center, Suite 1313
New York, NY 10048

Sluder Floral Co.
Rt. 2 (Highway 221)
Newland, NC 28567

Specialty Organics, Inc.
5263 N. 4th Street
Irwindale, CA   91706

U.S. Flavors & Fragrances, Inc.
511 Lake Zurich Road
Barrington, IL   60010

SSI Fragrances, Inc.
2581 S. Golden State Boulevard
Fowler, CA 93625

Vitamins, Inc.
200 E. Randolph Drive
Chicago, IL   60601

George Uhe Co., Inc.
12 Rte. 17 North
Paramus, NJ 07653

shipped and stored in burlap or polypropylene bags. Many states do not have fiber-drum manufacturers, often limiting markets with specific fiber-drum storage requirements. Some warehousing also requires pallet patterns on how the bags are strapped for storage. some crops will be able to be shipped in bales, since many bulk wholesalers prefer to process their materials from a bulk state, rather than from a cut form (see Chapter 7).

Once a bulk mailing list has been established for the crops desired, a bulk offering mailer should be prepared and sent to these prospective customers. Sample requests should be anticipated, most ranging from one ounce to one pound. If your product is in crude form, you should plan one pound samples as a minimum. Almost all of your advertising and marketing budget will go toward this mailer and toward sample requests. You should market your crops for three years before considering advertising in various source directories and magazines.

SOME FINAL COMMENTS

All products and crops are shipped either by common carrier (published rates) or a private carrier running a back-haul route. All spices and herbs are shipped Class 70 (Dried Herbs and Flowers), making the common carrier almost prohibitive in competition with landed import prices. Transportation can often make the difference between a bulk wholesaler buyer choosing domestic over imported crops. You must always remember that it is the customer who usually pays freight, so just because your selling price is less than import prices, this does not necessarily mean that the customer's landed price — total cost to his dock — for your goods is less than the import price.

There are always a number of transport brokering houses that specialize in organizing private owner trucks. If a trailer is returning home with only a partial load, and his destination is near your customer, then rates are often less than half those available from common carriers. This can make the difference in closing a sale. Rate breaks for bulk farm crops can even be better with

- FOR IMMEDIATE SALE -
November, 1997

RE: MONTHLY SALES SHEET OF CURRENT INVENTORY

Alfalfa Herb, dehy, meal 50# 60,000 lbs. $0.17/lb./truckload 18.5%+

Blue-Green Algae, 20/40-mesh 10.500 lbs. $48.00/lb./advance Freeze-dry

Blue-Green Algae, 70/90-mesh 10,500 lbs. $48.00/lb./advance Freeze-dry

Comfrey Leaf, c/s C/O 4,000 lbs. $3.20/lb. COG

Feverfew Herb, 1st cut, bale form 130,000 lbs. $1.40/lb./truckload 2%+ parthen.

Lavender Spikes, mix 3,000 lbs. negotiable

Mugwort Herb, bale 10,000 lbs. $1.20/lb. wildcraft

Oatstraw Herb, dehy, meal 50# 80,000 lbs. $0.17/lb./truckload 18.5%+

Prince's Pine Herb, whole 10,000 lbs. $2.20/lb. wildcraft

Sage, Dalmatian White, c/s and tbc 3,500 lbs. $3.20/ lb. COG/premium

St. John's Wort Herb, cut 20,000 lbs. $1.20/lb./truckload wildcraft

Wormwood Herb, bale form 74,000 lbs. $1.20/lb./truckload COG

CONTACT: Richard Alan Miller
      Agricultural Consultant

OREGANO
(*Origanum vulgare*)
Labiatae family

There has been some confusion over the years as to which species of *Origanum* is referred to by the common name oregano. It has often been confused with sweet marjoram (*Origanum majorana*), *O. heracleoticum* (native of Greece), and others. *O. vulgare* is also a perennial and native to the Mediterranean, and is the main product now used in most manufactured and processed foods using oregano.

Oregano can be started either from seeds or by cuttings. Good drainage and tilth are essential, although the soil fertility is minimal. Water is also minimal, although some irrigation is recommended. Cuttings planted in rows, 12 inches apart, is recommended since weed control is very important. Mulching the plants help keep them clean from grasses and other problems.

As soon as the flowers appear, oregano is ready for harvest. It should be trimmed about six weeks after planting, cutting off all shoots to within one inch from the growing center. This practice stimulates dense, bushy growth. Although it can in some situations be dried in the sun, it is best to dehydrate this product for higher oil retention. Oregano is then usually rubbed through a fine screen to prepare it for culinary use.

Last year more than 7,100 tons of oregano herb was imported into the United States, with more than 5 ton of oil. Mexican oreganos begin to be available in March while the more desired Greek and Italian products become available in June. In some situations, a special hybridization can be seen in flower stages even in December. The better grades of oregano begin their pricing at 90 cents per pound, with a processed cut beginning at more than $1.45 per pound.

Oregano is used extensively as a major flavor ingredient in pizza and other foods. The Mexican variety (*Lippia graveolens*) is more spicy and is used in prepared foods such as chili and relishes. Although mainly used as a spice, China has used this herb to treat fevers, vomiting, and other disorders. The thymol and carvacrol phenols in oregano have strong fungicidal properties.

larger shipments of 10 and 20 ton loads. Common costs can be as low as $1.30 per mile for full loads of 20 to 30 ton quantities.

The usual sales arrangements between markets and the small farm are c.o.d., based on sample approval. Some firms will offer a letter of credit (L/C) for your crop. This should be required from any firm outside your country. Most domestic market wholesalers will offer a purchase order, based on sample approval, the terms being either c.o.d., or net 30, meaning they have 30 days to remit payment. Very rarely does a farmer offer net billing.

Bulk wholesalers have their cash flow problems. Understanding their marketing often can help form a working relationship. For example, while most of a farmer's crops are harvested and ready for sale in the fall, most bulk wholesalers have their lowest cash flows during this period. The largest cash flows are during the cold winter months, when more people are drinking hot teas rather than juice.

If you have warehousing available on or near the farm, some of the larger crop sales include a provision for partial shipments, with prices reflecting amortizing expenses incurred by the farmer. An example is a peppermint farmer selling 200 tons of baled produce to a large tea manufacturer. Chances are, the bulk wholesaler does not have the warehousing to store this quantity for a year, nor probably the capital to buy all of the crop in the fall. He is, however, in a position to buy 20 ton loads each month. The farmer can be guaranteed payment for this lot before he commits to further shipments. Contracts are required for any marketing of this nature, of course.

Finally, there are some market games that the small farmer might want to consider. Rather than committing all of his crop to a single price, he might want to store some of it for later speculation during periods of shortages. For example, while a farmed catnip might market at a price of $800 per ton (40 cents per pound) in the fall, shortages often occur in the March through April periods. Tea manufacturers will buy catnip during these periods for more than $1,600 per ton, or 80 cents per pound — double what the farmer can contract for during the regular growing season. Some form of market plan for bulk marketing of each crop must be made.

Preserved Flowers

180

CHAPTER 10

The Cottage Industry, With Specific Examples

The emerging entrepreneur is a more truly thoughtful person who is changing products and services to fill the needs of a more thoughtful and caring audience than the world has previously known . . . This is what the young are saying: Don't make me an adjunct to the process; make me inherent in it.

Robert Schwartz, Tarrytown Executive House

The original concept of a cottage industry was one of a manufacturer in a rural setting, probably working from his home. The advantage to the community was seen on several levels. Not only did such industries broaden the marketing of local products, they also brought new money into the community because their marketing was primarily export. As the community grew, so did these private, home industries. Today, local entrepreneurs are considered critical to the health and growth of any rural community.

The diversity of marketing options available to farmers interested in herbs and spices in cottage industries is unbelievable. The small farmer who chooses not to market either by direct or bulk marketing channels can find a number of alternatives by helping form a series of cottage industries around his crops. Profit-margins can be increased by more than 400% in some situations. While these profit margins are necessary for most producer-manufacturer-distributor-customer structures of marketing, a number of other important benefits for the rural community also emerge.

Aside from the economic benefits to the community, there are the human development and community benefit aspects. It makes residents more aware of the natural resources available, thus creating further cottage industry opportunities. A number of technical information sources are created, usually including marketing and farm management training programs — usually through local County Extension offices or Community Colleges. Cottage industries also provide employment. They help build a community owned economic structure using local resources. This aids the community recapture its identity.

The best way to approach an understanding of these diverse opportunities is by example. The following are not meant to be inclusive. They are cited here to illustrate the diversity of opportunities. With a broader perspective, the small farmer now has options not previously available in his marketing plan. Cottage industries are a perfect way for the small farmer to market garden level production of herbs and spices while a definitive plan is being developed. With full production farm plans, the same cottage industries can provide stability in marketing from one year to the next.

GROWING HERB PLANTS FOR SALE

To grow herb and spice plants for sale, you will need a lath house for shade during the summer months, a greenhouse for colder spring areas of the country, and a good source of herb and spice seed. Once a good set of stock plants is established, propagation techniques become the only limiting factor for developing a growing business. It is surprising how much propagation material is created by a single two or three year old perennial plant.

For example, a two year old plant of lemon balm *(Melissa officinalis)* can be dug up, cut into as many as 100 cuttings, potted, and only take about two months before the finished plants are of a size ready for sale. When dealing with this many plants from a propagation source, you should avoid repotting. It is time consuming and unnecessary because rooted plants can be sold in their original container. The name should be written on each pot with a waterproof felt pen. It is cheaper than using labels, which have a tendency to fall out.

Pricing is established by comparing retail prices at local garden shops and other retail markets. Send for catalogs from a number of other herb farms and see what their prices are. With this information it becomes quite easy to set a good price on your own products. Most wholesale prices range from 50 to 60% less than retail as a rule of thumb.

When selling your plants on a retail basis, you will need to let the public know about your activity. An attractive sign outside your place of business is critical, especially when you are on a well traveled road. The wording should be brief and the lettering should be large enough to be read easily by passing cars, (see tables 20 and 21). The actual selling area should be away from the working garden and greenhouse. This keeps those plants not yet ready for sale away from those the public actually sees. Quality and cosmetic appeal are very important for a successful market, and first impressions make the difference.

When wholesaling your products, suitable outlets must have certain facilities to maintain continued sales of your products. This includes a place to hold the plants in good condition. Plenty of air, light, but not much sun, are required. Someone needs to be in charge who understands about watering and how to keep the plants healthy. Plant and garden stores work best with roadside farm markets and commercial greenhousing next in line. Some natural food stores can place the plants outside in favorable and attractive settings.

Most people, however, will grow their plants indoors, usually in 3 to 6 inch pots. This is the most labor intensive form of marketing, and includes transplanting plants into larger ones. This is for those customers who would like to cut fresh herbs and spices from their plants at once. Large clay pots are used in this instance and often requires an additional 4 to 8 weeks growth before they are ready for sale. If grown indoors, most plants require special fluorescent lighting or be near a window with good light, especially during winter months. Plants to be field grown are usually propagated from material too big to use for pot grown plants. These are usually offered for sale directly from the farm, unpotted. They are dug at the time of sale, not prior to a customer buying them. They can be lifted with a spade, keeping a good ball of soil on the roots. They are then put onto a sheet of thin plastic and gathered around the stem with a tie.

Propagation by layering and division will give you plants that are saleable to commercial growers more quickly than any other method. Herbs layer themselves naturally, putting down roots where their decumbent stems or branches touch the soil. Division is an excellent method for most perennial herbs and spices. In larger fields, a tractor can disc the rootstock into smaller plants. Rootstock suppliers will be needed as more and more small farmers grow herbs and spices as cash crops.

HERBAL SALVES AND LIP BALMS

Herbal salve combinations can be found in almost all drug sections of major mass market stores. Included are lip balms and sun screens. Included also are ingredients as collagen, elastin, vitamin E, Na-PCA, and aloe vera gel. These products are a perfect foundation for cottage industry because they are all essentially made from the same formula. By simply adding specific ingredients to the same base, new products can be created.

A *decoction* is made of the specific herbs to be used in the salve. This is done by boiling a single ounce of the botanical in 20 ounces of water for 20 minutes, usually in a closed enamel-type container. If the decoction requires several materials, put roots in first, since they require the longest period, 20 minutes, to remove the active principles. Barks, seeds, herbs, and flowers are added next for 10 minutes, and last, the spices are added for 5 minutes.

After each decoction is finished, strain the liquid into a larger pot and let it stand until you are ready to mix it into your salve base. The salve base is primarily a beeswax and oil combination. The highest quality, therefore the most expensive, is a virgin beeswax and cold pressed olive oil mixture. Other less expensive oils can be used, including sunflower oil, cottonseed oil, and wheat germ oil. Sunflower oil is almost as good as an olive oil, and is only half the price. Most formulas use one part wax to six parts oil.

Put about one fourth of the desired oil and wax into another large enamel or stainless steel container and melt the wax slowly. As the wax begins to melt, slowly add the rest of the wax and oil. The decoction is added when the wax is completely liquid, being stirred very slowly. Toward the end of preparation, take out a small amount of the mixture and let harden to check consistency. You may wish to add more beeswax at this time. The scented oils are added at the end, only when a final consistency is established.

The herbal salve is then poured into your final merchandising container before it begins to harden. While glass jars with metal caps have traditionally been used, their transportation costs is almost prohibitive. Today, most manufacturers use a plastic jar-lid container to minimize weight. When bought in gross quantities, these one ounce containers can be as low in cost as 15 cents per jar. They should have a sealing inner lid which forms when the lid is first placed on the new jar. Silkscreening is sometimes less costly than paper labels.

TABLE 34
*Partial List of Commercially Marketed Wildflowers
and Their Current Wholesale Price*

DRIED FLOWER	PRICE/UNIT
German Statice (*Goniolimon tataricum*)	$ 3.50/4 ounce
Baby's Breath (*Gypsophilla perfecta*)	3.25/8 ounce
Caspia (*Limonum bellidfolium*)	1.75/4 ounce
Gypsy Grass (*Lycopus virginicus*)	2.65/pound
Air Fern (*Selaginella lepidophylla*)	0.60/2 grams
Strawflower (*Helichrysum bracteatum*)	45.00/1,000
Spiral Eucalyptus (*Eucalyptus globulus*)	1.65/4 ounce
Cardoon Puffs (*Cynara cardunculus*)	0.12/head
Yarrow Flowers (*Achillea mullefolium*)	1.20/12
St. John's Grass (*Hypericum perforatum*)	1.25/12
Redwood Branches (*Sequoia sempervivens*)	4.75/pound
Pussy Willow (*Salix nigra*)	1.60/12
Wild Iris Pods (*Iris florentina*)	0.05/each

There are only two label requirements to meet FDA regulations. The net weight must be easily readable and the contents must be listed, each ingredient in order of decreasing amounts. Therefore, your oil will appear first, with beeswax second and the other additives in order of their total weights used in the manufacture of the final product. Usually the ingredient least used is the flavoring, so it appears last in the content list.

The following prospective costs are based on a 60 dozen batch (720 units) of herbal salves of one ounce jars. This represents approximately a 50 pound batch:

Sunflower Oil — 5 gal/$30 (7.6 pounds per gallon) $50.00
Beeswax — 7 pounds ($4.00 per pound). 21.00
Vitamin E — 250 milligram per ounce 8.00
Golden Seal Herb ⌐
Aloe Vera Gel   ├— decoction 14.00
Comfrey Leaf/Root ⌐
Flavor alternatives:
    Spearmint — 1.5 ounce
    Cinnamon
    Rosemary — 2.0 ounce
    Coconut
    Lemon grass $20.00
    Rose
    Wintergreen
    Total ingredient costs $113.00

This makes the cost of goods produced for the ingredients at 16 cents per ounce (50 pounds divided by 720 units). With the correct facilities, most people can produce five to six gross (144) units each per day. This includes preparing the salve, filling the jar, wiping any spillage, labeling, and packing the jars into a shipping box. The labor figure used represents only two gross per eight hour day at $4.00 per hour. The advertising figure represents a 600 mailing cost with 10% buy from mail order:

Container. $0.15
Label 0.02
Ingredients. 0.16
Labor 0.10
Advertising 0.10
Box shipping 0.02
Overhead 0.05

Total cost-of-goods produced (per 1 ounce unit). $0.60

This 60 cent per unit figure can drop 20% when producing 200 or more pounds of salve at one time. Suggested retail prices can range, depending on specific ingredients (such as vitamin E) from $1.95 to $4.00 per ounce. Wholesale prices could begin at 90 cents to retail chains, such as Safeway, to more than $1.25 to local health food stores and buying cooperatives. If your product is well labeled and the contents deliver, marketing is no problem. A typical supermarket chain of 40 stores will sell about a dozen salves of each flavor per week. This represents approximately 160 dozen one ounce salves per week, or about 150 pounds per week. The resultant salary is over $200 per week for labor plus a profit line for a growing small business.

Other marketing channels include —

Mail-order (retail/wholesale).

Distributors.

Supermarket warehousing.

Classified advertisements.

Private labeling (putting someone elses label on your product).

Terms can be offered, including consignment, with a 5% discount on six dozen quantities and 10% on gross quantities. Most also offer a net 30 day billing, with 2% discount if the bill is paid within 10 days (known as 2% net 10). Initial first orders could also be given a 10% discount with a c.o.d. order of two dozen assorted flavors. Sun screens could be marketed in the summer while herbal lip balms are winter markets. More oil is added to the salve to make sun screens more creamy, while less is used to make lip balms work as stick applicators.

EVERLASTING FLOWERS

Everlasting flowers are those varieties of flowers which hold their shape and color when dried. Their primary market is to the wholesale and retail florist. The actual market is quite large, and more extensive than most people might realize. Last year, for example, one rural county in Eastern Washington actually exported more than 400 ton of baby's breath as a foraged crop. This amounted to more than 600 partial summer jobs for that rural community. Most of those involved in the actual forage operation and marketing were not even from that county, representing tremendous losses in revenues for that community.

The list of diverse products which could be, and are, marketed in this area is rapidly expanding. Not only can individuals market directly to local wholesale and retail florists, export opportunities continue to expand as well. As a cottage industry, the potentials for supplementary rural incomes is excellent. Not only can these various products be sold in bulk, but manufactured arrangements offer even greater profits to the small farmer who wishes to deal with smaller quantities in marketing.

A partial list of varieties and their wholesale market price are given in table 34. These dried foliages, tree cones and other items are used in large quantities by wholesale florists, handcraft retail stores, nurseries, and allied industries. Some differences from the pricing in this table will be found, but it should be representative in fixing a price for marketing to local businesses as gift items and display. If your farm offers the correct conditions for growing, you really should consider them as a viable alternative to other crops.

There are several other varieties of flowers suitable for drying. They include *Gomphrena globosa*, Acroclinum *(Helipterum roseum)*, assorted variations of strawflowers (Helichrysum spp.), immortelle *(Xeranthemum annuum)*, and honesty *(Lunaria annua)*. This list includes a whole raft of forage crops (see Chapter 11) which grow wild in rural farm communities. The key to successful marketing is to blend the available foraged crops with those cultivated in your fields.

Cultural requirements for most of the everlasting flowers include a well drained soil of average fertility. High nitrogen should be avoided because it promotes a faster growth in the stem, making it weaker. Weak stems make collection and bundling more difficult. Also, flowers bloom with poor color and the plants dry more slowly. Fertilizers such as potash and phosphate are desirable, inducing sturdier stems and flowers with more intense coloring. They need full sun. Shading results in blooms with inferior colors and poor conformation. Everlasting flowers are sown and grown like any other annual flower. The soil needs to be deep-spaded and rototilled, then worked down into fine seedbeds. Furrows should be 18 to 20 inches apart with seeds planted one half inch deep, and then covered lightly. Thinning needs to be done when the seedlings begin to emerge, so that they stand four inches apart.

Flowers are ready to cut when they come into full bloom, and before seed formation. Harvesting should be done on a dry, sunny morning after the dew has evaporated from the blooms. When cutting, take as much of the stem as you can. This will induce young developing stalks to emerge from the base of the plant, producing a secondary crop during the same season. As the flowers are cut, they should be gathered in single handfuls, tied, and taken to cover away from the sun. Indoors is best, but they do need an air flow across them for faster drying.

For best results in drying, each bundle of flowers should contain between 10 and 20 flowerheads. By tying them at the end of the stem, the heads tend not to bunch together. This gives a better circulation of air around each flowerhead, especially when a box fan is used. The bundles should be hung upside down in a shaded area, such as a carport or barn. Often, when there are a number of flower bunches to hang, a support line is strung across the barn with several points tied to the roof. Once this line is full of flowers, a second line is strung directly below the upside-down flowers for another string of flowers. The most important factor in this drying is air flow.

Flowers can be preserved with a drying agent such as silica gel. Being light in weight, it flows easily and surrounds all parts of the flower. Hard to dry flowers such as the rose, daisy, or violet make excellent dried flowers with the use of silica-gel. Herbs such as lily-of-the-valley, passionflower, and Queen Anne's lace are often treated the same way. Silica-gel is a dessicant which draws moisture out of the plant material. A small amount is placed in the bottom of a plastic container, with the flowers placed on top and spaced so as not to touch each other. More silica-gel is then sprinkled over the top before the plastic container is recapped. The flowers will be dried within two days. The silica-gel can be reused by drying in an oven on a cookie sheet at a low temperature. Microwave ovens have been used to speed the drying.

The flowers should be arranged so that colors produce a harmonious effect. Always put the longer stemmed flowers on the outer circle of the bouquet and those with shorter stems toward the center. Wrap the finished product in a cellophane bag to protect the flowerheads from dust and shattering. A special box must be used for shipping and storage. Most florists need special packaging to protect their purchase and for display. A well designed package can be the detail that makes a sale. Bouquets can also be put into inexpensive vases made from reeds.

The best markets for dried flowers in bouquets are gift shops, flower shops, garden stores, supermarkets, and variety stores. You should always sell for cash. If the buyer is reluctant to buy, offer to consign them for a period of time, but be specific. Most retail stores will buy on consignment two or three dozen bouquets. Be sure to stress that they are from local growers, dehydrated and processed to last through the winter, when fresh flowers are not available.

Other good markets for dried flowers are department stores and other holiday decorations markets. Christmas wreaths made with baby's breath and gilded pine cones, wrapped around grape vine wreaths make excellent cash income products during the winter. A velvet ribbon makes a tremendous difference in appearance. Baby's breath also makes a garlic braid a wonderful addition to the kitchen almost any time of year. Color can be added by the addition of spices and red peppers.

ORNAMENTALS

Ornamental and tree farming, while labor intensive, are also high yield crops which have exceptional market potential. The first consideration with these forms of crops are the land's suitability for ornamentals. The property needs to be well-drained, cleared, and have a gentle slope with good exposure. Altitudes of 2,300 feet will encourage three growths a year for some evergreens, whereas 2,000 feet in altitude usually allows only two growths per year. The entire operation can be handled with a four-wheel-drive tractor with 20 hp. Other side tools would include a sprayer, mower, and rotovator. This keeps the operation small but profitable.

Some lath housing will be needed for starts and special ornamentals. Most successful farmers grow more than 20 different types of ornamentals. These usually include azaleas, rhododendrons, rock garden plants, tiger lilies, Japanese and other maples, hemlocks, firs, several spruces (Norway and Colorado blue), and junipers. The key to success seems to lie in the diversity of crops.

TABLE 35
Four Ornamental Crop Budgets (Approximate)

	COLORADO BLUE SPRUCE	EASTERN RED ELDER-BERRY	POTENTILLAM FRUITICOSA	MUGHO PINE (CONTAINER)
COST/ACRE				
Variable[1]	$ 1,000.00	$ 435.00	$ 6,500.00	$ 36,000.00
Labor	—	—	—	—
Fixed Equipment[2]	230.00	100.00	85.00	20.00
Overhead[3]	1,100.00	220.00	450.00	450.00
Stand Establishment[4]				
Total	$ 2,330.00	$ 755.00	$ 7,035.00	$ 36,470.00
INCOME/ACRE				
Yield 90% stand	4,350.00	31,000.00	15,500.00	44,500 pots
Price	4.50	0.15	1.00	1.50/pot
Total	$ 19,575.00	$ 4,650.00	$ 15,500.00	$ 66,750.00
INCOME OVER VARIABLE COSTS	$ 18,575.00	$ 4,215.00	$ 9,000.00	$ 30,750.00
RETURN TO OWNER LABOR AND MANAGEMENT	$ 17,245.00	$ 3,895.00	$ 8,465.00	$ 30,280.00
TOTAL RETURN/ ACRE/YEAR	$ 3,449.00	$ 3,895.00	$ 4,232.50	$ 15,140.00

[1] Fuel, oil, hired labor, materials, custom work.
[2] Depreciation and interest on investment, at 8% on field equipment.
[3] Utilities, taxes, insurance, automotive depreciation, interests on buildings.
[4] Estimated pro-rata cost of establishment.

Each may also have up to 20 or more crosses of the same species, broadening the market.

Markets include private customers, landscaping contractors, and local nurseries. Most ornamental farmers find that 80% of their sales are made to local residents. They are attracted not only to the size and appearance of these plants, but also by the value they receive for their money. The successful ornamental grower has found that he should charge one price to everyone, whether they are buying one plant or 100. Most of the plants are sold at four to five years of age. A rhododendron, for example, needs three years to reach market size, whereas a white pine needs five years before it is ready for sale.

Price generally range from $8 to $10 a plant, while the actual cost of producing the plant is approximately $1. This figure includes the cost of fertilizers, nutrient or chemical sprays, and potting materials, but does not reflect labor costs. A single contractor will buy more than 600 rhododendrons at a time at $10 each. A sale this size should represent 10% of a crop. Azaleas and white pines command about $8 each, and hemlocks go for about $2 a foot.

A beginning ornamental farmer should plan an outside income for the first few years while getting the operation off the ground. When growing ornamentals, you are still three to four years away from the market and a cash flow. The first years of operation are spent primarily performing nursery chores, such as placing the fledgling plants in containers, and putting them in sheds at night. Those of you planning to make a go of this form of small farm venture should cut your overhead to the minimum before become involved.

The table on page 189 is an overview of approximate ornamental crop budgets on several different crops. It should be remembered that most successful ornamental farmers grow more than 20 different crops, giving them not only diversity, but a broader market. Most have found that branching out into mail order is a waste of money and time. The cost of putting together a catalog that can attract buyers is almost more than can be returned via sales. Finally, the size of your operation should be small enough that you do not need to hire outside help.

DRIED CULINARY HERBS

In the high priced specialty food stores catering to the elite trade, culinary herbs and spices can be packaged in distinctive jars with artistic labels. This is a difficult market to get into because the larger companies have fairly well covered such stores. Also, the fancy glassware and labeling required tend to limit this market.

The beginner might first consider placing his products into small poly or cellophane bags that can be heat sealed and then stapled to a heavy cardboard display card. This is inexpensive packaging and if neatly assembled, it can be effective and will sell a lot of herbs. A display card, carrying 40 to 50 bags of herbs (one fourth ounce packs) will sell to the consumer for 35 to 50 cents per package. The store will want to make a minimum of 40% markup, so your price must be less than 25 cents a package.

A typical acre of land could make up as much as one thousand display cards, with some variation depending on the varieties offered. This estimate is based on an acre producing a minimum of 1,000 pounds dried herbs. Since each display card of 50 one fourth ounce packets takes less than one pound of herb material, 1,000 cards comes to about $12,000 per acre (gross). Most net returns in this form of marketing can yield approximately $6,000 per acre (net) when marketing flows smoothly.

HERB TEA BLENDS

Although tea bags outsell loose tea blends about 3 to 1, tea bags can be compared to instant coffee since the loose tea blend is comparable to fresh ground coffee in both flavor and quality. The 4 ounce blends usually can serve up to 48 servings and when compared to tea bag costs, blended teas cost about $4 per pound to the customer compared to $12 per pound for tea bags. Tea bag companies are primarily marketing paper and packaging rather than a quality blended herbal and spiced tea.

Herbal teas are considered to be the single fastest growing commodity in supermarket history, according to *Advertising Age Magazine*. Their popularity is seen to be a reflection of their nutrient value, price and flavor. There are numerous new companies springing up all over the country, with demand increasing for those flavor blends competing with the black tea and coffee markets. People are now interested in new flavor combinations and if the products are locally grown, markets increase even more rapidly.

The table 36 list of herbal tea blends are given only as an indication of the potential for this market:

HERBAL SMOKING MIXTURES

Nowdays, more and more people are looking for alternatives to those habits that give them trouble as well as pleasure. The alternative of herbal smoking

TABLE 36
List of Herbal Tea Blends and Their Ingredients

Alfalfa mint. alfalfa, peppermint, spearmint.

Cinnamon spice. black tea, cinnamon, clove, cardamom, anise.

Comfrey mint. comfrey, peppermint, spearmint.

Herbal coffee. roasted barley, dandelion root, roasted chicory, cinnamon, allspice, clove.

Jody's tea. rosehip, alfalfa, chamomile, raspberry leaf, dandelion root, comfrey root.

Lemon lime. lemon balm, lemon verbena, rosehip, lemon peel, lime peel.

Lemon spice. black tea, lemon peel, clove, cinnamon.

Licorice spice. licorice root, anise, cinnamon, orange peel.

Light lavender. comfrey, lavender, spearmint, red clover, lemon balm.

Nightcap. catnip, chamomile, scullcap, hops, valerian, strawberry, peppermint.

Obesity tea. alfalfa, comfrey leaf, kelp, lemon peel, elder flower, chamomile.

Orange spice tea. black tea, orange peel, cinnamon, clove, nutmeg, allspice.

Peppermint spice. peppermint, anise, clove, cinnamon, allspice, orange peel.

Pink tonic. chamomile, hibiscus.

Red racer. hibiscus, rosehip, lemon balm, lemon peel, orange peel, spearmint, wild cherry bark, comfrey leaf.

Spiced chamomile. chamomile, lemon balm, nutmeg, lemon peel.

Yogi tea. cardamom seed, ginger root, clove, peppercorn, cinnamon.

blends fit the bill for the man or woman who wants to rid themselves of the nasty nicotine habit. Many of the natural ingredients used in these alternative blends are perfect crops for the small farmer. Marketing them as cottage industry opens a number of alternative markets, such as tobacco stores, and the better department stores.

Made from such beneficial herbs as deer tongue, lavender, chamomile, coltsfoot, and mints, all are 100% free from nicotine. The herbs used in the recipes have traditional uses for cleaning the lungs! A box of rolling papers next to the display in a store only increases their sale. All the health conscious people who like to smoke will do nothing but keep your profits coming in from these farm crops. Tobacco stores and gift related businesses are a perfect first place to begin marketing. The following table list are ingredients used in a number of successfully marketed blends. They are given as an indicator of potentially viable crops which you might want to consider in your farm plan.

FROZEN PESTO FOR THE ITALIAN FOOD MARKETS

Most of us now realize that the Italian foods require a fresh basil, rather than one which has been dehydrated and powdered. There is no comparison in flavor when using a fresh basil from the garden in preparing pasta dishes. Most of the more exclusive Italian restaurants have a big problem during winter months, when fresh basil is only available from indoor grown facilities. Not only are these crops quite expensive, they seem to lack the oils found in field grown crops. The question is how to package basil so that it retains its important flavoring for winter use. The solution to this question could be a major cottage industry for almost all rural communities near large cities.

One suggestion offered is the manufacture of *pesto,* a combination of basil with other spices and oil. This preparation can be frozen, and has almost the

TABLE 37
List of Herb Tobacco Smoke Mixtures and Their Ingredients

English herbal. coltsfoot, eyebright, hyssop, rosemary, thyme, lavender, chamomile, buckbean.

Yuba gold. damiana, passion flower, scullcap, lobelia, peppermint.

American Indian herbal. damiana, strawberry leaf, comfrey leaf, coltsfoot, uva ursi, peppermint.

Deertongue smoke. strawberry leaf, deertongue, damiana, yerba mate, wild lettuce.

Early settlers remedy. coltsfoot, mullein, damiana, alfalfa, woodruff, raspberry leaf, horehound.

Ginseng tobacco. ginseng leaf, damiana, strawberry leaf, comfrey leaf, spearmint, uva ursi, passion flower, scullcap, hyssop, thyme, rosemary, chamomile, lavender, yerba mate, deertongue, wild lettuce.

TABLE 38
Frozen Pesto Recipe as a Cottage Industry

2 cups fresh basil leaves
1 cup fresh parsley (Italian)
$1/2$ cup pine nuts or walnuts
$1/2$ cup parmesan or romano cheese (mixed)
$1/2$ - $2/3$ cup olive oil
2 cloves garlic

Put all ingredients in a blender or food processor and mix thoroughly. It will expand a little when frozen, so make room in the container when packaging.

same flavoring as a fresh basil when mixed with pastas. It can be packaged in either a 12 ounce (net) plastic or cardboard container and frozen for storage. Most major supermarket chains are equipped to warehouse this as a frozen product, and would welcome it over the currently prepared canned spinach, also now marketed as pesto.

The above recipe comes from an excellent Italian homemaker, Margaret Sansone of Beavercreek, Oregon. She has successfully frozen this product, and the best culinary experts cannot tell the difference between this frozen product and one made from garden fresh produce.

DECOCTIONS, TINCTURES, ELIXIRS, AND ESSENCES

The potential for marketing unusual flowers and herbs and spices and byproducts is unbelievable. This is the primary area where most spices and herbs grown commercially are marketed. An example is peppermint oil, one of the major cash crops in Oregon and Washington. While byproducts as well as whole dill, spearmint, and other flavorings are grown and sold at large agribusiness levels, the potential for the small farm is quite impressive. Cosmetic industries and beauty aids are only one example.

A number of small scale extraction technologies exist for the small farmer (i.e., *Steam Distillation — Solvent Extraction Recovery of Volatiles from Fats and Oils,* by R. Teranishi, et al., *Agricultural and Food Chemistry,* volume 25, number 3, page 464, May-June, 1977). These type of designs, while they are fairly crude (using hot steam as a solvent), are perfect for extremely high oil spices and the active ingredients in other flavoring herbs. The prospects for the 40 to 80 acre farm producer in the international markets are increasing daily. Manufacturers of mayonnaise, pickle products, and relishes are only the tip of the iceberg.

For the small farmer, the options are also excellent. From supermarkets to the retail herb store, the market for tinctures, elixirs, and essences for health, cosmetics, and flavorings are only the beginning. What are tinctures? Assume you start with pure ethyl alcohol (95%), a *tincture* is defined as 50% alcohol, an

SWEET MARJORAM
(*Origanum majorana/Majorana hortensis*)
Labiatae family

This herb has been cultivated in Europe for centuries. As a tender perennial in Mediteranean climates, it must be grown in most parts of North America as an annual. The foliage is frost hardy and stays gray-green far into winter, the roots need protection from freezing. The root system is dense and shallow, utilizing only the top few inches of soil. It can be distinguished from the oreganos easily when both come into bloom. The scent and flavor are quite different.

Sweet marjoram is not the easiest herb to start from seed. The seed is extremely small and germinates in soils above 68 F., including night, in eight days. Because it is a slow grower, weeds are fierce competitors and need to be kept under strict control during the early growth. Plants should be spaced 6 to 8 inches in three plant clumps forest density-growth. The fairly rich humus soils are preferred and need to be kept moist with light irrigation via soaker-hose.

The first harvest of leaves should be made when the green ball-like tips appear at the end of stems. The entire plant should be cut back to 1 inch when flowers begin to appear. This stimulates a second growth which is considered the main crop. A third crop is often available with longer sun. The herb can not be sun-cured, but requires dehydration. It retains most of its oils when dry, although air-tight storage is recommended (like fiber-drum/plastic-liner packaging).

Extracts of sweet marjoram have anti-oxidative properties on lard, due in part to the presence of labiatic acid and the flavonoid present. The oil is used as a fragrance component in most cosmetic markets, including soap, detergents, creams and lotions, and some perfumes. The oil and oleoresin are used as a major food ingredient, especially baked goods, condiments and relishes, soups, and snack foods. Oregano is preferred in most medicinal preparations, although there is some recent documentation in its effective used with certain cancers.

Last year more than 630 ton of crude leaves of sweet marjoram imported into the United States from such countries as Egypt, France, and Chile. The spot price for sweet marjoram last year varied from $1.50 to $1.90 in tonnage, with processed prices beginning at more than $2.50 per pound. Since it will be fairly easy to match these prices in production, it is important to note that Europe uses more than twice our current domestic needs. And both figures are increasing.

elixir is 25% alcohol, an *essence* is 10 to 20% alcohol, and a *spirit* is 10% alcohol. If a pure grain alcohol is unavailable, you can use 150 proof gin or rum.

To make a tincture, add 4 ounces of a powdered botanical to 8 ounces of pure alcohol. You can use a 150 proof gin or rum in some situations. Then add 4 ounces of water and allow the mixture to steep for at least two weeks, shaking it daily. Strain and bottle the liquid in a dark colored glass bottle. Elixirs are made exactly like a tincture, except that an additional four ounces of water is added to the tincture immediately after straining.

Pharmaceutical grade essences are made by adding one part essential oil (usually from steam distillation) of the herb to nine parts alcohol. These are shaken thoroughly before use. Peppermint oil, taken in this manner, is better for an acid stomach than any other product on the market. Sold for centuries in China, *Po-Sum-On* also contains bloodroot and other important mineral containing herbs. Breath mints and other candy oriented markets show increasing demand for these types of products.

There are two basic ways that you may extract oil from seeds or beans. In the *pressure* or *expeller* method, ground or flaked seeds are fed into a large cylinder and driven against a back plate by a screw. Tremendous pressure squeezes out as much as 95% of the oil. In the *solvent extraction* process, ground seeds are bathed in a solution of hexane or other petroleum solvent. The resulting oil-solvent solution is then boiled to drive off the solvent. This method is preferred by oil producers because it extracts 99% of the oil from the seed. However, it reduces both the flavor and nutrient levels of the oil.

The terms *hot-pressed* and *cold-pressed* refer to the expeller press method of extraction. Hot-pressed sometimes refers to a higher pressure, more efficient process. These terms are essentially meaningless unless you know the exact temperature at which the oil is pressed. The term *cold-pressed* is especially misleading, because it suggests that the oil is not exposed to heat in the extraction process. In fact, all commercial oil extractions involve heats ranging from 120 F. to 150 F. Furthermore, many cold-pressed oils are refined, bleached, and deodorized after extraction, thus exposing them to even higher temperatures (up to 437 F.).

Far more important than the extraction process, in terms of nutritional value, is how much refining is done after the oil is extracted. An *unrefined* or *crude* oil is extracted, settled or distilled, and bottled. Nothing more is done to it. Unrefined oils that are pressure-extracted are sometimes called *natural oils. Refined* oils undergo a number of processing steps after extraction. The major purpose of these processes is to remove all extraneous materials that impart flavor or high color, affecting the character of the oil, even though they may be present in no more than traces.

To extract the odor of flowers, lay the petals out in a thin layer in flat enamel pans, approximately three to five inches deep. These are then covered with one to two inches of soft or rain water and set in the sun. Leave them undisturbed for a few days. Soon a film will be found floating on the surface. This is the oil

EUCALYPTUS
(*Eucalyptus globulus*)
Myricaceae family

There are approximately 600 species belonging to the Sweet Gale family, most are shrubs. Preferring an arid and temperate climate, eucalyptus can not survive extended freezing. It is cultivated in most parts of the world, with the largest plantations around the Black Sea of Russia and the Nilgiri Hills of India. As one of the fastest growing trees in the world, an average eucalyptus tree in northern California can grow up to 8 feet each year.

Between 15,000 and 18,000 seedlings will develop from 1 kg of seed. These can then be transplanted in rows 15 feet wide and apart for machine-harvesting of the leaf. India currently cultivates a rare species, *E. citriodora*, which yields the commercially important oil citronellol. The trees are kept as shrubs where limbs and leaves are taken as a coppice for the oil (steam distillation). In a typical year more than 1.3 million pounds of citronella oil are imported into North America at an average price of $1.90 per pound.

There are good markets for both eucalyptus leaf and eucalyptus oil (sometimes refined into eucalyptol or 1,8-cineole). Both oils have antiseptic (antibacterial) and expectorant properties, thus being used extensively as expectorants and/or flavoring agents in cold and cough medicines. These can include cough drops and syrups, vaporizer fluids, antiseptic liniments, ointments, toothpastes, and mouthwashes. The wood pulp is used in limited markets for scented papers such as toilet paper and tissues because of the fragrance.

Projected imports for 1985 eucalyptus oil is more than 1.6 million dollars. The primary producers now are China and Portugal, with leaf imports to be estimated at more than 400 ton. European markets are, of course, much larger. The price variation for eucalyptus leaf ranges from 35 cents per pound for overseas markets to more than $1.00 per pound when processed.

Eucalyptus looks to be the "tree of the future." Not only is it well-suited to reforestation projects, the entire tree can be used: the limbs and leaves yield a number of commercially important oils, and the wood pulp has potential futures markets. The key will be in developing machinery to harvest the limbs and leaves each year. Since the tree does grow so fast, yields-per-acre look excellent.

TABLE 39
List of Herbs and Spices commonly used in Sachets and Potpourris

Flowers. rose, hibiscus, elder, yarrow, chamomile, lavender, marigold, jasmine.

Herbs. thyme, rosemary, tarragon, lemon grass, lemon balm, basil, sage.

Fruits. lemon, lime, orange peel.

Mints. spearmint, peppermint, wintergreen, pennyroyal.

Spices. calamus, coriander, cinnamon, clove, allspice, nutmeg, cardamom.

Licorice. anise, licorice, fennel.

For Color. hibiscus (red), lavender (purple), fruit peels (yellow and green), nutmeg (orange), turmeric (bright yellow), clove (brown), sage (pale green), pennyroyal (mixed).

Essential oils. rose, lavender, carnation, almond, lemon, all mints.

and should be collected whenever it appears. This can be done with a cotton tipped wooden swab. The swab is then squeezed into a small amber colored bottle. The bottle is left open until all the water evaporates, and then capped and stored in a cool, shaded area.

SACHETS, POTPOURRIS, AND POMANDERS

A pomander ball is a dried orange (or other fruit) studded with whole cloves. It can be hung in a closet or room for its fragrance. While marketing is fairly limited to such outlets as gift stores and department stores which sell clothing, pomander balls broaden the marketing potential. *Potpourris* are clear bottles filled with dried flowers and herbs, arranged in layers for appearance. They are also usually scented with an essence oil. They are then opened to deliver a pleasant odor periodically. They market to the same stores as the pomander balls.

Sachets are mixtures of herbs and flowers, scented with essence oils and sewn into a square of cloth or net for placement in drawers or closets. The following list of herbs and spices may be combined to make potpourris and sachets. While sachets depend on fragrance alone, potpourris must also be visually attractive. Some department stores will buy more than 5,000 pounds of a given potpourris mixture, and some cottage industries offering more than a dozen different blends. The key to marketing lies in the packaging, and the fixing of a lasting odor. Fixing the odors is an art in itself.

Cottage industries are an excellent way for the small farmer to market his crops. The purpose of this chapter is primarily to overview the scope of possibilities available when growing herbs and spices on small acreages. The only limiting factor seems to be imagination. The profit margins available are excellent when you begin to add further processing to your crops. The advantages of these markets is that they allow you to begin marketing without large land commitments.

Oregon Grape

198

CHAPTER 11

Foraging as a Source for Supplemental Rural Incomes

If we see gain as a function of man's ability to think, and if we recognize the importance of the intellectual level on which the economy is based, then our prime interest will be oriented toward the development of this level . . . We can change our reality toward the goals we desire.

Eugene Loebl, Czechoslovakia

FORAGING AS A LIFE STYLE

Creative intelligence is the wealth of a modern society. The ability to recognize natural resources and then develop methods for harvesting and marketing them has been the backbone of American agriculture. Known as Yankee ingenuity, our desire to tinker with tools, making them useful for new applications, has given us the edge over foreign agriculture. Once a rural community recognizes these resources, new horizons for supplemental rural incomes becomes possible.

Among the wild plants of North America are many which have long been used in the medicinal, cosmetic and food industries. Some of them are used in sufficient quantities to make them commercially important. The collecting of plants or plant parts for these markets has long provided gainful employment for many people living in the rural sections of the country.

From the days of the early settlers, numerous native plants have long been credited with medicinal properties, eventually leading to their use as home remedies. Many have since become official pharmaceutical products. A growing number are purchased in substantial quantities, ranging from just a few tons to more than 2,000 tons annually. Wild plants have been with us long before cultivated crops arrived. They have been our food and medicines. For many years this form of natural resource use was the backbone of the pharmaceutical industry. Current prospects indicate a major industry trend to production of medicines and chemicals for diet and health use via raw material extraction, rather than by more recent synthesis technologies.

Among the plants utilized are common weeds, popular wild flowers, and various forest products. Common weeds include mullein and thistle, whereas popular wild flowers are such things as baby's breath and strawflowers. It would take a whole book to describe the various forest products now marketed, including such items as floral greens, cones (for seed and decoration), mushrooms, and a variety of mosses. A number of major drug plants are also harvested each year for export. Examples are cascara segrada bark from the West Coast, and sassafras root bark from the East Coast.

Although many of these products possess no real medicinal properties, their collection continues to be important because of established markets. Mullein and echinacea are typical examples. They contain chemistries associated with their use. Products which do contain specific chemistries have become cash crops in their regions of harvest. Another major market is that of the wholesale florist and decorative market. Dried flowers and unusual herb and spice byproducts are a very large business in North America.

Europeans have practiced these forms of natural resource use and agriculture for centuries. Several wholesale houses have been in business for more than 250 years, all family owned. Many of those wholesale houses are currently exporting botanicals to North America. The irony of this situation is that these products were originally harvested in North America, but collection was stopped due to World Wars I and II. During World War II, major pharmaceutical houses had their sources of supply cut off, and had to reorient their production to *synthesis* technologies, abandoning the traditional *extraction* processes. This trend limited the need for those raw materials and the market, and many of them went into a slump.

Today in North America, almost 80% of the currently used raw materials are imports. There are some botanicals, however, which have been exported for over 100 years. Such things as golden seal root and wild ginseng are typical products from the South, while cascara segrada bark has been an export laxative for more than 40 years from the Pacific Northwest. Other types of foraged products include mushrooms, sold to Japan, and picked fern, sold to West Germany.

Many new markets are now available again, due in part, to the revived extraction direction of the pharmaceutical houses and the health food boom of the 1970s. The domestic potential is open in the weed category again, since most are now imported into North America. It lies with the forager to consider creative ways of utilizing unproductive lands and recognizing the resources which they offer.

There is an increasing market for collecting plants suitable for use by the biochemical industries. This market is especially suitable for the small farmer who is either not fully employed, or has a farm which does not require his full time attention. Many of the so-called noxious weeds do in fact have good market potentials. While these crops vary from one community to another, their harvest considerations are quite similar. Once these natural resources have been recognized and markets identified, they can provide meaningful employment to those who need to supplement their agricultural incomes.

FIRST CONSIDERATIONS IN FORAGING

The first, and most important step in the collection of wild plants is to become familiar with market needs and seasonal demands. Most dealers in crude botanicals publish lists of plants they handle and often indicate the general range of prices offered to the forager. These are known as Forager Price Sheets. A good sheet will also include annual needs in terms of volume and form.

A prospective collector should be able to determine which plants found in the region offer the best opportunities for making a profit. Frequently a crop is overharvested, and the novice forager finds that the market is fully supplied. A knowledge of seasonal needs and demands will determine whether to hold the product, or sell it for less than the labor involved.

Such situations can be avoided by first submitting representative samples of the material to be collected, together with a statement of the approximate quantity that can be gathered. These should be sent to a number of reliable dealers. Purchase orders should always be obtained for quantities over 1,000 pounds. Since the crop harvested is usually in a crude or unprocessed form, samples must truly reflect the crop as it will be sent in terms of color, stem-to-leaf ratio, and other important factors.

The commercial value of wild plants depends to a large extent on the time and method of collection. The following categories are the major considerations for harvesting crude botanical plants from the wild —

1. Most forage crops are located in semi-inaccessible locations, where the crop has not been contaminated by dust, sprays, or road films. This demands a willingness to backpack into the brush, and in some instances, trailblazing.

2. Once a stand has been identified, it becomes a valuable resource for following years. You certainly would not tell any of your friends your secret mush-

201

room patch, neither does the forager divulge his sources of income to casual friends. These are the places you can go back to, year after year, to harvest your crop.

3. Brush permits or permission from land owners *must always be secured* before any harvest begins. The Bureau of Land Management (BLM), Department of Natural Resources (DNR), U.S. Forest Service (USFS) and most railroad companies issue brush permits for a number of non-timber forest floor products. They range in cost from free to 2 cents per pound (wet weight harvest). Some states charge 50 cents an acre per year to lease access and harvest rights for specific crops. While the usual access is for cattle forage, they do allow products with diameters less than .5 inches to be taken from the land.

4. If you plan a harvest in any area other than your community, you should contact the local police and forest rangers, letting them know what you are doing in their area. This prevents all sorts of problems, real and imagined. Oftentimes harvests occur during seasons which are also well suited to the poacher, for example. If the ranger is not notified as to what you are doing, you can draw your own conclusions as to what he will do.

5. When gathering botanicals from the wild, inspect your patch both for possible insect contamination, and to work out a re-seeding program for your next year's harvest. A few healthy plants should always be left to spread and continue natural production. While most forestry and agriculture departments do not have this type of information readily available, plant physiology departments at local universities near the harvest location will have good suggestions on regeneration programs. These must *always* be considered.

6. In order to make a good income, your stand or patch must be a minimum of 2 to 4 acres. The key is to be able to stay on the job, harvesting plants, rather than having to walk long distances between individual plants. The individual who takes foraging as a serious undertaking should prefer working out-of-doors and be prepared to spend 50% of his time actually searching for these likely patches worth harvesting. Only minimum harvests of 500 pounds dry weight are feasible. Smaller quantities severely limit marketing. A 2 to 4 acre stand puts you in the ball park.

THE FORAGE MARKET

There are three basic markets for foraged crops. The retail market is the smallest, requiring processing and some packaging. The wholesale or regional markets usually require packaging also, because of storage requirements. Export marketing often requires an organized group of 10 to 200 people for minimum quantity production. This means that there must be a central delivery point, usually a feed store in the area of harvest. Dehydration is required for almost all products, no matter what quantities are harvested. This requires further logistics and consideration.

The 2 ton prices (table 29) are slightly higher than a forager typically receives when marketing 500 pounds or less to regional wholesalers. The asterisk beside the herb (table 29) indicates it is already foraged, or has good potential as a foraged crop. The commercially marketed wildflowers, listed in table 34 are representative of the price you might ask a small florist, when buying 1 to 12 dozen "units" at a time. The large differences between what the forager receives and those at retail reflect processing labor, losses, and middlemen. Most milling operations experience 10 to 20% losses ("leavings"), and these prices reflect this kind of cost. Wholesale prices reflect warehousing costs, amortization of debt (storage and banking costs), and profits from sales. In addition, the forager's price is frequently constrained by current import costs and availability.

HARVESTING — THE COLLECTION AND
PREPARATION OF THE MATERIAL

Wild plants are collected as one of the following categories: roots, barks, herbs, flowers, or seed. There are always exceptions, aspen leaf being one of them. However, almost all botanicals are grouped into one of these five categories. As a category, the botanicals which fall into the same group are generally collected and prepared similarly.

Roots. Roots of annuals should be dug just before the flowering stage. Those from biennial and perennial plants should be gathered late in the fall or early in the spring. This is due to the fact that during the growing season, their active constituents are reduced and are therefore of poorer quality. In some areas, either a spade or potato fork is suitable for digging. A plow with a potato digger is more practical for larger stands. There are a number of different root-grappling devices on the market now, also.

Roots should then be washed and sliced to allow faster drying. When considering larger quantities, a rotating drum arrangement works best for cleaning and washing roots. They can then be cut into a chipped form with a mill. A composter or shredder tends to tear and powder the product, making it unsuitable for most markets. A sliced root should be at least 2 to 6 inches in length to be marketable to a processor.

Root harvest example. Oregon Grape Root *(Berberis aquifolium):* the principle alkaloids in this root are similar to those found in golden seal root *(Hydrastis canadensis),* berberine, oxyacanthine, and berbamine. It is considered anti-catarrhal (prevents mucous inflammation), and as a mild cholagogue (stimulating bile secretion). The root is now imported from Europe as a filler ingredient when used to cut golden seal. It thrives in coastal woods and thickets from British Columbia through Northern California.

Grown commercially as an ornamental, large nature stands can be found at lower elevations with western exposures. Since it propagates from a rhizome, harvesting parts of the root only stimulates the plant into further growth. It has a lateral rootstock with numerous taproots. By pulling this lateral root, where only one plant existed, 3 to 6 new plants emerge. Harvest of this plant is essentially similar to *coppicing.* This is a horticultural term used to describe the manner in which a shrub or tree is pruned, causing it to grow faster than if it were left to grow naturally.

The root is considered to be all parts of the plant up to the first leaf. This part is removed and then washed, chipped, and dried. Prices can range from 80 cents per pound in small tonnage as a "whole" or "chipped" product, to more than $1.40 per pound when sold as a C/S in 100 pound quantities. While most manufacturers do not buy more than 1,000 pounds on a single purchase order, it is a perfect crop to harvest during the winter months when farm work is at a minimum. An average forager can harvest up to 500 pounds (wet) in one day, resulting in over 300 pounds marketable product within four days if working in a good stand. The forager should look for stands where the root stems are over one foot high before the leaves develop. A brush permit from the land owner is required.

Barks. Barks should always be collected during the dormant season when the sap is not flowing. Vertical incisions a few inches wide are made. Depending on the nature of the bark, strips several feet long can then be pulled off the tree. The bark of branches and roots are removed by making long, lengthwise incisions, permitting the bark to be slipped off. When planning a harvest, trees should never be girdled or over-harvested. Some grow from rootstock. They should be cut above the crown before debarking, thus assuring that the tree will grow again. Many foragers neglect this important step, and strip small sections from rootstock type trees. Such trees die, of course.

Most of us have seen cinnamon sticks during Christmas or other holidays. This is a good example of how a bark should look when dried correctly. The bark tends to curl in on itself — which is known as a "quill" — when cut from 3 to 5 inch diameter limbs. Processors like to receive barks in semi-uniform lengths, allowing it to be milled with more uniformity. Therefore, most barks are chipped before sacking, often to speed drying times as well.

Bark harvest example. Cascara segrada bark — *(Rhamnus purshiana):* cascara bark is used in pharmacy as a cathartic. It not only acts as a laxative but restores natural tone to the colon. It is the most widely used laxative in the world, with the states of Oregon and Washington each exporting more than 400 tons each year. It is found along canyon walls, mountain ridges, and rich bottomlands in British Columbia, Washington, Oregon, California, Idaho, Montana, Colorado, and Arizona.

Collections are begun late in April and continue through the rainy season, because hot weather draws sap from the bark and forces it into the inner tree. The outer bark is easily stripped when the sap is rising along the inner wood. Since it is a member of the Rhamnaceae (buckthorn) family, it grows from rootstock. The tree should first be cut down. Then longitudinal incisions are made, after which sections are peeled off. These tend to roll into large "quills," protecting the rich oils on the inner sides of the bark. These quills are dried on large tarps in the sun and then milled into smaller pieces for sacking and shipment.

An average forager can peel as much as 300 pounds (dry-weight) per day. A number of collection points will buy the crude botanical from the forager at prices ranging from 12 cents per pound green or wet to over 40 cents per pound dried and ready for chipping and sacking. Export prices in large tonnages begin at 58 cents per pound for current-year harvests and more than 75 cents per pound for year-old bark. Aging increases the desired oils by as much as 100%, making it worth twice the current-year price in oil contents. A regional wholesale house will buy recently harvested cascara segrada bark at 80 cents per pound in 1,000 pound quantities, but most prefer the aged bark over newly harvested product. It is usually marketed as a powder so further economics can be realized by the forager willing to do the milling.

Herbs. An herb includes the leaf, stem, and flower of the botanical. They are usually harvested when the plant is in bloom, but before the seed head forms. The stalk or stem of the herb must be cracked, crimped, or split to reduce drying times and allow the plant to dry consistently and uniformly, stem and leaf together. The larger stems should be discarded, since they usually possess little or no value to the buyer. Leaves partially dried from age, or discolored by insects and disease, should also be excluded to get the best price in the market. Many herbs, like nettle *(Urtica urens),* should be harvested before the stem begins to turn woody. This allows several harvests of the plant during the season, with higher overall yields from the same area.

Herb harvest example — Prince's Pine Herb *(Chimaphila umbellata):* also known as pippissawa, prince's pine, it is now used as the principle ingredient in the manufacture of root beer. This is primarily because sassafras *(Sassafrass albidum)* root bark has been classified carcinogenic due to its saffol content. Most of the herb currently used is imported. However, larger domestic sources of supply are finding foragers willing to harvest it.

Prince's pine grows in mountainous country at altitudes over 2,500 feet. Since the market wants the root with the herb, the plant is harvested in a way basically similar to Oregon grape root. Having a similar root system, harvesting essentially prunes the crop for next year's growth: 300 pounds wet weight per day is common for most foragers, with a 65% weight loss in drying as a maximum.

Most regional wholesalers pay 95 cents per pound in 1,000 pound quantities, with larger wholesalers willing to buy at 80 cents per pound. This crop is usually sold "whole," so packaging is quite simple, use of burlap or polypropylene sacks indicated. Since the herb grows at high altitudes, snow dictates when the crop can be harvested. Due to distances involved, the forager should plan a minimum of 3 to 7 days in the field. Finding large stands seems to be no problem.

Flowers. Flowers should always be gathered when they first open. They can be gathered with a device such as a cranberry scoop or stripper, especially such small flowers as elder *(Sambucus nigra)* and yarrow *(Archillea millefolium)*. Passing them through the plant with the teeth forward causes the combs to snap the flowerhead off the stem which is then caught in a box. Red clover *(Trifolium pratense)* can be harvested in this manner using a rake on a tractor.

The dried flower markets have experienced an unusually large growth to provide materials for the potpourri and cosmetic products now on the market. Just the "color" market, where unusual colors of flower pieces is important, has an annual demand exceeding 200 ton dry-weight. Some commercial harvesters who are attempting to meet some of these domestic needs now use special vacuum systems connected to rakes and other harvest tools.

Drying the flowerhead for color requires some shade, as the long ultraviolet tends to fade colors. Flower pieces can be dried on tarps or racks in a heated shed, but flowers for the floral markets must be hung upside down in small bunches and dried slowly over a period of two weeks in the shade. While whole flowers bring more money from the market, it is their colors that are most important to the manufacturer.

Flower harvest example — baby's breath *(Gypsophyla paniculata):* the best, or most preferred baby's breath grows primarily in Washington and Idaho (although it can be cultivated in numerous parts of North America). Known as *G. paniculata,* this tiny white flower is sold all over the world in most dried floral arrangements. It requires dry, poor soils, and can be found growing as a perennial in 100 acre fields. It tends to grow as a large bush, sometimes as tall as five feet.

Permission to cut the flower from private land is common, paying the land owner 5 cents per pound wet-weight on the flowers removed from his land. Bundles are made, using the long stems (3 to 4 feet) to tie bunches for drying by hanging. Once cut, the flowers should be removed from the sun and dried upside down in the shade. They will dry within three days, although some usually take up to three weeks. A bunch should weigh somewhere between 4 ounces and a pound when dry. A bundle of wet bunches is made when transporting large quantities of bunches to a warehouse for drying. Bundles contain 10 to 20 bunches, end-to-end, and can be stacked as wet flowers for up to two days.

The marketing is retail and small wholesale florists in all major cities. Prices begin at $4.50 per 8 ounce bunch. There are usually buying stations which will buy the green baby's breath bunches (wet) for 25 cents per pound, also paying for access to the land and drying costs and losses. An average forager can make up to $75 per day selling his wet produce to buyers in the field. And, the forager has his money at day's end.

However, when drying and marketing your own forage or farm product, averages can be as high as $8,000 per acre. While a typical forager can harvest an acre in less than three days, drying and marketing takes time and some money. Most product is sold direct, requiring the seller to deliver the baby's breath in good condition. With further processing, with glycerine and dyes, the product will sell for even more. Farms in California currently raise *G. perfecta*, with a much larger flowerhead. It does not market quite as well as the smaller flowerhead of *G. paniculata*, but is representative of the futures for this foraged crop. More than 400 tons of baby's breath was harvested from Washington state in 1984, and there are still shortages for the domestic market. Japanese importers who have wanted this product for more than five years have yet to be able to buy baby's breath due to short supply.

Seeds. There are many methods for harvesting seed. Some species can be harvested with specially designed machinery such as vacuums and shakers, but most are still collected by hand. The seed of some conifers is harvested by tree climbers equipped with spurs, belts, and rope. Cones can always be obtained from logging operations where the trees cut have cones at the correct stages of development.

Elderberries and other terminal borne fruits can be harvested with pole pruners. Serviceberries and other berries are usually picked with special combs or stripped by hand. Some seeds cling tenaciously to plants while others readily dislodge at the proper state of ripeness into a bag or onto canvas spread out for that purpose. The artform is knowing when and where to harvest the seed.

Seed harvest example — seed cone: some 50 million acres in the United States need to be planted to trees because they can not restock themselves naturally. This replanting will require more than 25 thousand tons of forest tree seed. Although more than 600 species of woody plants are useful for conservation planting, only 130 species make up the bulk of the seed trade. Furthermore, some 25 species, mostly conifers, account for 90% of the area planted and seeded. The greatest users of reforestation seeds are the public forestry agencies, although there is a growing demand by the forest industries and commercial seed dealers. Prices vary markedly, ranging from 37 to 52 cents per pound for semi-dried cones. The seed is removed by specially designed machinery and eventually marketed to the various forestry agencies, usually via "bids." Each cone harvest has its own rules and requirements, but the money can be really good, especially when you live near logging operations.

Once the seed has been removed from the cone, temperature and storage become important factors in seed viability and hence marketing. When stored correctly, seed can be held for several years without any deterioration in quality and germination ratio. Labeling is a critical factor, specifying where and when the seed was harvested. A number of different agencies are monitoring this data for better understanding of the best seed sources.

HOW TO GROW GINSENG AS AN INTERCROP IN THE FOREST

American ginseng *(Panax quinquefolium)* grows wild in the eastern half of North America. This perennial herb inhabits hardwood forests on well drained, north and east facing slopes with soils which are porous and rich in humus. Ginseng can also grow on southwestern slopes when the soil is sandy or clayey, where the forests are primarily conifers and softwoods. It is the north and east facing woods, however, where ginseng thrive best. These slopes furnish the best shade and frequently have loamy soils.

Numerous efforts were made to cultivate ginseng in years past, but failed due mainly to the lack of knowledge of the plant and its requirements. The wild plant can now be semi-cultivated since we now have better information about it. Cultural techniques vary from simulating forest conditions to approximating the practices used in the commercial nurseries using artificial shade. As a prospective grower, you should adopt those procedures most compatible with your circumstances. The more limited your yearly investments in time and capital, however, the more money you will make.

Before you embark on a venture to cultivate ginseng, you must first consider the risks involved, the time and effort required, and a number of other important details. For example, not only must you have another source of income, you must also live next to the growing area to discourage potential vandalism, ranging from rodents to the "sang" hunger.

Then, of course, there are the diseases. Cultivated ginseng, whether commercially grown in lath houses or intercropped in a forest, is highly susceptible to a variety of diseases. When disease breaks out, the diseased plants must be destroyed immediately and the rest of the plants carefully washed and transplanted. Newer methods of disease control seems to work well in forest situations. Seed disinfection with such salts as potassium permanganate or tetramethylthiuram disulfide, and spraying with *Bordeaux* mixture two or three times during the season seems to be an inexpensive and effective means of control. A number of fungi can attack ginseng. These include *Alternaria panax* (the cause of Alternaria leaf spot or blight), *Phytophthora cactorum* (which attacks the stems and roots), *Rhizoctonia solani* (which attacks the bottom areas of the stem), Ramularia spp. (which causes the roots to become rotten), and Fusarium spp. (which attacks young seedlings).

To prepare the Bordeaux mix, dissolve 4 pounds of copper sulfate in 50 gallons of water, using a wooden or earthen bowl. Mix 4 pounds of quick lime under water in another container and let dissolve. Add the two together when you want to use them as a spray. They should be used only immediately after mixing them in water, since they lose their strength in a short period of time after being mixed. Seeds ready for planting should be dipped in this solution for about 10 minutes. They are then allowed to drain and then dusted in flour before planting. This treatment discourages fungus from beginning. The ground wants to be soaked and the plants sprayed with this solution about every three weeks during the growing season. Both the copper and the calcium in Bordeaux mixture are excellent nutrients, and it is nutritional self defense rather than toxicity that wards off fungus.

For the site, choose a well drained upland area with up to an acre of shade and slopes toward the north and east. The soil should be light and loose with rocky or porous subsoils, as that in limestone or sandstone areas. Avoid hardpan and sites lacking good soil moisture. These are areas which do not support other herbaceous growth. As a guide to appropriate habitats, look for indicator plants. Besides the usual deciduous trees, perennials which like these conditions include fern, Oregon grape, and wild ginger. The annual precipitation

TABLE 40

Native Plants of Commercial Importance by Region

Northeast	Midwest, cont.
Christmas Trees	Floral Pods
Elderberry	Horsetail Herb
Forest Tree Cones	Willows
Forest Tree Seeds	Scotch Broom Flowers
Mandrake Root	Wild Indigo Root
Stinging Nettle	
Pokeweed	Northwest
St. John's Wort Herb	California Bay Leaf
Sassafras Rootbark	Cascara Segrada Bark
Wild Cherry Bark	Douglas Fir Tree Pitch
	False Hellebore Root
South	Huckleberry Foliage
Black Cohosh Root	Mosses
Bloodroot	Oregon Grape Root
Blue Cohosh Root	Salal Foliage
Ginseng Root	Sword Fern
Golden Seal Root	Wild Ginger Root
Passion Flower Herb	
Prince's Pine Herb	Southwest
Slippery Elm Bark	Baby's Breath Flower
White Oak Bark	Chaparral Leaf
Wintergreen Herb	Chicory Root
	Dandelion Root
Midwest	Mormon Tea Herb
Black Haw Bark	Mullein Herb
Burdock Root	Pennyroyal Herb
Catnip Herb	Wildflowers
Coltsfoot Herb	Yarrow Flower
Echinacea Root	Yellow Dock Root

From Native Plants of Commercial Importance *by Richard Alan Miller, available from* Acres U.S.A.

should range from 28 to 51 inches of water with a mean annual temperature of 48 to 59 F. The pH needs to be 5.5 to 6.5.

A larger continuous area for intensive cultivation may be desirable, but a radical removal of small trees and even some of the larger ones may be necessary. A canopy shade of more than 70% must be maintained. The more intensive the culture, the greater the yields in a minimum time. Intensive cultivation minimizes competition from nature plant populations. Organic fertilizers are used to help prepare the seedbeds and root zones.

The soil is tilled to a depth of 8 to 10 inches, adding lime to adjust pH to at least 5.5. Some add a balancing fertilizer, such as 14-14-14 before planting, and 4 to 6 foot wide beds are elevated to at least 8 inches with a low walkway between them for maximum water runoff. The beds should slope gently downhill so that roots never stand in water. Beds should also not be elevated on steeper slopes where serious erosion could occur. Leaf litter is good for fertilizer and mulching as long as lime is present.

The seeds or seedlings are planted 6 inches apart in rows 6 to 12 inches apart at a depth of one half inch. A recent development, even more effective than stratification for germination, is a method that involves the use of a powerful plant hormone, *gibberellin*. The seeds should first be soaked in a .05 to .1% solution of gibberellic acid for a day which reduces the dormancy period to only six months, and improves germination. If this method is used properly, expect nearly a 100% germination from the viable seed within six months. By contrast, using older methods one could expect less than 60% germination over eight months to one year.

Beds should then be covered with 1 to 2 inches of leaf mulch or clean straw. Fresh or stratified seeds and seedlings are planted in the fall after disinfecting any stock purchased from commercial sources. Organic fertilizers enhance the plant growth, but also produce the lower valued field grown ginsengs. A top dressing of bone or blood meal can be added periodically during the growing season without affecting the plant, yet repel deer and rabbits. The beds — once the plants are established — must be covered annually in the fall with leaf mulch or clean straw, when freezing weather is imminent. Market size roots are not obtained until the fifth or sixth year from seed at the earliest. During this long growing interval, animals frequently become serious pests. Moles, mice and slugs can be destroyed with certain baits. It is often necessary to surround each site with a vertical metal shield, buried 1 to 2 feet into the ground and 2 to 3 feet above the ground, to keep most of these pests out of your ginseng. Daily attention to these immediate problems over this 6 to 7 year program requires the farmer to live near his crop.

Selling the seed can be quite lucrative. You can begin gathering seed the second season after planting. It has been reported that 25 to 30 pounds of seed is not uncommon for a bed 40 by 60 feet, with more than 8,000 seeds to the pound. Today's prices might surprise you. They are often more than $100 per pound. The seedling business is quite profitable, especially once a seed stock has become acclimatized and market established.

You can harvest the roots using a potato digger or by hand with an appropriate tool. The roots should be dug in the fall as the above ground parts die back. This is done by carefully exposing the underground rhizome at the base of the above ground portion, following the horizontal lengths until they join the top of the true root. The taproot is often forked and has many diffusely branched rootlets. With the rootlets attached, the root is worth considerably more money. Expose the whole root and rhizome intact, removing loose soil. Wash the roots as soon as possible, but do not scrub any remaining soil from the roots. A little soil left around the root rings is considered minerals, and may enhance the value.

The cleaned roots are then spread on screen racks for drying, turning them frequently and to assure good ventilation. Drying times vary, with larger roots taking up to three weeks or more to dry at room temperatures. Artificial heat can be used with temperatures up to 90 F. in conjunction with exhaust fans and other vapor-pressure techniques (outlined in Chapter 6). They must not be dried in an oven, which is too rapid and discolors the roots. The root is considered dry when it becomes brittle and snaps when bent.

In packaging for shipment, do not use bags or any containers that will crush or cause the roots to break in transit. Stiff cardboard boxes are probably the most efficient and inexpensive way to ship. With larger quantities, wooden boxes and barrels can be used. Taking these precautions is always worth this extra attention. The price for roots is best between November and April, fluctuating sharply with world events. The stock exchange in Singapore is based on this commodity, not gold.

Today, the market of American ginsengs, especially those collected from the wild, is increasing to such an extent that there are shortages and rising prices. Wild cultivated American ginsengs begin selling at more than $90 per pound. For those of us who can devote the required time and have access to timberlands, ginseng is a very viable and commercially feasible intercrop in the forests of North America.

The semi-cultivation of ginseng should open the eyes of small farmers to the possibilities of the semi-culture of other desirable wild plants.

SOME FUTURES WITH FORAGING

The concept of foraging is well suited to those who have chosen a rural style of living, but must augment sources of income until other farming plans are realized. By recognizing the natural resources in your region, you now have an immediate potential for supplementing your rural income in markets which will also eventually buy your field crops. Foraging cooperatives, organized along the lines of the local Grange, seem to be an excellent way for the community to develop their economy by creating rural jobs. A number of the foraged products are also well suited to cottage industries. With proper management,

TABLE 41
Some Common Herbs with Good Forage Potential

HERB/SPICE	PART USED	REGION	MAJOR USE IN MARKETING
Angelica (*Angelica atropurpurea*)	Root	East Coast	Food flavoring and fragrance in cosmetics
Bay (*Umbellularia californica*)	Leaf	West Coast	Common household spice — perfumes
Bergamot (*Monarda fistulosa*)	Herb	North America	Cosmetics — flavor additive for fruity citrus
Blackberry (*Rubus fruticosus*)	Leaf	North America	Food flavoring, tea ingredient
Black Cohosh (*Cimicifuga racemosa*)	Root	East Coast	Pharmaceutical — female disorders (menstrual)
Blessed Thistle (*Cnicus benedictus*)	Herb	North America	Pharmaceutical — increases gastric secretions
Blue Cohosh (*Caulophyllum thalicatroides*)	Root	East Coast	Pharmaceutical — female disorders (labor)
Borage (*Borago officinalis*)	Herb	North America	Pharmaceutical — increases milk in mothers
Burdock (*Arctium lappa*)	Root	North America	Major produce in Asia — antimicrobial activity
Calamus (*Acorus calamus*)	Root	North America	Major cosmetic fragrance — mild CNS-depressant
Cascara Segrada (*Rhamnus purshiana*)	Bark	Pacific Coast	Laxative — sunscreen preparations
Catnip (*Nepeta cataria*)	Herb	North America	Animal toys — tea flavoring — mild sedative
Chapparal (*Larrea mexicana*)	Herb	Southwest	Pharmaceutical — cancer
Chickweed (*Stellaria media*)	Herb	North America	Multi-vitamin additive (iron) — cosmetics
Chicory (*Cichorium intybus*)	Root	North America	Coffee substitute/additive
Coltsfoot (*Tussilago farfara*)	Leaf	West Coast	Tobacco substitute/additive
Dandelion (*Taraxacum officinale*)	Root	North America	Coffee substitute/additive
Devil's Club (*Oplopanax horridum*)	Root	Pacific Coast	Industrial grade panax ginseng
Desert Tea (*Ephedra nevadensis*)	Herb	Southwest	Pharmaceutical — bronchial dialator
Echinacea (*Echinacea angustifolia*)	Root	North America	Pharmaceutical — blood purifier
Elder (*Sambucus nigra*)	Flower	North America	Eye and skin lotions — food flavoring

Name	Part	Region	Use
Eucalyptus (*Eucalyptus globulus*)	Leaf	West Coast	Expectorant and flavoring agent
Ginseng (*Panax quinquefolium*)	Root	North America	Foods and cosmetics — longevity herb
Goldenseal (*Hydrastis canadensis*)	Root	East Coast	Pharmaceutical — eyewash, uterine hemmorhage
Horehound (*Marrubium vulgare*)	Herb	North America	Cold and cough medicines — food flavoring
Horsetail (*Equisetum arvensa*)	Herb	North America	Source for silica — pet food flavoring
Kelp (*Fucus versiculosus*)	Plant	Coast Regions	Food additive — high in potassium
Kinikinnick (*Arctostaphylos uva-ursi*)	Leaf	Mountains	Pharmaceutical — urinary antiseptic
Licorice (*Glycyrrhiza glabra*)	Root	North America	Food flavoring — cough drops and syrups
Lobelia (*Lobelia inflata*)	Herb	East Coast	Pharmaceutical — expectorant, CNS-depressant
Lovage (*Levisticum officinale*)	Root	North America	Food additive — fragrance (like celery)
Mandrake (*Podophyllum peltatum*)	Root	East Coast	Pharmaceutical — pain killer (danger)
Marshmallow (*Althea officinalis*)	Root	North America	Pharmaceutical — muccous inflammation
Mistletoe (*Phoradendron flavenscens*)	Herb	North America	Decorative — pharmaceutical, sedative
Mugwort (*Artemisia vulgaris*)	Herb	North America	Pharmaceutical — bring on menstrual period
Mullein (*Verbascum thapsus*)	Herb	West Coast	Ear drops, eye wash — bronchitis, asthma
Nettle (*Urtica urens*)	Herb	North America	Shampoos — food ingredient, tea
Oregon Grape (*Berberis aquifolium*)	Root	West Coast	Chemistry and use similar to golden seal
Pennyroyal (*Mentha pulegium*)	Herb	North America	Insect repellant — antispasmodic
Pippissawa (*Chimaphila umbellata*)	Herb	Northern (high)	Urinary antiseptic — food additive (Root Beer)
Plantain (*Plantago major*)	Herb	North America	Antiseptic, eyewash — flea repellant
Poke (*Phytolacca americana*)	Root	East Coast	Pharmaceutical — skin cancers, rheumatism
Queen-of-the-Meadow (*Eupatorium purpureum*)	Herb	East Coast	Pharmaceutical — breaks fever
Rosehip (*Rosa canina*)	Buds	North America	Vitamin C — bioflavonoid, food flavoring
St. John's Wort (*Hypericum perforatum*)	Herb	West Coast	Hypericum red dye
Sarsaparilla (*Smilax regelii*)	Root	Southwest	Food additive (Root Beer) — rheumatism, tonic

Includes the part used, where it grows (region), and major use in marketing.

TABLE 41

Some Common Herbs with Good Forage Potential

HERB/SPICE	PART USED	REGION	MAJOR USE IN MARKETING
Sassafras (*Sassafras albidum*)	Root	East Coast	Food flavoring — antiinfective
Scullcap (*Scutellaria lateriflora*)	Herb	North America	Pharmaceutical — nervine, sedative
Shepherd's Purse (*Capsella bursa-pastoris*)	Herb	North America	Pharmaceutical — stop hemorrhaging (birth)
Slippery Elm (*Ulmus rubra*)	Bark	East Coast	Laxative — food flavoring
Tansy (*Tanacetum vulgare*)	Herb	North America	Insect repellant
Valerian (*Valeriana officinalis*)	Root	North America	Pharmaceutical — sedative (valium)
Vervain (*Verbena hastata*)	Leaf	North America	Pharmaceutical — expectorant, tonic
Walnut (*Juglans nigra*)	Hull	North America	Brown dye
White Oak (*Quercus alba*)	Bark	East Coast	Pharmaceutical — burns and sore mouth
Wild Cherry (*Prunus serotina*)	Bark	East Coast	Pharmaceutical — worms and expectorant
Wild Lettuce (*Lactuca scariola*)	Herb	North America	Pharmaceutical — opiate compounds
Wintergreen (*Gaultheria procumbens*)	Leaf	East Coast	Methyl salicylate source — food flavoring
Witch Hazel (*Hamamelis virginiana*)	Bark	East Coast	Astringent and hemostatic ointments, washes
Woodruff (*Asperula odorata*)	Herb	North America	Cosmetic fragrance — food flavoring
Wormwood (*Artemisia absinthium*)	Leaf	North America	Food additive — pillows (sachet)
Yarrow (*Archillea millefolium*)	Flower	North America	Cosmetic — food flavoring, teas
Yellow Dock (*Rumex crispus*)	Root	North America	Red dye — skin disorders, iron source
Yerba Mate' (*Ilex paraguaiensis*)	Leaf	Mountains (high)	Coffee substitute
Yerba Santa (*Eriodictyon californicum*)	Leaf	West Coast	Pharmaceutical flavoring — food flavoring

Includes the part used, where it grows (region), and major use in marketing.

214

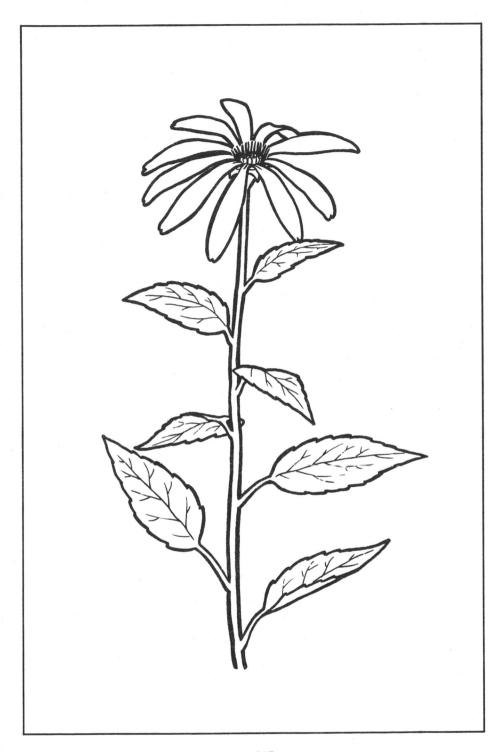

the community and social benefits are more far reaching than simple economic development.

To illustrate, take the case of mullein *(Verbascum thapsus)*. This herb is considered a noxious weed growing abundantly throughout North America. It is also an import from Yugoslavia. Last year, more than 400 ton was imported by just one brokerage house. It can be cut, conditioned and laid into a windrow, and then baled when dry. In this form, most processors will pay more than $700 per ton (or 35 cents per pound). If it is cut into a chip form and sacked, it begins selling at 65 cents per pound (or $1,300 per ton)!

In 1984 a feasibility study for harvesting mullein was made in a forest district in Southern Oregon. A number of years back, that district had a major forest fire. Reseeding programs proved almost futile in the poor, pumice soils. Only after a sixth reseeding was a *plantation* started. Unfortunately, one year after the successful reseeding program, the trees were invaded by solid stands of mullein. Herbicides had been banned several years prior, so the forest district assumed that they were going to lose their plantation because mullein grows to six feet, whereas the new trees were only 12 inches.

A number of members from a cooperative went in and cut the mullein with machetes. The herb was then trucked to lower fields for drying and baling. Not only did the forest district save the new plantation, it actually made a small amount of money from the brush permits issued. And, most importantly, a number of rural jobs were created, producing a product that was previously imported. It also provided a strong argument for alternative methods in weed control.

The future of foraging as a source of supplementing ones rural income lies with our ability to recognize natural resources. Each region of North America contain similar potentials and stories. It is up to us as individuals to realize these potentials. The forest can become more than just a source for timber. It can also be utilized as farm ground, perfectly suited for specific botanicals with existing markets. As one silvaculturist once said about foraging: "For the first time, I now see a way I can do what I went to college to study: *forest management rather than timber management!*"

Sources for Further Information

BIBLIOGRAPHIC DATA BASES

Depending on your information needs, a number of different bibliographic data bases for agriculture now exist. These should be used when you are confronted with a real technical problem, such as disease or insect problem. Here you will have to decide whether you want conventional answers —which usually include toxic chemicals of organic synthesis —or biologically correct information suitable to ecologically sound agriculture. Most technical information on herb and spice farming may not be immediately available from your local expert. But that information probably exists somewhere in the literature. You should ask you local librarian for more information regarding access and costs to these different resources. They are —

AGRICOLA. This is the largest of the agricultural data bases, covering economics, nutrition, rural sociology, plant sciences, agricultural chemistry, natural resources, entomology and agricultural engineering. It is updated monthly.

CAB (Commonwealth Agricultural Abstracts). Similar to AGRICOLA, it also covers a broad range of topics in agricultural sciences. It also includes an abstract (summary) of each article. While this makes this service more useful, it also increases your costs.

BIOSIS. Although this service is oriented primarily to the biological sciences, it does contain many useful references in agriculture. It is usually used as a second source for information.

CRIS/USDA (Current Research Information Service). This database contains agricultural research currently ongoing with USDA. This includes various research agencies, states agricultural experiment stations, state forestry schools and other institutions.

RESEARCH & PUBLICATIONS FOR SMALL FARMERS

A large number of agriculturally oriented groups have organized in different parts of North America. Each group is involved with more than one project, and have a variety of "doors" available to the small farmer. Some even offer newsletters and other resources. A few are . . .

Center for Rural Affairs
P.O. Box 405
Walthill, NE 60867

This group highlights political questions of importance to small farmers.

Community Alliance
   with Family Farmers
P.O. Box 363
Davis, CA 95617

Non-profit organization of urban and rural people working for family-scale, sustainable agriculture. Publishes *National Organic Directory*.

Ecology Action Network
5798 Ridgewood Road
Willits, CA 95490

Ecology Action conducts research into the biodynamic/French intensive methods and their potential for small-farm agriculture.

The Herb Growing
   and Marketing Network
P.O. Box 245
Silver Spring, PA 17575

Publisher, workshop sponsor, and online supplier of information regarding herb production and marketing.

Institute for Alternative Agriculture
9200 Edmonston Road
Suite 117
Greenbelt, MD 20770

This group disseminates scientific information on all aspects of alternative agriculture. Has a newsletter.

Kerr Center for Sustainable
   Agriculture
P.O. Box 588
Poteau, OK 74953

Non-profit group conducting research and presenting workshops teaching and improving sustainable and small-farm agronomical techniques.

The Land Institute 2440 E. Water Well Road Salina, KS 67401	Although its research is oriented toward prairie ecosystems, basic principles apply to all agriculture.
Organic Trade Association P.O. Box 1078 Greenfield, MA 01302	Membership-based group representing the organic industry. Publishes newsletter and conducts meetings.
Rodale Institute 611 Siegfriedale Road Kutztown, PA 19530	This is a non-profit Rodale organization.

With renewed interest in small-farm agriculture, a need for information sharing has also grown. The number of periodicals geared to small farmers has also steadily grown. The following list should illustrate the diversity of available publications, although it in no way attempts to be comprehensive. Subscription rates change too frequently to be published here.

Acres U.S.A. P.O. Box 8800 Metairie, LA 70011	The leading journal of commercial-scale ecological/organic farming. Features profiles of successful natural/alternative farm enterprises. Strong advocate for small, family farms. Also maintains an extensive catalog of books from around the world on organic farming and specialty crops such as herbs.
American Small Farm Magazine P.O. Box 1059 Delaware, OH 43015	Monthly magazine provides small farm operators with information on the business and science of agriculture.
American Vegetable Grower *and Greenhouse Grower* 37733 Euclid Avenue Willoughby, OH 44094	National publication for commercial vegetable growers. Features chemical controls, new varieties of plants, and modern machinery. A monthly.
Country Journal P.O. Box 420235 Palm Coast, FL 32142	A non-technical publication, emphasizing stories about happenings around North America which are revitalizing rural life. Monthly.

Growing for Market
P.O. Box 3747
Lawrence, KS 66046

Monthly newsletter written for market gardeners, cut flower growers, and more. Practical advice.

The Herbal Connection
P.O. Box 245
Silver Spring, PA 17575

Bimonthly trade journal published by the Herb Growing and Marketing Network.

The Herb Companion
201 E. 4th Street
Loveland, CO 80537

Bimonthly popular magazine in "celebration of useful plants." Beautiful, full-color magazine.

Herbalgram
P.O. Box 201660
Austin, TX 78720

Bimonthly magazine covering herb processing and marketing, with particular emphasis on the medicinal properties of herbs. Published by the American Botanical Council.

Maine Organic Farmer and Gardener
P.O. Box 2176
Augusta, ME 04338

Three to four good general articles and other useful data. Quality journalism, newspaper tabloid, bimonthly.

New Farmer and Grower
86 Colston Street
Bristol, BS1 5BB
England

Quarterly journal of the British Organic Farmers and the Organic Growers Association (U.K.).

Small Farmer's Journal
P.O. Box 1627
Sisters, OR 97759

Features practical horse farming. Quarterly.

BIBLIOGRAPHY AND SUGGESTED READING

Economic Outlooks

> *Economic Outlooks*, (regional) for current year. The local Cooperative Extension Service.
>
> *United States Condiment Imports*, (National) for current year. USDA Foreign Agricultural Service (FAS).
>
> *Chemical Marketing Reporter*, Schnell Publishing Company, New York.

Buying Land

> *How to Find Your Ideal Country Home*, 2nd edition, Gene GeRue. Heartwood Publications, Zanoni, Missouri, 1996.

Small Farm Agriculture

> *Research for Small Farms,* Howard Kerr, (ed). USDA document #MP 1422, Beltsville, Maryland, 1982.
>
> *Radical Agriculture*, by Richard Merrill, (ed). Harper and Row, New York, 1976.

Plant Identification

> *J.M. Nickell's Botanical Ready Reference.* Trinity Center Press, Beaumont, California.
>
> *A Field Guide to Medicinal Plants,* Arnold and Connie Krochmal. Times Books, New York, 1984.
>
> *A Modern Herbal* (2 volumes), M. Grieve. Dover Publishing, New York, 1971.

Agronomy and Farm Management

> *Eco-Farm — An Acres U.S.A. Primer*, Charles Walters and C.J. Fenzau. Acres U.S.A., Metairie, Louisiana, 1996.
>
> *The Albrecht Papers,* volumes 1, 2, 3, 4, edited by Charles Walters. Acres U.S.A., Metairie, Louisiana.
>
> *Production of Field Crops*, M.S. Kipps, McGraw-Hill Book Company, New York, 1970.
>
> *The Farm Management Guide*, 15th edition. Doane-Western, Inc., St. Louis, Missouri, 1982.
>
> *Soils and Soil Fertility*, Thompson and Troeh. McGraw-Hill Book Company, New York, 1952.
>
> *Organic Farming*, Wolf, (ed). Rodale Press, Emmaus, Pennsylvania, 1977.
>
> *Our Soils and their Management*, Donahue, Follett, and Tulloch. The Interstate Publishers, Danville, Illinois, 1976.

Use of Herbs

Encyclopedia of Common Natural Ingredients Used in Foods, Drugs, and Cosmetics, Albert Leung. John Wiley & Sons, New York, 1980.

Major Medicinal Plants, J. Morton. C.C. Thomas, Publisher, Springfield, Illinois, 1977.

Elementary Treatis in Herbology, Edward Shook. CSA Press, Lakemont, Georgia, 1974.

Advanced Course in Herbology, Edward Shook. Herbal Research Bureau, Los Angeles, California, 1974.

Physical Chemistry of Herbs

Magical and Ritual Use of Herbs, Richard Alan Miller, Destiny Books, New York, 1983.

Medical Botany, Lewis and Elvin-Lewis. John Wiley & Sons, New York, 1977.

Pharmacognosy, Pratt and Youngken. J.B. Lippincott Company, Philadelphia, Pennsylvania, 1951.

Herbal Medications, David Spoerke. Woodbridge Press, Santa Barbara, California, 1980.

Marketing

Current *OPD Chemical Buyers Directory*. Schnell Publishing Company, New York, annual.

Current *Source Directory*. Whole Foods Magazine, Irvine, California, annual.

The Annual Directory of Vegetarian Restaurants, L. Cronk. Daystar Publishing Company, Angwin, California, 1980.

Growing and Using Herbs Successfully, Betty Jacobs. Garden Way Publishing, Charlotte, Vermont, 1981.

Foraging Textbooks

American Medicinal Plants of Commercial Importance. USDA Miscellaneous Publication #77, July 1930.

Wild Harvest, Leonard Wiley, Portland, Oregon, 1966.

Ginseng and Other Medicinal Plants, A.R. Harding, Columbus, Ohio, 1972.

Goldenseal, Etc., Zarcor and Veninga. Ruka Publishing, Santa Cruz, California, 1976.

Pods — Wildflowers and Weeds in their Final Beauty, Jane Embertson, Charles Scribner and Sons, New York, 1979.

Native Plants of Commercial Importance, Richard Alan Miller. OAK, Inc., Grants Pass, Oregon, 1988.

INDEX